THE POETICS OF QUOTATION

IN THE

EUROPEAN NOVEL

THE POETICS

OF QUOTATION

IN THE EUROPEAN NOVEL

BY HERMAN MEYER

TRANSLATED BY

THEODORE AND YETTA ZIOLKOWSKI

PRINCETON, NEW JERSEY

PRINCETON UNIVERSITY PRESS

1968

Printed in the United States of America
by Princeton University Press, Princeton, New Jersey

This book has been composed in Linotype Caledonia

IN MEMORIAM

WOLFGANG KAYSER

*Nur aus innig verbundenem Ernst und Spiel
kann wahre Kunst entspringen.*

GOETHE

TRANSLATORS' PREFACE

THIS English translation, authorized and approved by the author, incorporates various minor emendations to the original German version. This explains any slight discrepancies between the text and notes of this translation and those of the German edition as published in Stuttgart by J. B. Metzlersche Verlagsbuchhandlung (1961; second edition, 1967).

With the exceptions noted below all translations from the cited literary and scholarly works are our own. Most of the German novels are not available in English translation. And because of the unique stylistic problems involved we preferred to make our own translations even for the passages from Thomas Mann's *The Magic Mountain* and *The Beloved Returns*, where we consulted but did not rely upon the standard translation by H. T. Lowe-Porter (New York: Alfred A. Knopf).

In Chapter I the two passages from Alfred Döblin's *Berlin Alexanderplatz* are cited according to the translation by Eugene Jolas (New York: Viking Press, 1931). The passages from Rabelais (Chapter II) and Cervantes (Chapter III) are quoted from the translations published by the Modern Library. And in Chapter X we have quoted Goethe's *Faust* according to the translation by Bayard Taylor, which is most easily available to American readers in a number of editions.

We are grateful to Professor Hermann J. Weigand for permitting us to use his translation of the chapter on *Tristram Shandy*, which was incorporated with only the slight revisions necessary for stylistic consistency.

The Princeton University Committee on Research in the Humanities and Social Sciences generously supported the preparation of the manuscript.

Finally, we would like to thank Lin Peterson for her careful and helpful editing of an unusually difficult text.

We undertook this translation with the strong conviction

that Meyer's study represents an exciting and original contribution to the theory and practice of the European novel. It is our hope that it will find, in America, the same enthusiastic response that it has encountered among scholars and friends of literature in Europe.

CONTENTS

ix

THE POETICS OF QUOTATION
IN THE
EUROPEAN NOVEL

CHAPTER I

Introduction

THIS introductory chapter offers a welcome opportunity to lay my cards on the table. The intentions of this study are manifold. The methodological starting point is structural analysis: to inquire what the literary quotation signifies and achieves as a structural element in the novel from Rabelais to the present, specifically in each of the novels to be considered here. In this connection structure may be defined as the pervasive order which is determined by the character of the work as a whole and of its parts in their reciprocal relationship, and which comprises in equal measure elements of form, substance, and content. It still remains to be considered in what direction it will be necessary to go beyond pure structural analysis.

Let us restrict ourselves for the time being to the structural-analytical aspect. The notion of investigating quotations with an eye to their structural effect may strike some people as an eccentric whim that would do credit to that unforgettable rider of hobbyhorses, Walter Shandy. For what more can the literary quotation—this little foreign element inserted into the narrative work—signify and accomplish than a statement of pure content or, at most, of contextual relevance? Of course, it is easy to see that it can have some significance for the spirit of a novel if the author appropriates words and sentences from the work of another writer. Certain connections can be established between the quoted matter and the new frame of reference in which it has been accepted, and this will have a certain bearing on the spirit of the novel in question. One can investigate, further, from what particular areas of literature the novelist borrows his quotations, and speculate about the conclusions that can be drawn with regard to his taste, his education, and his philosophical attitudes. All of this,

3

however, has very little to do with the structure of the novel. It concerns, rather, its substance or—even more precisely—the rudiments of substance that remain in our hands when we split into two isolated parts the primordial unity of substance and form through which alone the substance is realized. Can we go further and attribute to the quotation the significance of a true structural element? Or to put the question another way: Can the quotation, despite its natural limitations, play an essential role in the total structure of a narrative work? Are quotations anything more than simply the raisins in the cake, and can their aesthetic effect go beyond the momentary delight that the raisins offer the palate?

As a necessary implication of our definition of the concept "structure," structural analysis must include content and substance as well as form. At the same time, we must inevitably focus our view first of all on the formal nature of the relevant novels. Hence the interpretation of substance and content emerges primarily *sub specie formae*. This is not the result of any subjective caprice or formalistic bias; rather, it follows with logical consistency from the objective state of affairs that Goethe, with unequaled precision, once defined in this way: "Everyone sees the subject matter immediately before him; the substance is detected only by the man who has something to add to it; and the form remains a mystery to most people."[1] The last words of this sentence are surely not the product of any esoteric arrogance, but a sober assertion containing a challenge which must be taken with the utmost seriousness. In another place Goethe implies how the solution of the mystery is to be found. Here it is the creative artist rather than the reader who is placed at the focal point:

> The poet's reflection is directed primarily toward the form; the world supplies him with his subject matter all too liberally, and the substance rises spontaneously

---

[1] Goethe, *Maximen und Reflexionen*, ed. Max Hecker (1907), p. 55, No. 289; and in the edition by Erich Trunz (Hamburger Ausgabe), Vol. XII, p. 471, No. 754.

from the fullness of his heart; the two encounter each other unconsciously, and in the last analysis one does not know to whom this wealth actually belongs.

But form, although it is already latent in the poetic genius, demands to be recognized, to be considered; and here a certain reflection is required so that form, subject matter, and substance suit one another, adapt themselves to one another, interpenetrate one another.[2]

This refers to the poet, but a comparison of the two passages cited demonstrates how important Goethe considered the ontological analogy of creation and enjoyment, of poet and reader. With reference to *Wilhelm Meister* he once noted that "the reader must maintain a productive attitude if he wishes to participate in any production."[3] The concept of the "productive attitude" clarifies the phrase that the reader must have "something to add to it" if he wishes to find the substance. Without question, however, it is the form that places the highest demands on the productive capacity of the reader. It is binding on the reader, too, that the form demands to be "recognized" and "considered." And "reflection" is required of him also so that in his apperception "form, subject matter, and substance suit one another, adapt themselves to one another, interpenetrate one another." I can think of no better formulation to express the ideal that has hovered before me during this study, no matter how far the realization may lag behind the ideal.

The topic of inquiry is literally forced upon us by the wealth of factual data in narrative art. As we read certain novels, of whose typological nature we shall still have to speak, it strikes us again and again that the effect of the employed quotations is not limited to their statement of substance. They are put into overarching contexts of a formal nature and fulfill an essential function within them. This observation was the germinating source of the present

2 Goethe, *Werke* (Sophien-Ausgabe; Weimar, 1887-1920), Part I, Vol. 7, p. 100.
3 Goethe in a letter to Schiller, 19 November 1796.

study, and it inevitably became associated with more general reflections on the nature of narrative art and of the novel in particular. These reflections concern the problem of unity and totality in the narrative work. Speaking generally, the novel is not the mere product of organic growth from a simple seed. Rather, it arises through a complicated process whereby disparate elements are melted and welded together. The central, inchoate vision of the author attracts foreign subject matter, the whole fullness of empirical reality; and by this I mean not only the realm of external facts, but also the multiplicity of traditional cultural values. The artist's vision makes use of this foreign subject matter in order to realize itself in the work of art. The novel is thus a multiple totality, arisen out of multiplicity. It not only grows, it is also made. Its genesis is to a great extent a process of integration of heterogeneous elements.[4]

Now, the literary quotation is an element whose heterogeneity is far more obvious than is often the case; after all, it is a bit of preformed linguistic property shaped by another author. It is tantalizing to follow the ways and means by which the writer absorbs this foreign body into the totality of his novel until the two eventually merge. Now what is the optimal integration of this alien body into the new linguistic totality? One might believe that it should consist in the most nearly complete assimilation of the quotation. But this is generally not the case. If the quotation is blended into the new linguistic totality to the point of being unrecognizable, then it loses its specific character and its specific effect. In general it might be maintained that the charm of the quotation emanates from a unique tension between assimilation and dissimilation: it links itself closely with its new environment, but at the same time detaches itself from it, thus permitting another world to radiate into the self-contained world of the novel. Its effect is to

---

[4] See my essay "Zum Problem der epischen Integration," *Trivium*, 8 (1950), 299ff.

expand and to enliven the novel, contributing thereby to its variegated totality and richness.

This holds true not only for conspicuous quotations, but also for cryptic ones that remain hidden for the average reader and reveal themselves only to connoisseurs. In the case of the cryptic quotation we are dealing less with simple concealment than with an outright game of hide-and-seek. The point of the game is to discover the quotation, for only by being discovered can it achieve its specific effect. Between the conspicuous and the cryptic quotation there is, therefore, no difference of category but only of degree. Categorically, on the other hand, either kind of quotation differs from the hidden *borrowing*, for the discovery of the latter may result in a certain philological satisfaction, but no aesthetic delight. Two examples make this clear.

The anonymous author of *The Vigils of Bonaventura* characterizes the two hostile brothers, Don Juan and Don Ponce, with the following words: "In great indifference they lived side by side, and when they embraced, they seemed like two frozen corpses on the Bernhard, chest to chest, so cold was it in the hearts in which neither hate nor love prevailed."[5] This is a curious image, one that is not readily comprehensible. The riddle is solved if by chance we discover the source in Jean Paul's *Titan*, which had appeared shortly before *The Vigils*. There, in an exuberant conversation between Roquairol and Albano, we read: "Why do men always lie, like the corpses on the Bernhardus Mountain, frozen upon one another's chests, with fixed eye, with rigid arms?"[6] Even now the matter would remain puzzling if Jean Paul, following his usual practice, had not appended a scholarly footnote: "The unknown victims of freezing are left unburied by the monks, who prop them up chest to chest." The remoteness of the simile,

[5] *Die Nachtwachen des Bonaventura*, ed. Franz Schulz (1909), p. 40.

[6] Jean Paul, *Titan*, Part II, Cycle 55; in *Sämtliche Werke* (Akademie Ausgabe), Part I, Vol. 8, p. 324.

the verbal similarity, and the identity of what is meant in both cases by the comparison—namely the coldheartedness that exists among men—leave no doubt in our mind about the source exploited by the author of *The Vigils*, and it is clear that we can understand the comparison only on the basis of Jean Paul's footnote. Nevertheless it would be false to speak of a cryptic quotation. The borrowing is distinguished from the quotation by the fact that it has no referential character.[7] It does not aim to be related to its source, and this is appropriate since the return to the source may bring about a certain philological clarification, but no enrichment of the meaning and no added aesthetic value.

As a counterexample, let us consider the opening words of *Buddenbrooks*. Here Thomas Mann uses the naturalistic technique, patterned especially after the brothers Goncourt, of having the story plunge directly *in medias res* with direct speech. We hear a question and an answer:

> "What is that?—What—is that. . . ."
> "Oh, the devil, *c'est la question, ma très chère demoiselle.*"[8]

Not until then is the situation portrayed. The eight-year-old Tony Buddenbrook is sitting on her grandfather's lap, and we realize that she has asked something and he has answered. Only now do we find out that Tony is busy memorizing the Lutheran catechism. Now the reader understands—or to put it more cautiously, the reader is led to the point of comprehending—that the words "What is that?" are not, as he probably had assumed at first, Tony's own words. They belong, rather, to the catechism, where each article of the Ten Commandments and the Credo is followed by this question, whereupon the explanation of the relevant article is given. Only now does the reader also appreciate the ambiguity of the answer. The grandfather,

---

[7] Regarding the concept of referential character, see Albrecht Schöne, *Säkularisation als sprachbildende Kraft*, Palaestra, Vol. 226 (1958), *passim*, and especially the chapter on Gotthelf. This excellent work is quite revealing for the broader implications of our theme.

[8] Thomas Mann, *Buddenbrooks*, Part I, Chap. 1, sentence 1ff.

a mocking freethinker, intentionally misinterprets the question. Pretending that Tony herself has posed it, he answers rather blasphemously, "Oh, the devil, *c'est la question*." But even this blasphemy is revealed to the discerning reader only indirectly. The reader also must know his catechism by heart and must conclude from the words repeated by Tony ("I believe that God created me along with all creatures" and so forth) that she has just memorized the first article of the Credo ("I believe in God the Father, the Almighty, Creator of Heaven and Earth") and that the skeptical question of the grandfather refers to this article. The words "What is that?" have a clear referential character; despite the initial camouflage, they demand to be recognized as a quotation. For that reason the opening of *Buddenbrooks* belongs wholly in the thematic area of our investigation, whereas we shall exclude in general such borrowings as the one noted in *The Vigils of Bonaventura*.

Still a few more delimitations are necessary. In the technical language of literary criticism and also in popular usage, the word "quotation" is used in two senses. In the broader sense "quoting" can mean that one alludes to or cites not the literal words, but the content of specific literary passages or even of entire literary works. Reference, allusion, pastiche, parody, plagiarism—these are all somehow related to the quotation proper or have at least manifold and often compelling points of contact with it.[9] Precisely because the transitions are so fluid and the boundaries sometimes so uncertain, we consider it practicable to limit ourselves in general to quotations in the narrower sense of the word. Otherwise the danger arises that we will get lost in a limitless mass of material. So we shall restrict

[9] From the very voluminous secondary literature on these related concepts I shall cite only the following Dutch works, which might otherwise perhaps escape the reader's attention: A. H. van der Weel, *Vier vormen van nabootsing in de letterkunde*, Inaugural Lecture at the University of Amsterdam (Rotterdam, 1954); H. Wagenwoort, *Navolging en plagiaat in de litteratuur* (Groningen, 1958); and especially the informative and amusing book by Jan Grootaers, *Maskerade der muze* (Amsterdam, 1954).

ourselves to quotations that retain the wording of the original. This wording need not be absolutely precise. It can, for various reasons, deviate more or less from the original; as a matter of fact, these reasons are often rather interesting. The determining point in our delimitation is this: not merely is the content of literary passages referred to and to a certain extent faithfully reproduced, but also and above all the word order. However, we do not want to tie ourselves dogmatically to this criterion. In the interest of our theme it can be desirable here and there to go beyond the boundaries that we have established.

Structural analysis and literary history can proceed separately for great distances, but in many cases they are dependent upon each other in the last resort and must be united in some manner if they hope to reach valid results. It was Wilhelm Raabe and Thomas Mann whose willful art of quoting first fascinated me. But it soon became clear that this willfulness does not always signify something wholly unique and new, but that it is indebted to what could be called a tradition of willfulness. The material under investigation referred me imperiously to the great and exemplary antecedents, and especially to the three patriarchs of the humoristic novel: Rabelais, Cervantes, and Sterne. Thus, the formal analysis grew of its own accord and, as it were, without any intention on my part, into a history of form. Likewise, without any preconceived intention, the investigation had to transcend the boundaries of German literature. This does not mean that I am expanding into comparative literature for its own sake. The primary aim of this investigation is still to illuminate, analytically and historically, a certain formal trait of the German novel. If, in order to do so, it broadens out to a comparative scope, this should be regarded only as a means to the end.

It might be considered capricious to begin with German literature as late as Wieland, while in other literature we go back to the sixteenth century. The obvious reply is that the subject matter itself prescribes or, in any case, suggests this limitation. The development being traced is to a great extent the development of the humoristic novel, whose high road leads from Rabelais by way of Cervantes, Fielding, and Sterne to Germany, continuing there by way of Wieland, Jean Paul, and Wilhelm Raabe right down to Thomas Mann. I venture to suggest that the quotation has developed into a true epic artistic device of aesthetic significance in the humoristic novel. And it is perhaps not difficult to understand the logic of this circumstance. An autonomous epic art of quoting can originate only at the point where the narrative is borne by a personal narrator who can exploit the quotation in sovereign freedom, putting it into new and unique contexts of form and meaning. Wolfgang Kayser once brilliantly demonstrated that the presence of a personal narrator is the decisive factor in the origin of the modern novel in Germany. This contrasts with the baroque novel, in which the narrator "speaks as it were as an *anonymous* who has no individual point of view as a person."[10] The significance of this personal narrator, who should under no circumstances be identified with the author, since he is himself an element of the narrative fiction, emerges clearly from Kayser's juxtaposition of textual passages from a novel of the High Baroque, Lohenstein's *Arminius,* and Wieland's *Don Sylvio.* With Wieland, a process that had long been prepared abroad begins abruptly in Germany. Kayser rightfully points not only to Fielding and Sterne but also to Cervantes, and with equal justification one can single out Rabelais, in whose work the role of the narrator as a fictional element unfolds even more richly and shapes itself even more tangibly than in Cervantes.

What the sovereign freedom of the narrator implies with reference to the art of quoting will, I hope, become clear on almost every page of this book. The freedom of which the narrator makes use is the freedom of play. Here, of course, I do not mean by "play" any kind of irresponsibility.

[10] Wolfgang Kayser, *Entstehung und Krise des modernen Romans* (2nd ed., 1955), p. 9.

I think of it rather as a significant function of life that is basic to art—thus in that lofty sense which the aesthetics of Goethe's age lent to the concept and which we hear, for instance, in the words of Goethe set as a motto at the beginning of this study. Play may have a certain element of irresponsibility; but it is a paradoxical truth that the quotation, as an element of play, nevertheless arrives ultimately at aesthetic responsibility. The concept of play seems also to furnish the clear criterion by which we can distinguish the method of quoting in the German novel of the seventeenth century from the method employed in the period that we have chosen to investigate. In the novel of the High Baroque, quoting had a soberly learned and aesthetically unfree character. This may be illustrated by a little example which can of course raise no absolute claim to general validity, but which can cast some light on what is typical for the times.

One of the most learned products of the High Baroque art of the novel is Philipp von Zesen's *Assenat*.[11] If the text itself scarcely permits us to doubt the enormous polyhistorical learnedness of the author, it is revealed in oppressive abundance in the apparatus that he has added to the novel. The reasons and intention underlying this appendage are clearly stated in the preface. The book deals, as von Zesen emphasizes, not with an invented story but with one that is sacred and moreover true: "I didn't get it out of the clear blue sky nor did I dream it up solely from my own brain. I am able to cite the writings of the Ancients that I have followed." Von Zesen's chief concern is acknowledgment of authority; that is, factual substantiation. He needed, as he says, no "disguises" and no "distortions." "The naked Truth of these matters of which the present Story tells could suffice without all that. From the Notes appended at the end where I authenticate my composition from the Writings of the Ancients and Moderns, the Reader

---

[11] Philipp von Zesen, *Assenat* (Amsterdam, 1670). I quote from this first edition.

will see this. . . ."[12] The apparatus is called "Concise Notes," but this strikes us as an involuntary jest: including the appended alphabetical index these notes constitute more than two hundred pages, that is, almost two-thirds the volume of the actual text of the novel. Nevertheless the author explains with modest pride that he could easily have doubled the apparatus; only consideration for the patience of the reader prevented him from doing so! Let us see in one example how the text of the novel and the apparatus are related to one another. The opening sentences of the novel read as follows:

> The lovely Lily-Month had now passed; the solstice had occurred through the descendant Cancer: the Nile rose ever higher and higher; and Osiris began gradually to approach the Virgin Womb of his heavenly Isis when the woeful Joseph descried the Place of his misery. Memphis, the royal city, he regarded with plaintive eyes.[13]

These few lines inspire the author to eight pages of commentary. The very first substantive, "Lily-Month," is a neologism coined by von Zesen and thus requires explanation. Naturally he could have been content to note that the Lily-Month is June. Instead he expatiates for three pages on a whole nomenclature of months: the names given by Charlemagne; the Latin designations for the months with all possible (and impossible!) etymologies; the names of the months in the various Greek dialects, in Egyptian, and in Hebrew. All of this is larded with scholarly sources and liberal quotations from Ovid, Plutarch, Seneca, and so forth. We see the same thing in the even more extensive commentary on the place-name Memphis. The whole doxography of classical philology is requisitioned and offered by quotation and synopsis not only with reference to the question of whether Memphis really was the royal resi-

---

[12] The passages from the preface quoted here and below are to be found on (the unnumbered) pages iv-vi of the first edition.
[13] *Ibid.*, p. 1.

dence at that time, but also in connection with the etymology of this name. This moraine of pedantry strikes the modern reader as equally chaotic and superfluous. But this impression surely reflects in no way the intention that motivated the author. In his opinion the text of the novel and the notes belong inextricably together. He even goes so far as to implore the reader to read the notes first! "For if one has comprehended these well, one will read the Historical composition (which is to say, the Novel) itself with greater profit as well as understanding. Then one will know much more readily toward what goal I aspire. Then one will see that I did not write this or that in vain and without premeditation nor from my own inspiration. Verily, then almost no word will seem to have been written in vain." The scholarly cultural world which makes its appearance through quotation has absolute authority for the writer. It would be idle vanity to deviate from it and to allow one's "own inspiration" to come into play. Because of this the writer stands in a relation of intellectual bondage to the quotation, and takes it upon himself to impress this bondage upon the reader as well. Surely the quotation has in von Zesen's mind an integrating function, but this integration is of a purely factual sort and aims at the augmentation of the reader's knowledge. It differs radically from the aesthetic integration which comes about only through the author's free play with the quotations. Naturally what we have said should not be applied part and parcel to the whole art of the novel in the seventeenth century. It should be recalled that Grimmelshausen, in the concluding chapter of the fifth book of *Simplicissimus,* treats the long Guevara quotation ("Adieu World" and so forth) rather independently, subordinating it to his own purposes.[14] Nevertheless, I have the impression that even Grimmelshausen's serious treatment of quotations has basically little in common with the playful art of quoting which is our theme.

[14] See Günther Weydt, "Weltklage und Lebensüberblick bei Guevara, Albertinus, Grimmelshausen," *Neophilologus,* 46 (1962), 105-25.

14

The association of structural analysis and diachronic representation of historical connections is a question of tact and probably also of compromise. In the choice of the works to be treated I have consciously limited myself, in the opinion that the intensive must here take precedence over the extensive. Only nine writers, and by these altogether a dozen novels, are taken into account. In general, it has been my principle to treat only a single work by each writer: namely, such a characteristic one that whatever is found out about it should have a certain typical and thus representative significance for his entire work. Only in three cases have I deviated from this principle, for obvious reasons. In this way it seemed most easily possible to emphasize the main stages and the high points of the development. Naturally the choice is colored here and there by subjective preference and hence open to debate. Thus, for instance, a chapter on Fielding's *Tom Jones* might perhaps have been in order, and only because of the need for strong concentration did it seem feasible to focus all our attention on Sterne. It will perhaps strike some people as even more questionable that Goethe's novels were not taken into consideration. They seemed to me to lie somewhat outside the line of development traced here, which is on the whole the development of the humoristic novel.

Jean Paul has been omitted with complete awareness and conviction, no matter how strange this may seem at first glance. Contrary to my initial expectation and perhaps contrary also to the reader's anticipation, I ascertained that Jean Paul makes use of literary quotations here and there, but that they do not play a decisive structural role in his works. But what about the wealth of learned or quasi-learned notes with which Jean Paul accompanies his narrative and which, primarily in the form of footnotes, lend it such an unmistakably unique character? These footnotes ordinarily contain no direct quotations, but merely cite the sources for certain curious facts that occur in the text of the novel; or they clarify facts that are alluded to in the text of the novel in such a cryptic way that their meaning would remain completely obscure without the explanatory note. The facts utilized in this way have for the most part a highly esoteric and unusual character. They often scarcely clarify the sense of the narrative and can be justified only in part by the author's delight in displaying his knowledge. Their main function is radically to loosen up the narrative unity. The reader is constantly compelled to relate the content of the story to things that are far removed; he cannot permit himself to be carried along quietly by the stream of the narrative, but must as it were hop back and forth between the narrative and its scholarly apparatus.

One example can show the complicated relationship of tension created between text and apparatus as a result of this device. At one point, when Jean Paul is talking in an endlessly involved way about the phenomenon of the Court Favorite, contrasting him with his antipode, he uses the following words:

> Certainly there is in every country someone who—just as the goat in the desert or Adam in Halberstadt took all strange sins upon himself—in this very manner, as a plenipotentiary and representative of merit, is the levying agent and collector of all premiums that accrue to merit. This collector is better known under the name of Court Favorite.[15]

Obviously this passage is concerned primarily with the concept of the Favorite; the scapegoat has only a secondary analogical function. Nevertheless the writer is not satisfied with the paraphrase of the concept of scapegoat, which is clear enough in itself. He adds to it the rather puzzling allusion "or Adam in Halberstadt," which becomes comprehensible only through a footnote: "On Ash Wednesday the citizens of Halberstadt commissioned a fellow citizen, who was no angel, to go from church to church, black, barefooted, veiled, to do penance for the others." The footnotes teem with such curious bits of lore. Taken in their totality

[15] Jean Paul, *Der Jubelsenior*; in *Sämtliche Werke*, Part I, Vol. 5, p. 410.

they have a very peculiar but clear function. They add to the narrative that "colorful border and area of diffusion for strange associations" which in Jean Paul's opinion belongs essentially to "humoristic sensuousness" ("Humoristische Sinnlichkeit").[16] They are closely related to the quotation not only in their playful character but also through their formal origins. They extend the tradition of the parodistic pedantic commentary which, quite within the framework of our theme, will concern us in Rabelais, Sterne, and Wieland. For this reason it was necessary to linger somewhat more extensively on Jean Paul's footnote technique.[17]

Although we emphasize the history of form in our study, we must keep in mind the fact that literary phenomena do not develop in a vacuum, but that they are conditioned climatically by the cultural area surrounding them. Our theme leans strongly in the direction of intellectual and cultural history. It would be an artificial impoverishment if we tried ascetically to exclude this whole aspect. Perhaps it could be said quite generally that literature is not born out of pure spontaneity, but arises from the interplay of spontaneity and tradition. However that may be, the art of quoting substantiates the more general observation that literature is nourished by literature. Whether he is oriented toward tradition or against tradition, the writer is concerned with the management of a cultural inheritance that he himself absorbs, preserves, and passes along. Yet we understand the significance of this great process of *traditio* (which means a passing on) only in part if we view it solely from the author's point of view and do not give equal

[16] Jean Paul, *Vorschule der Ästhetik*, paragraph 35.
[17] Walther Rehm, in his learned and witty study of "Jean Pauls vergnügtes Notenleben oder Notenmacher und Notenleser," *Jahrbuch der Deutschen Schillergesellschaft*, 3 (1959), 244-337, has provided us with an exhaustive aesthetics of Jean Paul's footnote technique; his analysis does justice explicitly to the structural function of this "gelehrt-witziges Spielzeug." Note especially the eighth section, where the individual forms of the footnotes are distinguished or, as Rehm puts it in his Jean-Paulian idiom: "das Fuss-Noten-Volk . . . für die Parade geordnet wird" (p. 297). Our observation that quotations play no noteworthy role in Jean Paul's footnotes is wholly borne out by Rehm's thorough analysis.

weight to the role of the public. Precisely in the case of quotation it is of decisive significance whether there exists a literary and cultural background which the author shares with his public and to which he can appeal with full confidence that it will be understood. The quotation thus becomes an important indication for literary sociology, because in it the extent and nature of the literary culture of the public are reflected.

In this connection it is of central importance whether or not a people has at its disposal a national literature which it regards as classically exemplary and as the firm basis of its own culture. This point of view is of particular interest for German literature of the eighteenth and nineteenth centuries. The age of Goethe forms a kind of watershed. Whereas Wieland, for example, could not yet in his quoting draw upon an exemplary literature in his own language, the writers following Goethe—and even Goethe's younger contemporaries, along with their public—are in possession of a national literature with canonical validity. Above all, the works of Goethe, Schiller, and Lessing constitute the reservoir from which the cultivated German can draw. The quoting of one's own classic writers is a conspicuous characteristic of German bourgeois culture, which is reflected in the literature of the nineteenth century in all possible nuances. This reflection, however, is complicated in a fascinating way by the fact that precisely the most important writers take a critical stance with regard to the state of affairs we have just sketched. They see quite clearly that the general consumption of culture involves a rather dubious banalization of the product, and in their narratives they allow this view to appear openly. For this reason the use of quotations in E.T.A. Hoffmann, in Immermann, and especially in Raabe and Fontane takes on an unmistakable note of cultural criticism. As one element of mimetic social representation, it is an effective means of characterizing the satiated and shallow self-complacency of the culture of certain bourgeois circles. The cultured Philistine's passion for adorning his conversation with familiar quotations manifests itself as an alarming symptom of cultural weariness and debility.

We are convinced indirectly of the validity of that criticism if we cast a glance at the popular literature toward the end of the nineteenth century. Hedwig Courths-Mahler likes to give her novels "literary" titles, and we can be sure that in doing so she was catering to the taste of a broad circle of readers. She uses Biblical quotations ("Thy Brother's Wife," "What God Hath Put Together"); quotations from Goethe and Schiller ("Es irrt der Mensch," "Nur wer die Sehnsucht kennt," "Liebe ist der Liebe Preis"); and, with especial delight, quotations from songs ("Willst du dein Herz mir schenken," "Sie hatten einander so lieb"). These quotations are supposed to summon up a certain "romantic" mood and at the same time to give the reader the satisfaction of recognizing the quotation as such.[18] It is worth noting, moreover, that this literary-sentimental manner of giving titles is by no means restricted to popular or trivial literature. Think of the quotation-like titles that Paul Heyse is fond of giving to his dramas and novels: *Im Bunde der Dritte, Über allen Gipfeln, Zwischen Lipp' und Bechersrand.* In the case of both authors it is striking that the quotations are preferably given in fragmentary form. This makes them additionally piquant for the reader. It is supposed to flatter his self-esteem if he is able to complete the quotation from his own stock of literary culture, thereby proving to himself that he has literary history—as the cultivated narrator Eduard in Raabe's *Stopfkuchen* puts it so complacently—"at his fingertips."

It would be foolish, however, to forget the more significant positive aspect in view of this negative side. The author's art of quoting reveals his participation in the riches

[18] See Walter Krieg, *Unser Weg ging hinauf: Hedwig Courths-Mahler und ihre Töchter als literarisches Phänomen. Ein Beitrag zur Theorie über den Erfolgsroman und zur Geschichte und Bibliographie des modernen Volkslesestoffes* (privately printed in an edition of 145 copies, 1953-54). I did not have access to the book itself; Leonard Forster summarizes its contents in "Folk Reading Stuff," *German Life and Letters*, New Series 9 (October 1955), 26-29.

of the Western cultural tradition. He can refer to it and draw upon it with the justified confidence that his audience does not stand fully outside this tradition. The continuity of the cultural tradition guarantees a certain community of general cultural horizons, if not of philosophy or attitudes toward life. It is proper to ask whether this common horizon has perhaps in the last half-century lost in significance and in relative cohesion and stability, and whether this loss has perhaps had a reciprocal effect on literary production and helped to shape its features. The huge intellectual spaciousness of the narrative art of Thomas Mann, who, following Goethe's exhortation, is able to account for three thousand years and thereby, at one with the cultivated reader, to enrich his narrative, seems to constitute not only a *non plus ultra* but also a conclusion, whether temporary or final.

In this connection it is highly revealing to compare *The Magic Mountain* or *Doctor Faustus* with a novel like Alfred Döblin's *Berlin Alexanderplatz*. (I am not concerned with positing a difference in value; my admiration for Döblin's mighty epos is almost as absolute as it is for Thomas Mann's novels.) The humanistic-cultural world, which despite the sharp illumination of its problematic nature is still intact in Thomas Mann's novels, disintegrates totally in Döblin's portrayal of the social underworld. The radical decline of the humanistic-bourgeois ideal of the personality corresponds to a similarly radical depletion of the meaning of cultural possessions. In the stream of consciousness of the good-natured ex-convict Franz Biberkopf, bits and pieces of great literature, now grown meaningless, are mixed in a mad maelstrom with all conceivable linguistic tatters that roar into his consciousness from the tumult of metropolitan civilization: the catchy tags of advertising and songs, popular hits, and silly nursery rhymes. In a tavern he once repeats with genuine reverence a poem that he learned from a fellow inmate:

"If on this earth you want to be a creature, male and full of glee, be careful and weigh everything, before you let the midwife fling you towards the daylight, there to grow: Earth is a nest of grief and woe. Believe the poet of these verses, who often pines and often curses, while chewing on this iron crust—quotation pinched from Goethe's *Faust*: Man only relishes life's glow, in general as an embryo! . . . And now I ask you, friend, a-quiver: just what is man, what is life's river? Did not our great poet Schiller confess: 'It's not the highest men possess.' But I say: it's a chicken-ladder at best, up and down and all the rest."[19]

The same degeneration of quotation into silliness can be found repeatedly in the representational form preferred by Döblin, which intermingles reportage and inner monologue (italics mine):

Two new customers arrive. The girl sways daintily, then serpentines along the wall, and, dandling her buttocks, slithers sweetly across to Willy. He jumps up, grabs her for a brazen rollicking dance, after which they clinch in a ten-minute burner. *Deep immured beneath the earth stands the mold of dry-burnt meal.* Nobody looks at them. One-armed Franz starts tilting his third beaker and strokes his shoulder stump. The stump burns and burns. A clever hound, that Willy, a damned clever hound.

The parodistic Schiller quotation rams head-on into another "literary" product, the vulgar hit tune that someone sings to the accompaniment of the accordion: "My Johnnie, he's the one who can, my Johnnie's the essence of a man."[20] Here the final consequences are drawn from the motif that emerged in post-classical German literature with E.T.A. Hoffmann and reached its full development with Fontane: the deprivation of all meaning in literary culture. The kind of human existence portrayed in Franz Biberkopf's development surely has a value, but it lies completely outside the horizons of all that we know as "culture." Whether

[19] Alfred Döblin, *Berlin Alexanderplatz* (1930), pp. 98f. Quoted here in the translation by Eugene Jolas.
[20] *Ibid.*, pp. 286f.

Döblin's novel tolls the death knell of the art of quotation or stands, along with Joyce's *Ulysses*, at the beginning of a new development can probably not be decided. The three great writers who dominate the beginning of the development we have sketched, especially Rabelais and Sterne, teach us that the disintegration of a closed cultural world can often coincide with a fruitful new beginning. What we have said about Döblin, therefore, has for our presentation the function of an epilogue echoing away into open space. The study itself can be rounded off best by allowing it to culminate with Thomas Mann.[21]

The following chapters of this book have much the character of separate monographs, centered in themselves. To be sure, they are closely connected thematically and methodologically, but the connections are often of such a nature that they will become wholly apparent only to the reader who is willing to think them through for himself. For this reason the author hopes for readers who, in line with Goethe's expression, have "something to add" on their own!

[21] There are stimulating remarks on the quotation as a fermenting element in the modern novel in Walter Jens, *Statt einer Literaturgeschichte* (1957), pp. 15, 30ff.

PART ONE

EUROPEAN BASES:
THE ART OF QUOTING OF THE
GREAT HUMORISTS

CHAPTER II

François Rabelais

GARGANTUA
AND PANTAGRUEL

WHY does Rabelais' great narrative *Gargantua and Pantagruel*[1] have such a direct impact, and why does it strike us as being more lively and supratemporally modern than any other work of that century? The answer lies in its teeming fullness of life and the spontaneity of its astonishing linguistic power. This assessment is surely correct in general. But despite the almost overwhelming impression of immediacy that this work makes on any receptive reader, one thing must not be forgotten: it is at the same time the work of a *poeta doctus*, of a mighty polymath who places his scholarly learning at the service of his narrative art, causing it to enter into the work. One of the most competent Rabelais scholars correctly approximates the proportions when he sets up the following relationship of experience and book learning: "Autant que la vie, les livres

---

[1] The first four volumes—generally known as *Gargantua* (1534), *Pantagruel* (1532), *Le Tiers Livre* (1546), and *Le Quart Livre* (1552)—are designated in the following pages by roman numerals; the chapters are indicated by arabic numerals. Since the authenticity, or the degree of authenticity, of the posthumously published Fifth Book (1564) is debated, we have not taken it into consideration. *In dubiis abstine.* Cf. Georges Lote, *La vie et l'oeuvre de François Rabelais* (Paris, 1938), p. 84: "Nous ne pouvons juger Rabelais que d'après les quatre livres dont il est indubitablement l'auteur. Ainsi l'exige la prudence la plus élémentaire." For the first three volumes I have consulted the edition by Abel Lefranc and others, *Oeuvres de François Rabelais* (5 vols.; Paris, 1912-31); for the fourth volume I have used the edition by Robert Marichal, *François Rabelais "Le Quart Livre"* (Paris, 1947). In the following pages I have made grateful use of the rich factual commentary in Lefranc's edition, although I have not indicated the reference in each particular case.

ont apporté leur contribution à son oeuvre" ("Books, as much as life itself, have contributed to his work").[2] For more than half a century a horde of specialists has striven with great success to discover and chart the extensive areas that lie within his cultural horizon. This thorough source study, carried out with the techniques of often profound scholarship, has produced a rich harvest.[3]

It would shatter our framework if we attempted here to sketch Rabelais' cultural world in even its roughest outline. A few hints must suffice. To a certain extent Rabelais is a hybrid figure, due to the historical situation in which he is located. The words that Conrad Ferdinand Meyer coined for Luther would also be applicable to him: "His mind is the battleground of two ages." And this duality of his nature is ultimately connected to the wealth of his cultural world. For he is a modern humanist in every fiber of his being; he despises the "dark" Middle Ages and scourges the obscurantism of scholastic learning with scornful ridicule. But at the same time he is the rich heir of the entire medieval cultural domain. One Rabelais scholar suggests in lapidary formulation that "Rabelais connait à fonds toute la littérature du Moyen Âge" ("Rabelais has a profound knowledge of the entire literature of the Middle Ages").[4] He not only knows it, but he uses it as well. Both the poetic and the scholarly literature of the Middle Ages contribute in an essential way to the material fullness of his works. "A great taker"—this phrase coined for Goethe can be applied with equal justification to Rabelais. At the same

[2] Jean Plattard, *L'oeuvre de Rabelais* (Paris, 1910), p. xvii. See also the comprehensive work by L. Sainéan, *La langue de Rabelais* (2 vols.; Paris, 1922-23), *passim*, esp. Vol. 1, pp. 484ff.: "Sources livresques."

[3] This harvest is stored in the annual issues of the *Revue des Etudes Rabelaisiennes*, 1903-13 (later, 1914-32, entitled *Revue du XVIe Siècle*, and replaced in 1933 by the journal *Humanisme et Renaissance*); also in the introductions and notes to the critical edition by Abel Lefranc and his associates, as well as in a variety of voluminous monographs: e.g., those by Jean Plattard (1910) and by Georges Lote (1938).

[4] Lote, *La vie et l'oeuvre de François Rabelais*, p. 108.

time he shares fully in the achievements of the young humanistic sciences. The whole classical philological and historical knowledge of the day is accessible to him; he is familiar with Roman and canonic law; and as a doctor he is no less at home in the new natural sciences, which just at that time were in a state of fermenting growth, along with their occult offshoots. In his mind the scholastic system of knowledge is united with the universalistic cultural world of the Renaissance. Involuntarily one thinks of the enumeration in Faust's introductory monologue: "Philosophie, Juristerei und Medizin, und leider auch Theologie"—even the qualifying "unfortunately also" might have been phrased with specific reference to Rabelais! But Faust's tone of grievous enchantment ("Habe nun, ach . . .") is completely missing; moreover, Rabelais is not inclined, like Faust, to surrender himself to magic. On the contrary, he detests it heartily, as he proves in the satire directed against Agrippa von Nettesheim in the Third Book. Here we sense nothing of the Faustian disgust with knowledge, but on the contrary only an unfragmented joy in knowledge.

It is not as though this scholarly knowledge hovered more or less invisibly in the background of the narrative and had to be deduced indirectly. On the contrary: With the same abandon with which he gives free rein to his narrative fantasy, Rabelais opens at every step the floodgates of his erudition. His scholarly appetite for material is reflected in the exuberance with which he displays the heaped-up treasure of his knowledge. He is the typical polyhistor, the voracious reader who devours old and new alike, making many and exhaustive notes on his reading with detailed source references, and arranging them in folders or card files. Then if in the course of his narrative he happens to speak about a certain object, he can draw from his files abundantly and, in lengthy enumerations, append learned supplements to what has been said. These have a twofold character. We find either an enumeration of specific cases or facts that belong to one and the same category, or a concatenation of literary references that serve to

27

validate one definite fact or opinion. The first category embraces, for instance, the mention of all women who by unnatural love have made cuckolds of their husbands ("Semiramis, Pasiphaë, Egesta, the women of Mendes in Egypt who, according to Herodotus and Strabo, copulate with goats . . . and of sundry other bitches . . ." III, 34); all famous mourners (III, 48); all ancient oracles (III, 24); and so forth. An example for the second category: in I, 10, Rabelais polemicizes against a certain opinion regarding the colors white and blue. Although the occasion is quite incidental, he refers in his refutation to more than twenty sources—sixteen times with precise citation of the works that support his proof. Examples of this accumulation could easily be multiplied. The learned references and quotations, which often go on for pages, constitute a considerable part of the material from which Rabelais constructs his narrative work. But we have to ask what they imply with regard to the narrative attitude, and what they mean for the narrative form of his work. Does the polymath simply allow himself to be overwhelmed by the wealth of his material? Does his creative capacity capitulate here? Is measurelessness nothing but formlessness? Or is there here, despite all apparent formlessness, a definite formal intent and a specific realization of form?

The secondary literature on Rabelais has attempted primarily to establish the meaning of his work. The question of the contribution of Rabelais' cultural knowledge to the artistic form of his work plays at most a secondary role. It can be observed that the very sumptuous fullness of this work as such, which after all constitutes its chief characteristic, causes acute embarrassment to many French scholars as soon as they begin to talk about the artistic form. Lack of moderation must be considered a defect if artistic form is tacitly identified with measure and order. Thus Georges Lote characteristically begins his otherwise valuable chapter "Rabelais artiste" with a stern judgment regarding the shortcomings ("faiblesses") of our writer—especially his "désordre"—and summing up he concludes: "Il manque à la fois de goût, de délicatesse et de mesure" ("He simultaneously lacks taste, delicacy and moderation").[5] This verdict refers especially to the learned enumerations, where Rabelais is simply supposed to be hauling out his card file and where the scholarly humanist is assumed to be interfering with the narrative.[6] In Lote's opinion the frequent quoting is a relic of the Middle Ages, based on the need to support one's own opinion by the citation of authorities.[7] Certainly no one will claim that this view is totally unjustified. But one cannot get rid of the impression that here only one aspect of the complex phenomenon, and not even the most essential aspect, is being disproportionately emphasized. The use of the cultural tradition in enumeration, citation, and quotation is defined a priori merely as narrow pedantic gravity and thus as a symptom of intellectual and artistic bondage. As a result, there remains no latitude even for the question of whether and to what extent the specific freedom of the humoristic writer, who deals with his material in sovereign freedom, is preserved in these learned digressions.

And yet this very sovereignty is the important point! Let any reader surrender himself once to the episode where the conjuror Panurge is exploiting all means known to him in order to make invisible writing visible:

Panurge opined that, though the paper was blank, it had probably been written upon with invisible ink. So he pro-

[5] *Ibid.*, p. 397.

[6] *Ibid.*: "Ainsi beaucoup de ses récits sont coupés par d'inutiles digressions qui les alourdissent et les gâtent. Leur intérêt ne correspond certainement pas à l'importance qu'il leur accorde, et l'on est bien obligé de constater que trop souvent, chez lui, l'humaniste fait tort au conteur."

[7] *Ibid.*, p. 107: "Il lui faut des autorités et des textes, comme aux docteurs scolastiques; il suit volontiers ce qu'a dit un grand nom, et une vérité lui semble plus vraie qu'elle lui est attestée par un nombre plus imposant de témoignages. De là vient la lourdeur de ses démonstrations: il entasse les citations et les opinions, puis, quand il les a bien additionnées, il se figure trop aisément qu'il détient une preuve irréfutable. On sent en lui le clerc formé dans ces écoles et ces couvents ou l'on enseignait à énumérer, à colliger et à compiler, sans discriminations ni méthode."

ceeded to hold it close to the fire to see if the lady had used a solution of sal ammoniac steeped in water. Next he dipped it in water to see if she had used sugar of tithymales, a species of euphorbium. Next, suspecting it might be the juice of a white onion, he held it against a candle. Successively, he tested it for the lye of a fig tree by rubbing one part of it with oil of nuts . . . for the blood of a venomous toad by applying the milk of a woman suckling her firstborn daughter . . . for the dew found in *pomae Alicacabutae* or winter cherries, by rubbing one corner with the ashes of a swallow's nest . . . for the gall of a raven by applying earwax . . . for the acrid milk of a spurge by soaking it in vinegar . . . for whalesperm or ambergris by greasing it with the lard of a bat . . . for alum of lead by passing it evenly across a basin of cold water and very abruptly drawing it out. . . . (II, 24)[8]

That, of course, is pure polyhistory, but what a world of intricate and variegated images is conjured up here by a trivial instigation![9] It is a perfect case of the "humoristic sensuousness" that Jean Paul described so aptly:

If, as demonstrated above, seriousness always emphasizes the general and, for example, spiritualizes the heart to such an extent that in the case of an anatomical heart we think rather of the poetic one than vice versa, then the comic writer attaches us closely to what is sensuously definite, and he does not fall to his knees but rather to both kneecaps; why, he can even use the popliteal space.[10]

One must simply have a feeling for the fact that a certain *vis comica* is latent in fullness as such. This is often even intensified by the glaring disproportion between the expenditure of pedantry and the negligible incentive. This becomes

---

[8] Passages from Rabelais' works here and elsewhere are quoted by book and chapter according to the translation by Jacques Le Clercq (Modern Library edition).

[9] Lote, *op.cit.*, finds the quoted passages "lourds et pénibles, avec une accumulation de détails sans intérêt" (p. 394).

[10] *Vorschule der Ästhetik*, paragraph 35.

particularly clear when Rabelais lets himself go in seemingly pedantic enumerations of scholarly sources of reference.[11] A telling example is offered in the delightful legal satire in the Third Book, where Judge Bridlegoose painstakingly demonstrates why he first allows the cases to devolve in all proper form and "to mature," but nevertheless ultimately decides them simply by casting dice. His senseless demonstration of proof is spiced from beginning to end with references to standard works in the area of canonic and Roman law. Once he finds it necessary to support a very simple and obvious statement by the verses much quoted at the time:

Saepe solet similis filius esse patri,
Et sequitur leviter filia matris iter.

(The son is wont to be more like his father,
The daughter following her mother, rather.)

But the authority requires in turn a documentation on its own, for he continues:

Gl., VI. q. I c. : Si quis; g. de cons., d. v. c. I. fin.; et est no. per doct., C. de impu. et aliis subst., l. ult. et l. legitmae. ff. de stat. hom., gl. in l. quod si nolit, ff. de edil. ed., l. quis, C. ad le. Jul. majest. Excipio filios a moniali susceptos ex monacho, per gl. in c. Impudicas, XXVII q. I. (III, 41)

And on it goes, page after page. Here Rabelais is obviously parodying the abuse of pedantically scholastic quoting along with its monstrous external form: the extreme heaping up of abbreviations that no reader can possibly understand. Notice how cleverly the crude joke "with the exception of the sons of a monk and a nun" is smuggled into the learned apparatus! In *Tristram Shandy*, Laurence Sterne

[11] Cf. the pertinent comment by Plattard, *op.cit.*, p. 271: "Il est évident que l'effet visé par Rabelais est précisément dans le contraste entre cette science, si copieuse et si précise, et le rôle dérisoire ou la fin ridicule que l'écrivain lui assigne. Il s'amuse lui-même de l'éblouissement que produit sur le lecteur cet étalage intempestif d'érudition."

later gratefully appropriated this very form of ridiculing pedantic quotation from Rabelais, intensifying it wholly into the realm of the illusory. It is astonishing with what diversity Rabelais develops the humoristic contrast between pedantic display and actuality. During the terrible storm on the sea voyage in the Fourth Book the craven Panurge wishes, in his fear of death, to make his last testament. He refuses to be persuaded of the senselessness of his undertaking; a well-meaning wave, he says, will cast his testament on the beach, and some princess, finding it, will erect a cenotaph to him,

... just as Dido did, for her husband Sychaeus ... as Aeneas did, for Deiphobus, on the Trojan shore, hard by Rhaete ... as Andromache did, in the city of Buthrotum, for her husband Hector ... as the Athenians did for the poet Euripides ... as Aristotle did, for Hermias and Eubulus ... as the Romans did, in Germany, for Drusus, and in Gaul for the Emperor Alexander Severus ... as Argentarius did, for Callaïschrus ... as Xenocrates did, for Lysidice ... as Timarus did, for his son Theleutagoros ... as Eupolis and Aristodice did, for their son Theotimus ... as Onestes did, for Timocles ... as Callimachus did, for Sopolis ... as Statius did, for his father ... as Catullus did, for his brother ... as Germain de Brie did for Hervé, the Breton sailor.... (IV, 21)

Remember that poor Panurge is screaming out all this book learning into the roaring storm while gripped by a paroxysm of fear. The comedy of the contrast between the real situation and the content of the pedantically circumstantial digression is obvious. Even these few examples should make it sufficiently clear that it is no slavish worship of facts that causes Rabelais to spread out his knowledge in such exuberant abundance. Rather, standing freely above his erudition, he lets it achieve its effect in multiple contrastive figures, thereby making it one of the chief means of shaping his humor. This is not contradicted by the fact that the narrative integration of the cultural matter does not always succeed to the same degree.

What has been treated up to this point is the "art of quoting" in a broader sense, namely the use of cultural knowledge including learned citations and allusions. We now arrive at our special theme: true quotations in literal (or at least approximately faithful) reproduction. Our analysis must do justice to the thematic and formal multiplicity of the means that Rabelais employs. For it is precisely in this multiplicity, as we shall see, that the freedom of the writer, who manipulates his stock of quotations in sovereign fashion, is preserved. It is particularly the subtle and also very conscious dosage of seriousness and jest in which this sovereignty reveals itself. This dosage in itself suggests that we should treat the two main areas of his art of quoting separately: namely the pagan and the Biblical-Christian quotations.

When the young giant Pantagruel begins his studies at the University of Paris, he receives from his father Gargantua the famous admonitory letter in which Rabelais, through the mouth of his gigantic protagonist, sings the joyous praise of the new century. With deep indignation he looks back at the dark times when the "Goths" (which means quite generally the medieval barbarians) had destroyed the entire "good literature." As an energetic contrast he juxtaposes against those times the intellectual spring of the present: "Now, by God's grace, light and dignity have been restored to letters, and I have lived to see it." He sings the praise of the "rehabilitated" humanistic sciences:

> To-day, the old sciences are revived, knowledge is systematized, discipline reëstablished. The learned languages are restored: Greek, without which a man would be ashamed to consider himself educated; Hebrew, Chaldean and Latin. Printing is now in use, an art so accurate and elegant that it betrays the divine inspira-

tion of its discovery, which I have lived to witness. Alas! Conversely, I was not spared the horror of such diabolic works as gunpowder and artillery. (II, 8)

It is the same cultural enthusiasm that resounds from Ulrich von Hutten's famous letter to Pirkheimer in which, praising the times and literature, he notes that studies are thriving and minds flourishing: "O seculum! O litterae! Juvat vivere, etsi quiescere nondum juvat, Bilibalde! Vigent studia, florent ingenia." The art of printing assumes for Rabelais the significance of a divinely inspired invention, because it again makes accessible the treasures of antiquity and thereby disseminates light and dignity among men. And Rabelais for his part wants to collaborate in this reconstruction of human dignity by allowing the voices of the ancients to resound again in his work. Whatever one may conclude in other respects regarding the faith of this great mocker, his relation to antiquity is thoroughly and unambiguously faithful and reverent. (In this connection Rabelais can be distinguished from the great humorists of later date, Cervantes and Sterne.)

To be sure, this faith is not equivalent to any dogmatic bondage; Rabelais is not exchanging an old thralldom for a new one. Instead the feeling of liberation is basic.[12] Classical tradition has no rigid authority in his eyes—this again contrasts with the classicistic attitude—and it is also symptomatic that he by no means accepts it part and parcel as authentic truth. Rather, conventional opinions that he regards as somewhat farfetched are repeatedly rejected as mistaken. Thus without wasting a word he judges Plutarch's report about the ostensible soothsayers on the Ogygian Isles as an old wives' tale: "C'est abus trop evident et fable trop fabuleuse" (III, 24). But again and again one senses what a great exemplary splendor is radiated by the sayings handed down from antiquity—especially those of the philosophers and historians. Where he takes over their

[12] See in this connection Erich Auerbach, *Mimesis. Dargestellte Wirklichkeit in der abendländischen Literatur* (Bern, 1946), pp. 250ff.

words, he does so in order to lend greater solidity to his own statement and to raise it into the realm of the objective. Friar John does not want to accept the gift of money that the noble Grangousier wishes to give him for his services in the war with Picrochole, because the king could use the money better for his war: "Coin is the sinews of war" (I, 46). Through his reference to a saying handed down from antiquity in many variations (for instance in Tacitus, *Hist. Roman* II, 24: "Pecuniae belli civilis nervi sunt"), which is emphasized by his use of the Latinism "pecunes," Friar John's behavior is seen in the light of the exemplary, namely of Roman virtue, and the specific case receives the stamp of general validity. Parodistic distortion of the meaning of classical quotations occurs only by exception, and it should be noted that the poet does not put these distorted quotations into the mouths of the noble figures in his novel, but attributes them to the impudent scoundrel Panurge. The latter, appealing to the authority of Seneca's verse "Nemo tam divos habuit faventes/crastinum ut possit sibi pollicere" ("No one can be sure enough of divine favor/ To know that he will live until the next day," *Thyestes* 619), seeks to justify his measureless extravagance as an emanation of the cardinal virtue *prudentia*. No less parodistically, he claims *justitia* as a justification for his squandering by interpreting Cato's "Patrem familias vendacem, non emacem esse oportet" ("It behooves a family man to be a seller rather than an avid buyer," *De Agricultura* II, 55, 7) to mean "The father of a family must be a perpetual seller" (II, 2).

In general, however, it can be said that a relationship of simple consonance exists between the spirit in which Rabelais quotes and the original sense of the quotation. The effect of the classical quotation is emphasized even more strongly when it serves, at the conclusion of a chapter or even of a series of chapters, to sum up in a valid formula the sense of what has been narrated. Thus the satire on the judicial system, which embraces several chapters through part of the Third Book, closes with an utterance from Cato which once again highlights the whole unreliability and uncertainty of the exercise of justice: the law courts ought to be paved with caltrops (II, 44; after Pliny, *Hist. Nat.* XIX: "Catonis Censorii, quo aternendum quoque forum muricibus censuerat"). A similar effect is achieved by the quotation from Aesop in III, 15, which sums up in one impressive image the sense of a whole series of chapters. Of still more general validity, however, is the quotation from Plato's *Republic* (473D) at the close of I, 45. After Grangousier has informed the foolish pilgrims of the senselessness of their superstition and evangelically given them a tenable precept for life, it is stated in conclusion: "Commonwealths will be happy only when rulers philosophize or philosophers rule." The quotation has the effect of a resounding pedal tone because, transcending all specific cases, it embraces and defines the meaning of the figures of Grangousier, Gargantua, and Pantagruel: they represent precisely the embodiment of the Renaissance ideal, sage and ruler in one!

So it comes as no surprise to us that Rabelais refers by quotation to Plato in the prologue of the First Book, where he hints at the deeper meaning of his narrative and the difference between its exoteric and its esoteric meaning. The point of departure is the well-known passage in the *Symposium* (215A) where Alcibiades compares the ridiculous and ugly external appearance of Socrates to the figurines known as Sileni. If one takes apart the two sections of the statuette, one finds the image of a god inside. In Rabelais it is not the sense but the specific image that is slightly distorted when he compares these Sileni to apothecary jars that are decorated on the outside with frivolous scenes but which contain precious herbs within. This comparison serves to stress the esoteric significance of his own work. If one looks only at the outer covering ("l'ensigne exteriore"), one finds only mockery and jest ("derision et gaudisserie"). As far as the concealed content is concerned, however, "the topics treated are not so foolish as the title suggested at first hand." He then combines the Silenus image with a

36

statement from Plato's *Republic* (376B) to the effect that
dogs are by nature truly philosophical. For, Rabelais con-
tinues in an independent extension of the thought, the dog
sucks the marrow, which alone matters, from the marrow-
bone (*os medullare*). Similarly, the reader should "break
the bone of my symbols to suck out the marrow of
my meaning," or less metaphorically: he should find the
"doctrine plus absconce" which will reveal "the deepest
mysteries, the most agonizing problems of our religion,
our body politic, our economic life." Lefranc takes Rabelais'
distinction between exoteric and esoteric and his image of
the "os médullaire" in this prologue as the starting point
for his basic thesis, so consequential for all Rabelais schol-
arship, of Rabelais' anti-Christian, deistic-naturalistic
"esoteric doctrine."[13] His thesis as such is not at issue here,[14]
but its point of departure again illustrates quite clearly
what an important role the classical quotation plays in the
network of meaning of Rabelais' work. Rabelais uses it for
nothing less than the designation of the esoteric-exoteric
basis of his work altogether, and the literary quotation thus
has actually a key function as an element of meaning.

Since the quotation borrowed from Greco-Roman an-
tiquity possesses in general for Rabelais the value and dig-
nity of the purely exemplary, the parodistic reshaping of
these sources and the distortion of their sense is generally
prohibited. His sense of play could find here only a very
limited area of freedom. The situation is completely differ-
ent with quotations from the Christian realm, from the Bible
and other sacred literature. Here the parodistic element
plays a very great role. It is difficult to determine how this
parodistic element ought to be interpreted "ideologically."
Ever since Lefranc's sensational introduction to the third
volume of his critical Rabelais edition (1922), the relation-
ship of our writer to Christianity has been the great point

[13] Introduction to Vol. 3 of Lefranc, *op.cit.*, pp. xlff.
[14] Cf. the brief summary in J. Plattard, *Le vie et l'oeuvre de Fran-
çois Rabelais* (Paris, 1939), Chap. 3 ("Interprétations diverses de
l'oeuvre de Rabelais"), pp. 70ff., 131f.

of debate that has kept Rabelais scholarship in motion. Lefranc advocated the thesis that Rabelais in his novel was promulgating a skillfully disguised hermetic doctrine, which however was clearly enough recognizable for the initiates; its content was "la foi rationaliste," "la penseé indépendente." According to this theory Rabelais, consciously and resolutely emancipating himself from Christianity, was a deistic freethinker, a pupil of Lucian and Lucretius, and an adept of a radical movement whose adherents constituted a secret sodality. In this extreme form Lefranc's view did not make any headway. Perhaps its great merit consisted in the fact that it summoned up opposition.[15] Lucien Febvre supplied the most thorough refutation:[16] here the argument with Lefranc's thesis grew into one of the most profound and richest books in existence on the thought—and in particular on the religious views—of the sixteenth century. According to Febvre, Rabelais was a devout Christian with certain pronounced affinities to the evangelical movement, though he did not share its views in the most essential matters. Rather, he proclaimed a Christian humanism strongly reminiscent of Erasmus.

This shall suffice to indicate briefly the amplitude of standpoints represented in Rabelais scholarship; for it is not our job to take issue with them in more detail. It is obvious that any discussion of Rabelais' attitude toward religion and of his position in the conflict between Catholic tradition and Reformation must attribute a central and decisive significance to the examination of his references to articles of belief and his borrowings from the corpus of sacred writings. But because this whole question is of an ideological sort—what did the author "actually" mean and believe—it is not the narrative work of art as such that

---

[15] Cf. the circumspect treatment of the question by Plattard, and especially the sharp refutation by Etienne Gilson in "Rabelais Franciscain," *Les Idées et les Lettres* (Paris, 1932), pp. 197ff.

[16] Lucien Febvre, *Le problème de l'incroyance au XVIe siècle. La religion de Rabelais* (Paris, 1942). Febvre, to be sure, exaggerates Lefranc's opinion when he recapitulates it as follows: "Dès 1532, le père spirituel de Panurge était un ennemi du Christ, un athée militant" (p. 15).

stands in the focal point of observation: the work is considered interesting above all as the container of a philosophical content. This also has an effect on the treatment of quotations and on the discussion of their possibly parodistic nature. The question is not what they achieve as an element of his narrative art, but rather what they prove regarding the ideology of the author. It is possible, however, that certain matters interpreted as statements of opinion cannot be seen in their proper light until one examines them to determine whether and how they are conditioned by the inner exigencies of the narrative art as it is practiced here and by the author's narrative attitude, which is to a certain extent a priori; and until one determines whether these matters contribute to the realization of certain purely narrative possibilities. Thus it might be that by isolating the element of meaning one does not do justice to the meaning in that narrow sense: the "opinion" of the author. Then the question regarding the specific narrative form remains of far-reaching significance also for the interpretation of meaning.

This consideration is supported by the following observation. There is a clear (but, as far as I can see, scarcely heeded) discrepancy between the way in which Rabelais *literally* quotes the corpus of sacred writings and his *other* references to the contents of this corpus. The latter—general references to the Bible and especially to the Gospels— are rendered in a tone of genuine serious enthusiasm. Listen to the tone in which Pantagruel prays before the decisive battle with the giant werewolf: "Lord God, who hast always been my preserver and protector, behold the peril that now encompasses me." Continuing, he vows, "In Utopia and in all lands over which I may hold power and sway, I will cause Thy holy gospel to be purely, simply and entirely preached" (II, 29). The same pure earnestness is evident in Grangousier's prayer when he hears the report of Picrochole's aggression (I, 28), and especially in the oft-quoted strophe of the inscription above the gate of the abbey of Thélème (I, 54):

39

Here enter, all ye loyal scholars who expound
Novel interpretations of the Holy Writ.
Here is a fort and refuge; from this favored ground
You may confound the error that is elsewhere found,
You may found a profound new faith instead of it,
Sweeping away false teachings, bit by fallacious bit.
Come unto us and make your cogent meanings heard:
Destroy the foes of God and of his Holy Word.[17]

In the ordinary quotations, however, this serious tone is an
exception; the bulk of the material has to a greater or lesser
degree a parodistic touch. It is perhaps not too bold to sug-
gest that this discrepancy is in the last analysis not condi-
tioned by ideology but above all by aesthetic exigencies.
The humor of our writer is preeminently of a verbal sort:
it specifically refers to words and is catalyzed by words.
No wonder that it is precisely the firmly molded formulas
of the sacrosanct text which challenge the humoristic lan-
guage-virtuoso irresistibly to draw them into a turbulent
game of parodistic perversion of meaning, thereby unset-
tling their steadiness of meaning.

For the modern reader one of the most striking charac-
teristics of Rabelais' Bible quotations is surely their blas-
phemy, which is as frequent as it is crass. We can see from
his parody of Christ's last words from the Cross that he
does not hesitate to drag into the dust even those Bible pas-
sages that are most sacred to the Christian. In "The Pa-
laver of the Potulent" (I, 5) a voice can be made out in
the bacchantic euphoria of the drinking companions: "The
Saviour's words are on my lips: *Sitio*" ("I am thirsty," John
19:28). In similar fashion the last utterance of Christ,
"*Consummatum est*" ("It is finished," John 19:30), is put
into the mouth of the manic wastrel who has squandered
his entire fortune and even reduced his own house to ashes
(III, 2). Now it must be kept in mind, of course, that the
blasphemous impression depends largely on an illusion of
perspective and that such parody, being very widespread

[17] Further references in Febvre may be found on pp. 271ff.

at the time, was in all probability hardly felt to be objectionable.[18] This is explicitly proved for the two *Novissima Verba* just mentioned.[19] But one cannot get rid of the impression that the satirical sharpness of Rabelais' parody often goes far beyond what was customary in those days.[20] And this impression is strengthened the more we consider the context in which the quotations occur. In the difficult hour when Gargamelle is bringing Gargantua into the world, Grangousier consoles her with the words of Christ (John 16:21): "A woman in travail hath sorrow because her hour is come; but as soon as she is delivered of the child, she remembereth no more the anguish" (i, 6). At first glance the quotation seems merely to reflect the meaning of the situation, but the context reveals its parodistic character. In the mouth of Christ the comparison with the woman in labor refers to his grief at his own death and his joy at his resurrection; for Rabelais the future joy is sexual pleasure, as becomes evident with an obscene clarity from the passage directly following. Especially revealing is the unrestrained lamentation of the cowardly Panurge in the face of the threatened shipwreck in IV, 19 and IV, 21: "*Consummatum est*," "*Adieu, in manus*" (an abbreviated form of "in manus tuas, Domine, commando spiritum meum," Luke 23:46), and so forth. Here, too, one should keep the situation in mind. Naturally it is not Panurge himself who intends the parody. But the very fact that the coward is char-

---

[18] Concerning this theme generally, see Paul Lehmann, *Die Parodie im Mittelalter* (1922) and *Parodistische Texte* (published as an appendix to the preceding work, 1923).

[19] Cf. the notes in Lefranc, *op.cit.*, Vol. 1, p. 61; and Vol. 5, p. 41.

[20] J. Plattard's thorough study, "L'écriture sainte et la littérature scripturaire dans l'oeuvre de Rabelais," *Revue des Études Rabelaisiennes*, Vol. 8, pp. 257ff., has the thesis that Rabelais' *applications bouffonnes* of the sacred texts remain within the limits of what was customary at the time and that they did not constitute an affront in the eyes of the Sorbonne. "Ces familiarités qui nous paraissent choquantes étaient d'usage dans le monde des clercs" (p. 292). Febvre agrees with this (*op.cit.*, p. 161). But the examples adduced by Plattard and Febvre for "plaisanteries" that were ostensibly widespread among the clergy and laymen of the time are far more innocuous and moderate than much in Rabelais.

acterized by his mouthing of the words of Christ in all seriousness while, on the other hand, the brave stoicism of Friar John is expressed in boorish language, represents basically a more malicious debasement of the Biblical expression than many a more obvious *application bouffonne*!

At one point Rabelais' Bible quotations are of heavier caliber, inasmuch as they permit him to deal mockingly with the relationship of reason and faith and thus with the very essence of the Christian religion. In I, 6, the marvelous birth of Gargantua is depicted with juicy vividness— *naturalia non turpia*. The excessive gluttony of the mother accounts for the fact that the birth cannot take place in a normal way; instead "the cotyledons of the placenta of her matrix were enlarged. The child, leaping through the breech and entering the hollow vein, ascended through her diaphragm to a point above her shoulders. Here the vein divides into two; the child accordingly worked his way in a sinistral direction, to issue, finally, through the left ear." And then the author asks why we should hesitate to believe this strange nativity.

> Does not Solomon say in *Proverbs* Fourteen: "*Innocens credit omni verbo*, the innocent believeth every word," and does not St. Paul (I *Corinthians*, 13) declare: "*Charitas omnia credit*, Charity believeth all."
>
> Why should you not believe what I tell you? Because, you reply, there is no evidence. And I reply in turn that for this very reason you should believe with perfect faith. For the gentlemen of the Sorbonne say that faith is the argument of non-evident truths.

In the edition of 1542 this passage was deleted. We surely do not need to believe, as Lefranc did, that the miraculous birth of Gargantua is direct persiflage on the birth of Christ. And when Febvre objects that Christ, after all, did not come to the world through his mother's left ear, we have to agree with him. But if we relate the story to the "scholarly" theological digression, then we can not avoid interpreting it as a conscious travesty of the Christian faith in miracles as such. And how slyly Rabelais has constructed his jesting pseudo-argumentation, relating his quotations to one another with a stealthy perversion of their meaning! For Solomon (Proverbs 14:15), *innocens* means the same as "foolish," the opposite of *astutus*: "Innocens credit omni verbo: astutus considerat gressus suos" ("The simple believeth every word; but the prudent man looketh well to his going"). Rabelais, however, attributes to the word the other meaning of "innocent" (related to the immediately preceding passage in his work: "an honest and sensible man always believes what he is told and what he finds written"), whereby it becomes a parallel to the Pauline "Charitas omnia credit" (I Corinthians 13:7). No less crafty is the shift of meaning in the formula "foy est argument des choses de nulle apparence," which goes back to Hebrews 11:1: "Fides est substantia rerum sperandarum, argumentum non apparentium" ("Now faith is the substance of things hoped for, the evidence of things not seen"). There *non apparens* means "unseen," "not appearing"; but Gargantua's strange birth, in the eyes of doubters, has *nulle apparence*, that is to say, no probability.[21]

The whole passage is certainly a rather indigestible chunk for those who rise to the defense of Rabelais' orthodoxy. Even Febvre, in his highly learned excursus,[22] does not succeed in whitewashing his hero. Is it to be taken as additional proof for Lefranc's freethinker thesis? Perhaps not, if one recalls only for a moment that it is, first and last, a poet who is here giving free rein to his parodistic genius. I have no desire to attempt any lame justifications. But should it not be permissible for parody also to be a form of specifically *poetic* activity? And do we do justice to the poet if we accept his parodistic caprioles at face value ideologically, interpreting them as a valid expression of opinion that holds true even outside this specifically narrative context? In order to clarify this important point we

---

[21] Cf. Plattard's proof in *Revue des Études Rabelaisiennes*, Vol. 8, pp. 275ff.

[22] *Ibid.*, pp. 171ff.

must now pose the question more resolutely than before: What is the *structural* contribution of the quotation to the narrative whole? What does it *accomplish* as an element of humoristic form? Let us try therefore to illustrate the formal wealth of this parodistic quoting. The charm of parody, one might say in general, is based on a sharpened contrast between the original sense of the quotation and the meaning newly attributed to it by the act of quoting. If we cling to this as a guiding point of view, then the contrast can be shaded in a series of gradations, according to its constitutive elements.

The gentlest form of contrast is found in the tension which results when the quoted words as such are used in the original sense but, through their *context*, collide with meanings of an opposite sort and are themselves dragged over into a contrary sense. This collision can be primarily in form or in meaning. The following passages illustrate both. After Gargantua has taken away the great bells of Notre Dame in order to hang them around the neck of his giant mare, the theological faculty of the Sorbonne sends Master Janotus de Bragmardo to demand the return of the bells. He bases his address upon Christ's well-known saying (Luke 20:25): *"Reddite que sunt Cesaris Cesare, et que sunt Dei Deo. Ibi jacet lepus"* (I, 19). One must concede that the master has used great skill to find his saying; it applies with the most precise correspondence of meaning to the given situation. But what a parodistic effect it has, nevertheless, because of its collision with the macaronic expression "Ibi jacet lepus!" ("That's where the hare lies!" "There's the rub!"). The essential thing here is the glaring discrepancy between levels of style. More strongly colored by the meaning is the collision between the sacred expression and the cruder earthiness in Friar John's answer to Panurge's constant deliberations about marriage. Naturally he ought to get married: "How would you feel on the day of judgment—*dum venerit judicare?* when He cometh to judge—if He found you with the genitals filled to the stopcock" (III, 26; a reminiscence of Psalm 96:13,

44

"Quoniam venit judicare terram," and of the Office of the Dead in the liturgy).[23] Yet here, too, the original sense of the quotation is simply preserved, and the parodistic effect is based on the contrast between text and context.

If we go one step further, the quoted words themselves are given a meaning that is conditioned by the new context and deviates from their original meaning. When Panurge, with that Eulenspiegel-like cruelty which in those days obviously seemed like harmless fun, has allowed the merchant and his sheep to drown in the ocean (IV, 8), Friar John speaks the closing words: "It is written: *Mihi vindictam, et caetera.* Holy stuff, that, breviary matter!" (Romans 12:19). The antecedent of the personal pronoun is no longer God but Panurge. This sense-perverting use of the *matiere de breviaire* has the structure of the monastic jokes that were apparently still quite common in those days. We also sense the monastery in the homely meaning attached to the psalm verse "Beati immaculati in via" (Psalm 118:1): "Blessed are they who do not defile themselves when they visit the kitchen" (IV, 10; this too is spoken by Friar John). It is clear, moreover, that the parodistic use of Christ's last words, mentioned above, belongs in this category.

The freedom in using quoted material increases considerably when not just the content but even the form of the words and sentences is implicated. Only at this point can Rabelais' verbal impulse to play develop fully. From the language itself new substances are created that have a remarkably iridescent relationship to extra-linguistic reality. As an abortion of language they have their most immediate reality within the realm of the language itself. More an abortion than a birth: language prostitutes itself and the result is a rabble of verbal cobolds and changelings. What is produced when a sentence of the Apostle Paul ("Multi . . . quorum deus venter est," Philippians 3:18) and the words of the Credo ("Patrem omnipotentem") are coupled? A race of giants with bellies like barrels is born, of whom it is written: *"Ventrem omnipotentem"* (II, 1). This sort of

[23] Cf. Lefranc, *op.cit.*, Vol. 5, p. 206.

patchwork can also invalidate normal syntactical links. From an exhortation of the Lord ("Crescite, et multiplicamini," Genesis 1:22) and a sentence fragment ("nos qui vivimus," II Corinthians 4:11), Friar John brews his suggestion "*Crescite, nos qui vivimus, multiplicamini*" (II, 26). Even more vivid: Psalm 123 begins, "Ad te levavi oculos meos." The first three words are taken out of the sentence, their original object is suppressed, and with an obscene imputation of meaning they become the subject of the syntactically "impossible" monstrosity "*Ad formam nasi cognoscitur ad te levavi*" (I, 40), which is supposed to mean, in line with popular belief, that a strong nose implies something positive about the masculine virility of its possessor. This is the same shattering of the linguistic unit that also occurs frequently in such "para-etymological" play as when, for instance, the name "Beauce" is "explained" as a segment extracted from the judgment "(je trouve) beau ce (pays)" (I, 16). And "Gargantua" is traced back to "Que grand tu as (le gousier)" ("What a grand gullet you have!" I, 7).[24]

The impact of the quotation on the narrative structure becomes most conspicuously clear when the quotation actually constitutes the starting point for narrative invention and supplies the germ of the episode.[25] An example for this exaggeratedly "literary" manner of invention, which begins with a coined expression, can be seen in the episode dealing with the letter that Pantagruel receives from a lady in Paris whom he has left without a word of farewell (II, 24). Apart from the address, the letter contains no writing, and nothing can be done to make letters appear on the white paper. But it does contain a ring set with a diamond and bearing as an inscription one of the *Novissima Verba* of

[24] Cf. Leo Spitzer, *Linguistics and Literary Theory* (Princeton, 1948), pp. 15ff., 49; and L. Sainéan, *La Langue de Rabelais*, Vol. 2, pp. 417ff.

[25] Plattard, *L'oeuvre de Rabelais*, pp. 276ff., makes a nice distinction between "érudition assimilée" and "érudition adaptée." Whereas the latter is nothing but supplementary ornamentation, the former supplies the idea, and in part even the subject matter, for certain episodes. Only the designation "assimilated" strikes me as less felicitous; the expression "productive" might be preferable.

Christ (Matthew 27:46): "Lamah sabacthani." Panurge finds the solution of the riddle. The diamond is a fake ("un diamant faux"). The lady's message therefore means: "Say, false lover (Dis, amant faux), why hast thou forsaken me?" The Biblical text combined with a rather rational play on words produces a rebus which in turn provides the basis for the invention of the episode.[26] It is therefore nothing but linguistics that gave birth to the forlorn lady of Paris.[27]

The same technique, much more elaborately executed, underlies the episode "How Gargantua Ate Six Pilgrims in a Salad" (I, 38). During a sumptuous meal Gargantua has an uneasy feeling in his stomach, and in order to soothe it he makes himself a salad of huge lettuce plants, unaware that six poor pilgrims have hidden themselves among the lettuce and are stuffed into his mouth with the salad. When he washes the snack down with a draught of red Burgundy, they are almost swept down into his stomach by the torrent. But a marvelous coincidence of circumstances frees them from their ordeal. Escaping, they must wade through the pond produced when Gargantua, to ease his discomfort, urinated. Thereupon they get caught in a wolf trap, but one of them knows how to tear up the snares, so that they get away without a scratch. Up to this point one would believe that the whole episode is nothing but an abortion of grotesque fantasy without any "literary" connection. But then there follows a long Bible quotation. One of the pilgrims consoles his companions with the assertion that David, in Psalm 123 (actually Psalm 124) had already prophesied their whole adventure:

Cum exergerent homines in nos, forte vivos deglutissent nos, then had they swallowed us up when their wrath was kindled against us (in other words, when we

---

[26] It is known that Arnaud de Villeneuve supplied the writer with the idea for the Hebrew inscription. Cf. Plattard, *L'oeuvre de Rabelais*, p. 276.

[27] Regarding the share of linguistic motives in the grotesque invention, see Leo Spitzer, *Die Wortbildung als stilistisches Mittel, exemplifiziert an Rabelais* (1910), pp. 58ff.

were eaten in salad with salt, oil and vinegar) . . . *cum irascaretur furore eorum in tuos forsitan aqua absorbuisset nos*, then the waters had overwhelmed us, the stream gone over our soul (that was when he took the deep draught of wine) . . . *forsitan pertransisset anima nostra aquam intolerabilem*, then the proud waters had gone over our soul (that was when he took the piss!) . . . *Benedictus Dominus qui non dedit in captionem dentibus eorum*, blessed be the Lord who hath not given us as a prey to their teeth (alas, the mandibulary nerve we struck!) . . . *Anima nostra sicut passer erepta est de laqueo venantium*, our soul is escaped as a bird out of the snare of the fowlers (when we fell into the trap!) . . . *laqueus contritus est a Fournillier et nos liberati sumus*, the snare is broken by Fournillier and we are escaped . . . *Adjutorium nostrum*, etc.; Our help is in the name of the Lord, etc.

Apart from the interruption for the "exegetical" interpolation, this is a literally precise and complete reproduction of the Vulgate text. Here, of course, the medieval practice of interpreting Bible passages as a prophecy of events in everyday life is held up to ridicule.[28] But the function of the quotation is not yet exhausted. Though it seems at first glance to be a dispensable afterthought, the psalm text, viewed clearly, is the primary fact from which the grotesque narrative has been retroactively constructed. Only in this way can it be explained why the prophecy agrees so precisely with the adventure. Because in this episode the narrative construction is so calculatedly precise or even contrived, it makes the freedom with which meaning is humorously distorted all the more emphatically visible. Characteristically, Rabelais imputes two new meanings to the single concept *aqua* (both the flood of wine and then the puddle of urine) although he saw, of course, that the double occurrence of this word is only a rhetorical repeti-

[28] See the note in Lefranc, *op.cit.*, p. 328, which cites pertinent passages.

tion. But this playful freedom does not affect the rational basis of the witty procedure practiced here.

It casts some light on this circumstance if we consult, for the sake of comparison, the episode "Geschichtsklitterung" in Fischart's German adaptation (Chapter 41). Fischart retains precisely the details of the plot, elaborating them even more fully. (His chapter is exactly twice as long as his source.) At the end, however, he does not quote the entire psalm, but abridges it selectively, whereby such an essential element as the double reference of *aqua* disappears; and he adds a digression of his own, spiced with jocular quotations, on the absurdity of such Bible exegeses. The specific characteristic of Rabelais' narrative, the precisely calculated "agreement" of the quoted Biblical text and the plot, is lost in the process. It should not be assumed that Fischart was not aware of it; rather, he probably regarded the rational precision of the correspondence as unsuitable to his style and thus intentionally destroyed it. However that may be, in the episode of the six pilgrims we have a story which is actually conceived from a Biblical quotation and whose structural uniqueness consists in the total dependence of the story upon the concluding quotation. In Sterne's *Tristram Shandy* we shall later encounter related devices, most probably inspired by Rabelais.

The same compositional principle is employed on a much greater scale in the Third Book, which was intentionally neglected in the treatment of classical quotations. In comparison with the first two books, the third has a unique narrative character. The adventure stories disappear completely, and in their place a "theoretical," "ideological" question constitutes the thematic center. Just at that time the "anti-feminist" *Amye de Court* by La Borderie (published in 1542) and its pro-feminist refutation *La Parfaite Amye* of Antoine Héroët (also of 1542) had acutely renewed the "querelle des femmes." The theme is not new: it is a question of the centuries-old conflict between the aristocratic, courtly veneration of woman (now

49

supported in the Renaissance by impulses of Platonic idealism) and the much more folksy contempt of women which was deeply rooted in medieval life.[29] This literary dispute stands in the background of the Third Book, and it is partially for this reason that the whole inventive procedure in this book, much more pronouncedly than in the preceding ones, has a specifically cultural, even bookish tone.[30] Hence it is particularly engrossing to consider how the epic narrator manages to contend in narrative fashion with this booklore; how he transmutes it into narrative. For the question is not answered by stating generally that Rabelais uses the occasion to make his contribution to the dispute, taking up an anti-feminist position. Let us first summarize how, in the Third Book, Rabelais fits the theoretical material into the epic framework of his work. At the end of the Second Book (II, 34), he provides a preview of the future continuation. The enumeration of the adventure stories to be expected is bombastic enough, and one can reasonably doubt whether this preview is to be taken in complete earnestness or to be read as boastful irony with no serious implications. The truth probably lies somewhere in between. At the beginning of this enumeration stands a promise closely related to the content of the Third Book: Panurge will get married and, in the first month of his marriage, will become a cuckold. Perhaps Rabelais really had such a continuation in mind. But he took his time with its realization. For throughout the entire Third Book the big question is still simply *whether* Panurge wants to get married or not, and the oracle of the *Dive Bouteille*, which is supposed to answer this question once and for all, has not even been cited at the end of all the sea adventures of the Fourth Book. This oracle is not consulted until the end of the Fifth Book. With some justification, therefore, one can regard the entire Third and Fourth books as a colossal re-

[29] For the history of the dispute cf. esp. Lefranc's introduction to Vol. 5 of his edition, and Lote, *op.cit.*, pp. 140ff.

[30] Plattard, in *L'oeuvre de Rabelais*, finds a felicitous formulation: "C'est à son érudition qu'il demande de nouveaux thèmes à développer" (p. 277).

tardation. In any case, it is certain that the plot as such does not move a single step forward in the Third Book. Instead, a question is debated. But how is it debated? How does the discussion achieve a genuinely epic substance despite all lack of a consistent plot?

In this connection it is revealing to take a look at two of Rabelais' main sources and to see how he used them. One is a work of satiric-moral content, the *Sylvae nuptiales libri sex* of the jurist Jean de Nevizan (1521). The material, for the main part ribaldly lascivious tales of love and marriage, is organized in an academically irreproachable manner. The first two books, under the title "Non est nubendum," treat all arguments speaking against marriage, while the two following ones advance arguments for marriage under the heading "Est nubendum." The other source, "Le Songe du Pantagruel" by François Habert (1542), is a verse narrative based on the first two books of Rabelais' work; it subsequently helped to direct the development of Rabelais' continuation. In Habert's poem, Pantagruel dreams that he asks his table companions at a banquet to reveal to him the great truth that he strives to discover. Making note of their answers, he decides the following night to interrogate his father Gargantua. The latter appears to him in a dream and earnestly implores him to get married.

Now the manner in which Rabelais has used this suggestion is a classic example of epic assimilation. At the very beginning (that is, in the ninth chapter; the preceding ones have a different content), the skeletal contrast of "est nubendum" and "non est nubendum" is delightfully transposed into narrative. Panurge informs Pantagruel of his decision to wed. But he is obviously not sure of himself, for at the same time he asks Pantagruel for his opinion. Of course you should get married, says Pantagruel; that is the best advice I can give you.—But what if it were better to remain a bachelor?—Then don't get married!—But to be alone my whole life long? It is not written in vain: *Vae soli!* —Then get married!—But one thing gives me pause: my

51

future wife might make me a cuckold!—Then don't get married! and so forth.[31] The conversation ends without any conclusions whatsoever, but now Pantagruel reveals his resourceful genius. Again and again he comes up with new authorities to be consulted by Panurge, which should bring about a decision regarding his burning problem. But although no fewer than fifteen "consultations" are carried out, each even wilder than the preceding one, all is in vain, for they all fail as a result of the fact that the pronouncements are open to various interpretations. Rabelais uses his enormous polyhistorical knowledge to intermingle, from one consultation to the next, the whole cultural store of his age—philology and theology, medicine and law, the natural and occult sciences—in a veritable Witches' Sabbath of pedantry.

Let us restrict ourselves to the first consultation that Pantagruel urges upon his friend, namely the questioning of the Virgilian book oracle (Chapters 10-12), which, as we shall see, also supplies a sort of directive for the following consultations. After the procedure has first been briefly outlined in the tenth chapter—the works of Virgil are opened three times at random, and it is agreed in advance that such and such a verse on the page in question shall be considered as an oracular pronouncement—Pantagruel enumerates in detail all persons known to him who made use of the book oracle (Homer or Virgil) in antiquity: Socrates, Opilius Macrimus, Brutus, Alexander Severus, Emperor Hadrian, and so forth. One almost believes that the whole production is nothing but an idle display of pedantry. But its function consists in its contrastive effect. For although the book oracle was generally meaningful in the cases known to antiquity, it becomes absolutely meaningless in Panurge's hands (Chapter 12). As the first oracular dictum he finds the concluding lines of the famous Fourth Eclogue: "Nec deus hunc mensa, dea nec dignata cubili est" ("No god deemed him worthy of his table, nor goddess of her

[31] This abbreviated recapitulation is taken from H. Hatzfeld, *François Rabelais* (1923), p. 91.

bed"). Very impropitious, says Pantagruel on the basis of learned hermeneutics: Panurge's wife will be a lecherous wench and will make a cuckold of him. On the contrary, replies Pantagruel with no less crafty reasoning: the oracle says that she will be demure, chaste, and faithful. In the same way the two following sayings—"Membra quatit, gelidusque coit formidine sanguis" ("My limbs tremble, and chilled with fear my blood curdles," *Aeneid* II, 30) and "Foemineo praedae et spoliorum ardebat amore" ("She was ablaze with a womanly love of booty and spoils," *Aeneid* XI, 782)—however catastrophic they may sound, result in no decision, for here too Panurge's sophistry is capable of enticing from the rough shell the sweet kernel of his propitious interpretation.

Though it is generally true that Rabelais, in quoting, is dependent on secondary sources[32]—the third of the Virgilian oracular sayings actually can be found in the works of many anti-feminist writers, e.g., in Tiraquaeus' *De legibus connubialibus*, to which Rabelais frequently owes tribute—the chapter on the *Sors Virgilianes* still shows clearly that this dependence impedes in no way the freedom of the narrator. With an impressive artistic sense, he selected his quotations with an eye to revealing in them and through them the humoristic motif of ambiguous interpretation, which also dominates the following chapters. In another sense, too, the three quotations prepare what follows, for Pantagruel derives from them the conviction that Panurge will be "deceived, beaten and robbed" by his wife. (The three qualifications naturally correspond precisely to the three Virgil quotations and keep the same order of succession.) And this formula becomes a leitmotific *ceterum censeo* inasmuch as it repeatedly concludes the debates about the various consultations as a sort of pedal note. Whereas in other cases (most conspicuously in the chapter

[32] Cf. Plattard, *L'oeuvre de Rabelais*, p. 261: "Mais la plupart des citations textuelles de l'Iliade, de l'Odyssée et de l'Enéide que nous trouvons dans son livre ont été empruntées à des ouvrages d'érudition anciens ou modernes. . . . Elles ne sont point des indices d'un commerce intime de Rabelais avec les poètes épiques anciens."

about the six pilgrims mentioned above) the narrative construction beginning with the quotation is restricted to the chapter in question, the structural effect of the three Virgil quotations in III, 12 extends beyond the limits of the chapter to a long series of chapters comprising the essential content of the Third Book.

Let us try to summarize the results of this study. In Rabelais' work the quotation does not have merely a material character. It serves to enrich the meaning and, going beyond that, constitutes an important structural element. In the shaping of the narrative, two opposing forces become evident. At times an irrational play of fantasy predominates, bestowing upon the quotation, by distorting its meaning, previously unsuspected new implications. At other times it is a rational consideration which makes of the quotation an auxiliary device or even the basic element of a calculatedly precise narrative construction. It was our concern to show that the narrator in both cases subjugates the quotation in sovereign freedom to his specifically narrative purposes, and to indicate by what means he does so.

CHAPTER III

Miguel de Cervantes

DON QUIXOTE

CERVANTES' *Don Quixote*[1] matches Rabelais' novel in its inexhaustible wealth of invention and diversity in execution. The great difference—one might even say Cervantes' great advance beyond Rabelais—lies in the fact that *Don Quixote*, despite all its diversity, is at the same time an impressively unified work and, despite all its elaborate playfulness, simple in the best sense of the word. *Simplex sigillum veri*: Critics have rightfully praised the natural consistency as well as the vigorous and logical straightforwardness with which the entire narrative invention proceeds from the simple initial fact that the Hidalgo loses his head while reading his involved courtly romances. This straightforward consistency is of course somehow related to the unity of the meaning embodied in the figure of the Hidalgo and his squire, who complement each other in their polar-

---

[1] The passages from *Don Quixote* are quoted by page number from Ozell's revision of the translation of Peter Motteux (Modern Library edition). The author is himself unfortunately not sufficiently at home in Spanish to be able to read *Don Quixote* in the original. To his delight and reassurance he found a well-informed reader in Dr. Mia I. Gerhardt, author of the excellent study *Don Quijote, La vie et les livres*, Mededelingen der Koninklijke Nederlandse Akademie van Wetenschappen, Afdeling Letterkunde, Nieuwe Reeks, deel 18, Nr. 2 (Amsterdam, 1955), who criticized and approved this chapter. To the titles of secondary works cited in the notes should be added that of the highly stimulating study by Leo Spitzer, "Linguistic Perspectivism in the Don Quijote," *Linguistics and Literary History* (1948), pp. 41-73. Cf. also the study by Käte Hamburger, "Don Quijote und die Struktur des epischen Humors," *Festgabe für Eduard Berend* (1959), pp. 191-209, which is related both thematically and methodologically to my undertaking, but which became accessible to me only after I had completed the manuscript.

ity. This meaning, however, is not only unified but also multilayered. Here we must distinguish between conscious ideology and *meaning* in a broader sense. The former is aggressively satirical and time-bound inasmuch as it is directed against a specific phenomenon of the times; it lampoons the hollow mendacity of the courtly romances which, in the wake of the *Amadis* of Garcí Ordóñez de Montalvo (1508), had held sway for a century. This ideology is unambiguous and constant from beginning to end: from the prologue to the last chapter, where Don Quixote, on his deathbed, becomes aware of his erroneous fixation and abjures the false ideals of the romances.[2] This satirical tendentiousness, however, is only superficial; on a deeper level it in reality produces something that can be designated roughly as the eternal conflict between "idealism" and "materialism." As far as this deeper level is concerned, one can speak less affirmatively of an unambiguous attitude in the author. From the first to the second part of *Don Quixote*, a subtle but incessant shift of perspective takes place. It goes hand in hand with the clearly growing personal commitment of the writer to the nature and destiny of the Hidalgo as well as of his squire. Don Quixote's superior and inwardly victorious purity of heart becomes ever more strongly apparent; similarly, the figure of Sancho assumes clearer delineations, becoming more human and wiser. Behind the satiric gaze a milder humoristic view emerges—a kindly attitude of live-and-let-live in the face of the irreconcilable antinomies of existence and human

---

[2] Cervantes' opinion of and attitude toward the courtly romances is of a complex nature. This complexity is instructively treated by Salvador de Madariaga in *Don Quixote. An Introductory Essay in Psychology* (2nd ed.; Oxford, 1948), pp. 11-37: "Cervantes and Chivalry Books." Especially fruitful is the distinction between Cervantes' literary criticism and his creative artistry. I am not convinced, to be sure, by its thesis that the battle against courtly romances was from the very beginning at most an unimportant secondary motif and even that "Cervantes' first idea must have been that of writing a model Chivalry Book" (p. 37). In particular I fail to understand how the author is able to detect a clear praise of the courtly romances in the—in my opinion—totally unambiguous diatribe of the curate against courtly romances (Bk. I, Chap. 6).

values that obtain even in the imaginary realm of the purely abstruse. But it never comes to a radical rupture between satire and humor. The literary satire does not revolve hermetically in itself, as is so often the case in romantic literary satire, for instance. It spreads out organically of its own accord to embrace all that is human. For the relationship of man's everyday reality to the imaginary world of his books is both a literary *and* an eminently existential problem.

The great miracle of this novel, however, is not the depth of its meaning in itself (even if such a thing existed), but the meaning *in* its realization as an artistic form. How is that basic antithesis of humor between the finite and the infinite, between realism and idealism, transmuted into epic form? The humoristic manner of narration is subjective. The author is present in the work as the leader of a game that the reader plays and imitates. At the same time the author stands above his work with sovereign detachment, committed and indifferent alike, bending down to the world of his own creation like the puppeteer over the marionette stage. This all holds true, it should be emphasized again, if we are willing to take the concept "play" (*Spiel*) in the lofty and comprehensive sense bestowed upon it by the aesthetics of the age of Goethe—above all by Goethe and Schiller themselves—and expressed in Goethe's formulation in his essay "Der Sammler und die Seinigen": "True art can originate only from an intimate union of seriousness and play." Play is no less "serious" than seriousness, and above all it is no less existentially valid.

Now what are the elements, the pieces with which the game is played? It is not only, and perhaps not even primarily, through such pragmatic narrative contents as persons and events that the narrative is realized, but above all through the literary *forms*. The available literary styles and their individual stylistic forms—and this is what strikes us as astonishingly new about this novel—become, so to speak, part of the "subject matter" of the poetic work. And in their capacity as subject matter they are juxtaposed in unsuspected new relationships of form. The style of *Don Quixote* is thus to a certain extent a style magnified to the second power. The forms themselves, as it were, become dramatis personae: they come into conflict, bump into one another, are reconciled, and reflect one another reciprocally. This is possible, of course, only insofar as the poet maintains an attitude of free detachment with regard to these forms. And this attitude in turn is possible only because he has lost his absolute faith in them. If here the fashionable and traditional forms of Renaissance poetry are "parodied," it means that they are no longer a vehicle to which the poet confidently entrusts himself, but rather the passengers whom he, the driver of his own vehicle, causes to climb on and off at will. They are subservient elements under the domination of a will which makes of its own subjectivity the bearer of a new, more complicated, and more comprehensive form. Naturally these forms are debased in the very process of appropriation. The reader becomes aware that they all have a bookish character and, tied down to the paper as they are, no validity in real life.

Even in the prologue this transposition gets under way, and the reader is impelled to participate in carrying it out. The ceremonious scholarly form "Prologue," sanctified by tradition and fashion, itself becomes by an ironic reversal the content of the prologue and is made the object of a sublime ridicule. The author makes the reader a witness of his ostensible perplexity as he writes his prologue. He would have preferred, he avers, to offer his novel to the public "as naked as it was born, without the Addition of a Preface, or the numberless Trumpery of commendatory Sonnets, Epigrams, and other Poems that usually usher in the conceptions of authors: For I dare boldly say, that tho' I bestow'd some Time in writing the Book, yet it cost me not half so much Labour as this very Preface." For our theme it is important to note how the ironic *testimonium paupertatis*, prepared in this manner, particularly affects the use of scholarly or pseudo-scholarly quoting. His narrative, so he reproaches himself, is as "dry and insipid" as a weed,

> ... wanting good Language as well as Invention, barren of Conceits or pointed Wit, and without either Quotations in the Margin, or Annotations at the End, which other Books, tho' never so fabulous and profane, have to set 'em off. Other Authors can pass upon the Publick, by stuffing their books from Aristotle, Plato, and the whole Company of ancient Philosophers; thus amusing their Readers into a great Opinion of their prodigious Reading. (p. xx)

But fortunately, succor appears in his moment of distress. A friend instructs him how to insert, on occasions both appropriate and inappropriate, the well-known *loci communes* from the literature of classical antiquity and the Bible. Moreover, tradition requires that he should append an alphabetical index of quoted authors, and he should feel free to appropriate this index from any book he chooses. After all, not a soul will check up on him and notice the deception.

It is clear that the device of pedantic quoting, which in countless works of Renaissance and Baroque poetry belongs to the reverently venerated set of decorative literary forms, has become meaningless for the author of *Don Quixote*. It has been debased to the function of a piece in a puzzle of literary fictions, along with—their range can only be briefly indicated here—the panegyric dedicatory poems at the conclusion of the prologue which are attributed to famous figures from the *Amadis* cycle and even to Rosinante; the frequent references to the ostensible Arabic "source" *Cid Hamet Benengeli*; and, most delightful of all, the use of two existing books (namely, the first part of *Don Quixote*, which appeared in 1605, and the "false" continuation, in 1614, by Avellaneda of Tordesilles) as pragmatic elements of motivation in the second part of the novel that appeared in 1615. Several adventures in the second part grow out of the literary fame enjoyed by Don Quixote and Sancho Panza thanks to "their" romance, that is to say the published first part. Through this collision of the empirical book and the imaginative world within the book, the fictive quality of the literary imagination is not lessened, but on the contrary vigorously underscored.[3]

It is demonstrated once and for all, then, that the literary quotation is for the author of *Don Quixote* far more than a mere ornament attached to or imposed upon his novel with no organic connection. We shall see that he finds, rather, a much more artful possibility of exploiting the quotation, one which adapts itself organically to the overall style of the novel and contributes essentially to its structure. To make this evident, let us begin with the fundamental stylistic fact of this novel: the tension between two levels of style, the "lofty" and the "lowly," and the constant antithetical play among the various stylistic elements proper to these levels. From a genetic point of view, of course, this contrast consists by no means only of a simple opposition. It embraces the most varied shadings of influence from the entire Spanish literature of the day— from the realism of the picaresque novel to the idealistic sublimity of the Arcadian novel and the strident bombast of the courtly romances. To these are joined no less disparate elements from classical literature and Italian Renaissance poetry.[4] But from a structural point of view this whole variety can be reduced to the simple contrast of high and low or, in other words, of pompous and simple. Yet these two styles are not equal partners. In the prologue

---

[3] Thomas Mann expressed his delight with the "epic wit," the "romantic vexation," and "ironic magic" of this narrative motif in "Meerfahrt mit Don Quijote," *Adel des Geistes* (Stockholm, 1945), pp. 621f.

[4] Cf. in this connection the penetrating analysis by Helmut Hatzfeld, *Don Quijote als Wortkunstwerk* (1927), esp. pp. 1ff. and pp. 222ff., as well as the same author's summary in the following study, in the series edited by Oskar Walzel, *Handbuch der Literaturwissenschaft*: Viktor Klemperer, Helmut Hatzfeld, and Fritz Neubert, *Die romanischen Literaturen von der Renaissance bis zur französischen Revolution* (1924), pp. 175ff.

the simple style is clearly represented, through the mouth of that "friend," as the true one that best serves the purpose of narrative:

> And since this Writing of your's aims at no more than to destroy the Authority and Acceptance the Books of Chivalry have had in the World, and among the Vulgar, you have no need to go begging Sentences of Philosophers, Passages out of Holy Writ, Poetical Fables, Rhetorical Orations, or Miracles of Saints. Do but take care to express your self in a plain, easy Manner, in well-chosen, significant, and decent Terms, and to give an harmonious and pleasing Turn to your Periods: Study to explain your Thoughts, and set them in the truest Light, labouring, as much as possible, not to leave 'em dark nor intricate, but clear and intelligible. (p. xxiv)

The simple style is the one with which the poet feels at home; in the high style he generally speaks, as it were, with a borrowed voice. Naturally one should not oversimplify to the point of implying that Cervantes was a genuine "opponent" of the high style. This would not agree with the obvious pleasure with which he composes such rhetorical models as Don Quixote's speeches on the Golden Age (p. 8), and on weapons and the sciences (pp. 327-30). It must be stressed, however, that in the contextual and formal texture of this novel the statements in high style represent a world devoid of meaning in which one no longer believes. This explains the paradox that the same author who works out the speech to the Golden Age as a proud sample of his rhetorical ability immediately thereafter characterizes it as "a speech which might very well have been omitted" and as "pointless words." Furthermore, in the high style it is not difficult to distinguish between a relatively straightforward and a bombastic type; the writer regards the latter in a completely negative light. Early in the exposition of the novel it is said:

> But among them all, none pleas'd him like the Works of

the famous Feliciano de Sylva; for the clearness of his Prose, and those intricate Expressions with which 'tis interlac'd, seem'd to him so many Pearls of Eloquence, especially when he came to read the Challenges, and the amorous Addresses, many of them in this extraordinary Stile. "The Reason of your unreasonable Usage of my Reason, does so enfeeble my Reason, that I have Reason to expostulate with your Beauty": And this, "The sublime Heavens, which with your Divinity divinely fortify you with the Stars, and fix you the Deserver of the Desert that is deserv'd by your Grandeur." These and such like Expressions, strangely puzzled the poor Gentleman's Understanding, while he was breaking his Brain to unravel their Meaning, which Aristotle himself could never have found, though he should have been rais'd from the Dead for that very Purpose. (p. 2)

The stylistic parody with its empty display of rhetorical splendors—hyperbole, polyptoton, *annominatio,* and so forth—lets the reader conclude by the principle of contraries what is meant in the prologue by "significant" and "decent" words.

The use of borrowed language, expressly satirical and with index finger raised in admonition, is at this point not yet very artful. It is adapted much more skillfully to the epic movement in the second chapter. During his departure, Don Quixote describes his setting out as he imagines that his future biographer will describe it:

"Scarce had the ruddy-colour'd Phoebus begun to spread the golden Tresses of his lovely Hair over the vast Surface of the earthly Globe, and scarce had those feather'd Poets of the Grove, the pretty painted Birds, tun'd their little Pipes, to sing their early Welcomes in soft melodious Strains to the beautiful Aurora, who having left her jealous Husband's Bed . . ." (p. 8)

and so forth. The fictitious description which activates the whole cosmic apparatus of classical mythology contrasts quite effectively with the realistic description of the actual departure. We see here—and in general this holds true with very few exceptions—that the narrator does not move on his own into the lofty tone, but bestows it upon his figures in the reproduction of their speech or thoughts, thereby giving a pragmatic justification for the change in style. This motivation of stylistic shifts is not a restricting fetter. On the contrary, it enables this stylistic device to be spread out in inexhaustible epic variety. In order to bring about an interplay of two levels of style, Cervantes invents delightful interlacing or reflecting figures. In one instance Sancho must recapitulate from memory his master's letter to Dulcinea, composed in the sublimely lofty epistolary style of the time, and in doing so he distorts it grotesquely (pp. 195-96, 204). On other occasions the author hands over his role of narrator for a moment to the fictive narrator of the "source," permitting the latter to speak in a superlative bombastic style that contrasts with the plaintiveness of the actual situation. A perfect example of this can be found in the adventure with the African lion, with its glaring mixture of genuine heroism and burlesque pitifulness. Still dripping with the curds that ooze down from his helmet, Don Quixote has taken a stand before the dangerous animal. At the moment of greatest tension the narrator interrupts himself:

Here the Author of this faithful History could not forbear breaking the Thread of his Narration, and, rais'd by Wonder to Rapture and Enthusiasm, makes the following Exclamation. O thou most magnanimous Hero! Brave and unutterably Bold Don Quixote de la Mancha! Thou Mirror and grand Exemplar of Valour! Thou Second, and New Don Emanuel de Leon, the late Glory and Honour of all Spanish Cavaliers; What Words, what Colours shall I use to express, to paint in equal Lines, this astonishing Deed of thine! What Language shall I employ to convince Posterity of the Truth of this thy more than human Enterprise! (p. 548)

The laudatory speech flows along at this stylistic level until the "real" narrator again takes over and reality sets in again with stark words. The king of the desert yawns, sticks out his tongue, and turns his rear to the challenger.

In this alternation between simple realism and ironically employed "high" speech, the literary quotation—and this means primarily the quotation in Don Quixote's own speeches—plays a key role. It is not dragged in but existentially determined as a natural emanation of his nature. For we should keep in mind that the whole existence of our hero is to a certain extent a quotation, a quoting *imitatio* of the form of existence "realized" (that is to say: imagined) in the courtly romances, and hence prescriptive for him. With reference to psychoanalysis Thomas Mann once brilliantly demonstrated to what a great extent "character" is only apparently a spontaneous uniqueness, since in reality it is determined by the *imitatio* of a prefigured model:

> His character is a mythical role which the actor just emerged from the depths to the light plays in the illusion that it is his own and unique; that he, as it were, has invented it all himself, with a dignity and security of which his supposed unique individuality in time and space is not the source, but rather which he creates out of his deeper consciousness in order that something which was once founded and legitimized shall again be represented and once more for good or ill, whether nobly or basely, in any case after its own kind conduct itself according to pattern.[5]

Men "quote" this given form, so to speak, in their lives and through their lives, thereby celebrating a mythic role.[6] Thomas Mann does not mention *Don Quixote* in this connection, although the Hidalgo might have been his prize witness. For in the "character" of Don Quixote the "quota-

---

[5] Thomas Mann, "Freud und die Zukunft," *Adel des Geistes*, pp. 592f. Translated by H. T. Lowe-Porter: "Freud and the Future," *Freud, Goethe, Wagner* (New York: Alfred Knopf, 1937).
[6] *Ibid.*, p. 596.

tive life"—as a form of life and, by analogy, as a form of the novel—has come more completely into its own than almost anywhere else.

The fifth chapter provides a good example. Badly beaten by a mule-driver, Don Quixote lies in misery on the edge of the road. "Don Quixote perceiving that he was not able to stir, resolv'd to have recourse to his usual Remedy, which was to bethink himself what Passage in his Books might afford him some Comfort" (p. 26). Because of the similarity of the situation, he identifies himself with the wounded Baldwin from the popular Romance of the Marquess de Mantua, and in a weak voice quotes the latter's lament of love:

"Alas, where are you, Lady dear,
    That for my Woe you do not moan?
You little know what ails me here,
    Or are to me disloyal grown!" (p. 27)

The stages of identification with the model can be clearly distinguished here. At first it is said only that Don Quixote finds the romance "as if made on purpose" for his circumcumstances: the relationship is still only analogical. But immediately afterwards he reaches a complete identification with the pattern, for when a sympathetic peasant wants to help him he mistakes him for "his" uncle from Mantua.[7] Nevertheless, this celebration of the mythic role contains an element of conscious choice. When the perplexed peasant raises a protest, Don Quixote answers:

"I know very well who I am; and what's more, I know that I may not only be the Persons I have named, but also the Twelve Peers of France, nay, and the Nine Worthies all in One; since my Achievements will outrival not only the famous Exploits which made any of 'em singly illustrious, but all their mighty Deeds accumulated together." (p. 28)

[7] The entire episode goes back to the parodistic work *L'Entremés de los Romances* (1957); cf. Paul Hazard, *Don Quichotte de Cervantes* (Paris, n.d. [*ca.* 1938]), pp. 119ff.

Since the awareness of "as though" does not disappear entirely, the identification is ruptured and the *imitatio* takes on an artistic quality. When Don Quixote decides to imitate the penance of Amadis in the desert and play the role of the desperate madman, Sancho asks him what his reason is, for his model certainly also had a reason. But Don Quixote gives him to understand that the *imitatio* is pure art for art's sake:

> "For, mark me, Sancho, for a Knight-Errant to run mad upon any just occasion, is neither strange nor meritorious; no, the Rarity is to run mad without a Cause, without the least Constraint or Necessity: There's a refin'd and exquisite Passion for you, Sancho! for thus my Mistress must needs have a vast Idea of my Love, since she may guess what I should perform in the Wet, if I do so much in the Dry." (p. 186)

Now whether Don Quixote draws his quotations from the courtly books or—what is much more frequently the case—from the national store of romances, they all embody the world of chivalric illusion with which plain reality collides head-on. Thus they contribute to form that stylistic high level which, as we indicated above, sets itself in contrast to the low level of the realistic style of speech. One might ask whether this simple and direct contrast of reality and illusion and of high and low speech is not all too self-evident to be put through its paces for well-nigh a thousand pages. But the fluctuation between the two never becomes monotonous, thanks to the epic variety with which it is transformed. This is achieved especially by the sophisticated adaptation and assimilation of quotations in their new context. The second chapter offers a splendid example. Don Quixote comes into a miserable inn, which he takes to be an elegant castle. The innkeeper cannot even supply him with a bed. But that does not matter. Don Quixote answers magnanimously with the beginning lines of the well-known romance, "La Constancia":

"For Arms are the only Things I value,
And Combat is my Bed of Repose."

The inn keeper obviously knows the romance also, for he is able to weave the next lines skillfully into his own answer:

"At this rate, Sir Knight,

Your Bed might be a Pavement
And your Rest a constant Waking;

you may then safely alight, and I dare assure you, you can hardly miss being kept awake all the year long in this house, much less one single Night." (p. 11)

It is obvious that the primordial antithesis between the heroic world of fantasy and miserable reality has here been reduced to the specific contrast between idealistic asceticism and hardship from indigence, with the humoristic twist that the sly innkeeper goes so far as to capitalize on the opportunity he can offer for not sleeping! In the same hostel Don Quixote is disarmed by two slovenly but good-natured whores. He mistakes them for ladies of nobility and, while he is being disarmed, recites the Romance of Lancelot, adapting it slightly to the situation at hand:

"There never was on Earth a Knight
So waited on by Ladies fair,
As once was he, Don Quixote hight,
When first he left his Village dear:
Damsels t'undress him ran with Speed,
And Princesses to dress his Steed." (p. 12)

The antithetical device of high and low is rather simple here—poor camp followers instead of the illusory noble ladies—but it is enriched by an almost mirror-like correspondence in the thirty-first chapter of the second part, where knight and knave enter the ducal palace. In all innocence Sancho exhorts an aristocratic old duenna to go out before the gate and lead his dear ass Dapple into the stables. When she becomes highly indignant at his imputation, he quotes the same romance: "Damsels look'd after him, and Waiting-women after his Horse" (p. 643). The only result is that she berates him as the rascally son of a whore and garlic-eating stinkard. Again we find the antithesis of high and low, but the components have been turned about: the one who is addressed is now really a noble lady, but the peasant and his donkey have taken the place of the knight and his stallion. Figure and counter-figure, like a musical theme and its inversion, are related to one another by remote control over the space of a thousand pages.

Such thematic long-distance responses, which overarch the entire work with invisible bridges, are not at all rare. In the first part, as a confirmation and corroboration of his challenge to any man who might cast a dishonorable aspersion on his high mistress, Don Quixote cites the inscription on Roland's escutcheon (*Orlando Furioso*, Canto XXIV):

> "Let none but he these Arms displace,
> Who dares *Orlando's* Fury face." (p. 79)

When, having been defeated in a duel at the end of the second part, he has had to vow that he will refrain from further adventures and return to his village, he decides that now *his* weapons should be hung up on a tree and that the motto from Roland's escutcheon will stand beneath them (p. 889). Here the contrast between quotation and reality has been intensified. The first time, Don Quixote still had the right to speak in this manner. Now the challenging expression is highly out of keeping, because he has just lost the right to take any combat upon himself. This destroys the basic impulse of his life, and the whole bitter melancholy of the end of his life is concentrated in the inappropriately haughty quotation.

But even when a quotation is used only once, a rich elaboration of the basic antithesis is possible by means of parallel and contrary references. In the courtyard of an aristocratic house Don Quixote glimpses a row of earthen wine jugs which, because they come from Toboso, summon up in his mind the memory of his "enchanted" Dulcinea. In an ecstatic frame of mind he recites the introductory lines of a sonnet by Garcilaso de la Vega:

"O! Pledges, once my Comfort and Relief,
Though pleasing still, discover'd now with Grief!"

(p. 553)

To the association based on the place of origin, Toboso, is added the aural association "*dulces prendas*"—"Dulcinea"; further, the comic parallel between the squat wine jug and the robust peasant maid ("Dulcinea" in the state of enchantment); and finally, the contrast of these two with the ethereal image of the beloved in his imagination.[8]

The use of quotations has shown us that the constant joining of elements related to one another by parallel and antithesis produces a finely balanced harmony of contrasts, by means of which the crass basic antithesis of delusion and reality is toned down. It is also part of this harmony of contrasts that Don Quixote's quotations find their antithetical correspondence in Sancho's brilliant use of popular expressions and proverbs. Quotation and proverb have as a common denominator the fact that both are preformed linguistic material. Proverbs in their totality constitute an unwritten literature, as it were, and represent a popular analogue to the quotations from written literature. Now, whereas Don Quixote's quotations are in general eminently inappropriate, Sancho's proverbs—despite their variegated disparity and apparent foolishness—are actually with few exceptions quite relevant to the matter at issue. In Sancho's conversation with the duchess regarding the promised governorship, the whole pages-long potpourri of folksy say-

[8] This is not the only time that Garcilaso de la Vega, who was after all Cervantes' "pronounced and venerated favorite among the poets of Spain" (Hatzfeld, *Don Quijote als Wortkunstwerk*, p. 144), is treated parodistically. Here again is an indication that parody by no means requires a "hostile" attitude toward the object of parody and that it is misleading to conclude automatically that such an attitude exists.

ings constitutes in essence nothing but an elaboration of his one main thought: that the distinction between poor and rich, lowly and aristocratic, is only vain appearance, for which reason he is gladly willing to renounce the governorship (pp. 663ff.).

But even the contrast between literary quotation and proverb does not remain wholly at odds. Cross-connections emerge which are associated with the interlacing figures treated above. On the one hand Don Quixote condescends to express himself idiomatically in Sancho's fashion, although he does so only with a borrowed voice in order to make himself more comprehensible to his squire. When the latter wants to leave his master because he has not been paid, Don Quixote answers: ". . . and remember this, that if there be Vetches in my Dove-House, it will want no Pigeons. Good Arrears are better than ill Pay; and a Fee in Reversion is better than a Farm in Possession. Take notice too, there's Proverb for Proverb, to let you know that I can pour out a Volley of 'em as well as you" (p. 487). Conversely, Sancho, at the peak of his emotion in his lament after the supposed death of his master, imitates the latter's lofty manner of speech, only to slide back into his everyday language (p. 435). Likewise, he also makes occasional use of literary quotations, to which especially the popular literature of romances is suited. In these cases there is no lack of bowdlerization, but it affects only the outer form. Even when he mutilates the Latin text of the Mass, the contextual reference is astonishingly appropriate. Sancho's most brilliant achievement comes toward the end of the novel. Don Quixote tries to take off his trousers while his squire sleeps so that he can undertake the scourging which is supposed to release Dulcinea from the enchantment. But Sancho, overpowering him, kneels on his master and makes him promise to desist from his attempt. Otherwise:

> "Here thou diest,
> Traitor to Donna Sancho." (p. 848)

The eminently adapted and even more precisely literal quotation from the romance is disconcertingly appropriate, and the only impropriety lies in the contrast of its heroic atmosphere to the slapstick comedy of the situation.

We must forego any attempt to treat Don Quixote's "quoting" in a broader sense. There are many cases in which he ornaments his language with classical *topoi* or commonplaces or, in free form, summarizes large chunks of his courtly romances. It would turn out that the principle underlying these ornamental forms is the same as that in the literal quotation. They, too, are fitted consistently into the balanced harmony of contrasts that emerges from the interplay of antithetical elements. It suffices if we have succeeded in showing that the quotation in Cervantes' novel is a direct and pure expression of meaning, and that it succeeds in contributing to the establishment of that harmony of contrasts dominating the whole, in which the intended meaning finds its appropriate total epic form.

CHAPTER IV

Laurence Sterne

TRISTRAM SHANDY

As AN artistic creation in the form of the novel, *Don Quixote* stands out in well-defined contours. Turning now from Cervantes to Laurence Sterne, we are confronted by a very different situation: uncertainty and disagreement becloud the literary image of *Tristram Shandy*. No less confusing than the "opinions" advertised by the gentleman autobiographer, is the welter of opinion regarding Sterne's novel. Is *Tristram Shandy* really a novel? That is the question that readers have pondered with diffidence and bewilderment from the date of its first publication to the present day. During half a century the English novel as an art form had undergone a magnificent development from Defoe and Swift to Richardson, Smollett, and Fielding. Then Sterne came along and tossed all their achievements onto the scrap heap: the clear and richly variegated train of the action, the consistent development of character, the thoroughly realistic depiction of milieu, and so forth. The development from Defoe to Fielding appears like the mighty swell of a tidal wave that in *Tristram Shandy* (1760-67) crests, breaks, and shatters in a mad whirl of spray. Sterne as the destroyer of "genuine" novelistic form and his book as an improvised extravaganza of utter formlessness—this is approximately the line established by nineteenth-century criticism. Surely his contemporaries, schooled in the great tradition of Pope and Swift and the other "wits" of their Augustan Age, were not wanting in perceptiveness in honoring the author of *Tristram Shandy* with the eponym of "an English Rabelais." But the century that followed did not know what to make of Sterne. Taine's

72

judgment may be quoted as typical: "Son livre est comme un grand magasin de bric à brac où les curiosités de tout siècle, de toute espèce et de tout pays gisent entassées pêle-mêle" ("His book is like a great bric-a-brac shop where curios of every sort, from every century and every country, lie heaped up pell-mell").[1] And even today the general verdict seems to be not very different.[2]

Nevertheless, during the last few decades other voices, contradicting this view and ranging as far as extreme dissent, have been heard. Obviously it is the avant-garde experimental novel of our own day which has cleared the way for a more positive approach, even if its appearance leaves unsettled the hotly debated question of whether Sterne is really to be hailed as the great and legitimate precursor of such authors as Proust, Joyce, and Virginia Woolf or even as the true initiator of the stream of consciousness novel. *Tristram Shandy* no novel? On the contrary, it has been called "the most typical novel in the world." The ostensibly absolute disorder turns out, on a higher level, to be absolute and conscious order, provided we grasp what "order" means to Sterne. "To him, this was preeminently a novel *of* form and *about* form, and Sterne is everywhere a *conscious* innovator and experimenter."[3] Thus speaks an exponent of Russian formalism. Similar conclusions have resulted from an investigation of the apparently inextricable mix-up of the novel's time sequence, for analysis has shown that despite the disconcerting shifts from one time level to

---

[1] Hippolyte Taine, *Histoire de la Littérature Française*, IV, 146f.; quoted from A. de Froe, *Laurence Sterne and His Novels Studied in the Light of Modern Psychology* (Groningen, 1925), p. 193.

[2] Cf. J. A. Work's introduction to his excellent critical edition of *Tristram Shandy* (3rd ed.; New York, 1940), p. xlvi: "A recent critic, who echoes the general opinion, writes of 'the absolute disorder of *Tristram Shandy* . . . an indefinite theme, worked out by a verve that has not the slightest concern for order, unity, or logic.'" Quotations from *Tristram Shandy* in this study follow J. A. Work's edition, citing book and chapter. (In one case the page number is cited.)

[3] Victor Shklovsky, *Tristram Shendi: Sterna i teoriya romana* (Leningrad, 1921). This work was not available to me; I quote here and above from p. 94 of the report of Kenneth E. Harper, "A Russian Critic and Tristram Shandy," *Modern Philology*, LII (1954), 92-100.

another, the whole is governed by a pedantically sustained sense of time.[4] Many readers now look upon *Tristram Shandy* as the Bible of novelistic art, the *summa* of its higher mathematics. A more moderate variant of the vindication, while declining to explain away all "disorder" as a kind of higher order, sees the disorder substantially reduced. Straightforward chronological sequence does, after all, play an essential part in the structural scheme of our novel, it is quite properly argued; although two strands of action, that of Father Shandy and his family and that of Uncle Toby, are mixed up together, each of them is cast in a clearly traceable time sequence.[5] So there is something "normal" about this novel after all! All such controversy has not prevented one recent study of Sterne from hewing to a quite different line. It centers the discussion on Sterne's philosophical rhetoric, on the ground that "he was a rhetorician and not a 'novelist.' "[6] Thus, there seems to be no real consensus of opinion on the basic question of whether *Tristram Shandy* is an authentic product of narrative art. For this reason our study, concerned as it is with the functional uses of quotation in narrative art, will have to train an even more critical focus on this feature of Sterne's narrative practice, if possible, than is turned upon the other writers included in this study.

There is one point, after all, on which the divergent opinions register agreement: that the sustaining element on which the whole movement of the novel is based is the principle of the subjective association of ideas, regardless of whether it be construed as a foundation of genuine order or simply as sanction for wanton license; regardless also of whether this principle properly derives from an application of Locke's theory of the association of ideas,[7] or whether Sterne merely lampoons it. Inasmuch as the two

[4] A. A. Mendilow, *Time and the Novel* (London, 1952). See Chap. 12, "Time, Structure and Tristram Shandy," esp. p. 169.

[5] Work, *op.cit.*, pp. xlviiif.

[6] John Traugott, *Tristram Shandy's World: Sterne's Philosophical Rhetoric* (Berkeley: University of California Press, 1954), p. xiii.

[7] John Locke, *Essay Concerning Human Understanding*, Bk. II, Chap. 33.

most conspicuous formal features of our novel, the lush pro-
liferation of digressions and the crass shifting of the tem-
poral planes, can readily be accounted for by the process
of subjective association, it seems eminently probable that
this procedure also governs Sterne's use of quotations. To
avoid misunderstanding, however, a second observation
must be added: subjective association is not offered to us
in its true guise as a product of mad caprice, but rather,
by way of humoristic distortion, as a means and con-
sequence of subtly methodical erudition. The same spirit
of shrewd reasoning and fussy accuracy that is character-
istic of Father Shandy also guides the pen of his son
Tristram. Again and again, Tristram represents the setting
down of his "opinions" as a rigorously scientific undertak-
ing. He poses as a "historiographer," a "researcher." To
cite one instance of this among many, he advertises his
account of Uncle Toby's adventure with Widow Wadman
as "one of the most compleat systems, both of the elemen-
tary and practical part of love and love-making, that ever
was addressed to the world" (VI, 36). This humoristic
avowal of exact research is also responsible for the citation
of many learned "authorities" in support of both Father
Shandy's opinions and his own. But they are not only
"cited"; they are also ridiculed. Rabelais' parodistic wit
made a shambles of scholastic learning. Sterne applies the
same treatment to scholastic pseudo-science in its widest
sense—that abstract, unempirically-oriented type of knowl-
edge distinguished by bold speculation on the one hand
and slavish dedication to authority on the other. For
Sterne this mode of thought, which continued to hold sway
long after the passing of the Middle Ages, constituted an
inexhaustible supply of material that could be exploited in
parody. In this respect he carries on a tradition which in-
cludes such works as Swift's *Tale of a Tub*, Pope's *Art of
Sinking in Poetry*, and the satirical *Memoirs of Martinus
Scriblerus*.[8] This tradition owes much to Rabelais. Sterne,

[8] Cf. D. W. Jefferson, "Tristram Shandy and the Tradition of
Learned Wit," *Essays in Criticism*, I (1951), 225-48.

75

in particular, is in his debt and acknowledges this by repeated laudatory references to him in *Tristram Shandy*. He has an even greater fondness, however, for Cervantes. He swears "by the ashes of my dear Rabelais, and dearer Cervantes" (III, 19) and recalls with tenderness the Knight of La Mancha, "whom, by the bye, with all his follies, I love more, and would actually have gone further to have paid a visit to, than the greatest hero of antiquity" (I, 10). The conception of the two brothers, Walter and Toby, as a pair of polar opposites would probably not have been possible without the precedent of Don Quixote and Sancho Panza. It is a creative variation on these prototypes.

That Cervantes and Rabelais turned quoting into a literary game and played it with gusto was not lost on Sterne. Cervantes and Sterne have this in common, that the basic characteristic of their quoting is the humoristic inappropriateness of the quotation. But an essential difference must be stressed: despite all the wealth of narrative invention, the incongruous application of quotations in *Don Quixote* follows a simple standard pattern. The author subordinates his quotations imperiously to the thematic contrast between high and low, delusion and reality, that was discussed extensively in the preceding chapter. This original antithesis was the firm and abiding principle that forced the most extravagant arabesques into a symmetrical scheme of architecture. No such unifying principle is encountered in *Tristram Shandy*. The incongruity of quotation does not conform to any principle of head-on antithesis. Sterne's use of quotations is not characterized by any straightforward contrast, but by an obliqueness of reference. It is infinitely variable, embracing potentially all possible and impossible curves and convolutions. The symmetry of monumental Baroque that still dominated *Don Quixote* has yielded in *Tristram Shandy* to the asymmetric play of line found in rococo ornamentation.

This may be illustrated by a relatively simple example. Near the outset Tristram pridefully asserts that he has begun his story and intends to continue it "as *Horace* says, *ab*

Ovo" (i, 4). In two respects the quotation has an incongruous slant. As we know, Horace, in the *Ars poetica* (pp. 146ff.), observes that Homer begins his story of the war of Troy not "ab ovo," not with the egg hatched by Leda and the birth of Helen, but by taking us straightway into the middle of the resulting war. Whereas Tristram seems, on the immediate level, to be employing only a pale stock metaphor ("from the very beginning"), the original specific image latent in the phrase is necessarily activated by the three preceding chapters, all of which had been concerned with the moment of Tristram's conception. The mischievously oblique use of the quotation consists in the fact that Tristram, determined to go Horace one better, reaches back to the more original point of origin with the spermatozoon, the "homunculus," who had so lamentable a time of it during Tristram's conception, as circumstantially reported in the earlier chapters. (As the actual protagonist of the introductory narrative, "homunculus" easily outtrumps Leda's egg!) But there is a catch in our phrase, even in its use as a bland metaphor. As regards the narrative technique, the phrase "ab ovo" suggests a regular and chronological progression, and this is precisely what Tristram does *not* employ, to an extreme degree.

Even more manifest is the humoristic incongruity of quotation in the passage where the confusion that reigns in Uncle Toby's head is discussed (ii, 2). In a lively interchange with readers and critics, Tristram goes far afield by citing, once again, Locke's *Essay Concerning Human Understanding*. After characterizing the book in general terms, he goes on to reproduce in detail the three factors that are responsible for the obscuring of thought. In Locke's essay we read: "The cause of obscurity in simple ideas seems to be either dull organs, or very slight and transient impressions made by the objects, or else a weakness in the memory, not able to retain them as received."[9] Tristram renders this passage as follows:

[9] *Essay Concerning Human Understanding*, Bk. II, Chap. 29, No. 3.

Now if you will venture to go along with me, and look down into the bottom of this matter, it will be found that the cause of obscurity and confusion, in the mind of man, is threefold. Dull organs, dear Sir, in the first place. Secondly, slight and transient impressions made by objects when the said organs are not dull. And, thirdly, a memory like unto a sieve, not able to retain what it has received.

We see that Locke's conceptual terms are retained verbatim despite the picturesque embroidery of Tristram's phrasing; and a dramatic touch is added when the comparison of the human consciousness to a piece of wax brings the maid Dolly to life. Starting from her trance, she fishes in her pocket for a piece of red sealing wax to seal the letter to her admirer. Notwithstanding the elusive complexity of the form, the reader follows along, fancying that he is getting enlightened as to the cause of Uncle Toby's confusion, only to be brought up short by Tristram's matter-of-fact explanation: "Now you must understand that not one of these was the true cause of the confusion in my uncle Toby's discourse; and it is for that very reason I enlarge upon them so long, after the manner of great physiologists,—to shew the world what it did *not* arise from." The real reason is revealed as altogether different. It is "the unsteady uses of words," a formulation that also seems to be suggested by Locke,[10] even though in a much more general sense. The whole of the preceding discourse owes its origin to that "Liebe zum leersten Ausgang," that trick of maximum deflation which Jean Paul ascribes to the humorist as a type and to Sterne in particular.[11] The long disquisition was a mere feint, retaining the character of a pure digression.

That this does not result from narrative impotence is proved by the shrewd artistry with which Sterne in another place blends a theory of Locke's into the pragmatic con-

[10] *Ibid.*, Bk. II, Chap. 29, No. 6.
[11] *Vorschule der Ästhetik*, paragraph 33.

text. In Book Two, taking his cue from the time elapsed between Father Shandy's ringing for his servant Obadiah and the arrival of the obstetrician Dr. Slop, he has so inextricably mixed up the time span of the events reported with that of their reporting, that the reader loses footing and flounders helplessly. Then, as a saving straw, Sterne tosses to the reader the theorem extracted from Locke's chapter "Of Duration and its Simple Modes,"[12] namely "that the idea of duration and its simple modes, is got merely from the train and succession of our ideas" (ii, 8). This theorem, offered at first as a purely digressive byplay, turns up after twenty-seven additional chapters, now delightfully transposed into action. Since Dr. Slop's arrival, not more than two hours and ten minutes have elapsed, by Father Shandy's precise calculation; yet, as he exclaims in astonishment: "I know not how it happens, brother Toby,— but to my imagination it seems almost an age" (iii, 18). His astonishment, however, is not entirely genuine. He protests that he cannot understand how this can be, only because as a seasoned philosopher he *does* understand and burns with eagerness to treat his brother to a subtle explanation "by a metaphysical dissertation on the subject of duration and its simple modes." But what a disappointment for him when Uncle Toby, this *anima candida*, suddenly anticipates his explanation with the remark: " 'Tis owing, entirely, . . . to the succession of our ideas." Is this a flash of inspiration of his own, or did he pick up the phrase on some other occasion from his brother? Be that as it may, Father Shandy does not let the matter rest: "Do you understand the theory of that affair? replied my father. Not I, quoth my uncle.—But you have some ideas, said my father, of what you talk about.—No more than my horse, replied my uncle Toby." And it is this honest answer that enables Walter to drive home his metaphysical point in a disquisition that fills a whole page, exactly following Locke as to its conceptual context and quoting verbatim whole sentences and phrases from the philosopher. But with what consum-

[12] *Essay Concerning Human Understanding*, Bk. II, Chap. 14.

mate art that severely sober philosophical text is enlivened by small additions and slight rearrangement, and transformed thereby into a genuine conversation rooted in the concrete situation! Father Shandy talks completely past his brother. When, at last, he trots out Locke's formula "train of ideas," he is driven to despair by the fact that this phrase calls forth in Uncle Toby's mind the associated idea of a "train of artillery." At this he recognizes that his love's labor is lost and is silenced. This time it is that "unsteady use of words" that leads to the "maximum deflation." It may be supposed, by the way, that Locke's favorite phrase "train of ideas"[13] stimulated Sterne's visual imagination, and that this chapter owes its existence to the potential distortion latent in the term's range of association.

The "unsteady use of words" is a theme that is vividly embodied in Toby's endless misunderstandings. But beyond this it has a much more far-reaching significance for the whole novel. Sterne's relation to words and to language is one of deepest skepticism. The problem of language, a matter of passionate interest to him as the source of many of his digressions, is the desolating lack of connection between word and thing. Language is unreliable and full of holes. Between this skeptical attitude and Sterne's humor there is a structured relation similar to that we have shown to be present in Cervantes. But in his case the disbelief was only partial; it concerned the ornamental forms of elevated literary language, the hollow emptiness of which his gaze penetrated and exploited humoristically. Sterne's skepticism is more comprehensive and radical. It relates to language as such and to everything transmitted by means of words—to the whole treasure of learning and wisdom stored up in writing in the course of centuries and handed on to posterity. This state of affairs must concern us if we are to come to an adequate understanding of Sterne's art of quotation. We cannot shirk facing up to a disquieting question: To what extent are quotation and plagiarism identical in

[13] Cf., for instance, the title of Bk. II, Chap. 14, paragraph 9: "The Train of Ideas Has a Certain Degree of Quickness."

Sterne? To what extent is a quote a quote and to what extent is it a lift? Sterne's younger contemporary John Ferriar, in his *Illustrations of Sterne*,[14] demonstrated with great acumen and a ranging knowledge of sources countless silently lifted passages in *Tristram Shandy*. Since that day the charge that Sterne was fundamentally a highhanded plagiarist has never been wholly silenced. This verdict, to be sure, was occasionally mitigated to a concession that it is a question of "le plagiat d'un grand artiste."[15] But the matter cannot be disposed of in that way. There simply is no hiding the fact that many such borrowings, from an external point of view of form, reveal the character of plagiarisms. The matter is of importance to our inquiry, not primarily because we should attempt a vindication—he himself is equal to vindicating his honor as artist—but because in the actual or alleged plagiarisms the very essence of Sterne's art of quoting is displayed. We shall attempt to get to the bottom of this matter by scrutinizing the borrowings with a view to asking whether and how they have been integrated into the narrative web. This aspect of the problem is of very special importance, because the decision as to the justification of a borrowing must be weighed in scales of the most delicate balance.[16]

In Book Five Father Shandy receives the news that his son Bobby has died in France. How does he get over his grief in the following chapters? We must indeed ask whether there can be any question of his "getting over" his grief, because he never allows the final reality of his loss and his pain to approach him. What he does is to benumb

[14] John Ferriar, *Illustrations of Sterne* (London, 1798; 2nd ed. 1812).

[15] Paul Stapfer, *Laurence Sterne, sa personne et ses ouvrages* (Paris, 1882), Chap. 19.

[16] Rodolf Maack, *Laurence Sterne in seiner Zeit* (1936), makes a praiseworthy effort to repudiate Ferriar's charge of plagiarism against Sterne (pp. 97ff.). However, he approaches Sterne's relation to his sources by way of ideas rather than of narrative technique. This makes his vindication weaker than need be. The following statement by Maack: "Nirgends[!] suchte er in der Kunst die artistischen Werte, sondern überall den Ausdruck des Seelischen" (p. 102) seems to me to miss the point at issue.

81

his consciousness by a flood of rhetoric, by an excessive cumulation of arguments for taking comfort, all of which are variations of the platitudinous fact that all men must die.

'Tis an inevitable chance—the first statute in Magna Charta—it is an everlasting act of parliament, my dear brother,—*All must die.*
If my son could not have died, it had been matter of wonder,—not that he is dead.
Monarchs and princes dance in the same ring with us.
—*To die*, is the great debt and tribute due unto nature: tombs and monuments, which should perpetuate our memories, pay it themselves; and the proudest pyramid of them all, which wealth and science have erected, has lost its apex, and stands obtruncated in the traveller's horizon. (My father found he got great ease, and went on)—Kingdoms and provinces, and towns and cities, have they not their periods? (v, 3)

These comforting sentiments, the reader discerns at once, are by no means Father Shandy's own thoughts. They are not the offspring of the specific situation. They are, all of them, commonplaces picked up at random. In very fact Father Shandy (or Sterne) here plunders the rich treasury of the ancient and Christian discourse of solace, the *consolatio*.[17] That is to say, he plunders a plunderer, for his direct source is that curious monster of a book, *The Anatomy of Melancholy* by Robert Burton. Since its appearance in 1621 it had been widely read, and for a century it enjoyed a high reputation as a treasury of humanistic learning. Great minds at that time admired Burton's intellect and wit, whereas the work affects us today in the main as a jumble of undigested and ill-assorted scraps of

[17] E. R. Curtius, *Europäische Literatur und lateinisches Mittelalter* (1948), pp. 88-90, succinctly discusses the commonplaces of the consolatory oration, which in reduced form constitute the letter of condolence. A characteristic feature of the *consolatio* is the enumeration of many famous persons who despite their power on earth had to die.

knowledge. In the chapter entitled "Against Sorrow for Death of Friends or Otherwise, Vain Fear, etc.,"[18] we find in the midst of a heap of similar pronouncements such sayings as: " 'Tis an inevitable chance, the first statute in Magna Charta, an everlasting Act of Parliament, all must die"; and "Tombs and monuments have the like fate, *data sunt ipsis quoque fata sepulchris*, kingdoms, provinces, towns, and cities, have their periods, and are consumed." It is obvious at first glance that Sterne copied Burton almost word for word. For long stretches he quotes the sentences in the sequence of his source. Only now and then is the scrap heap stirred about once more.

Yet it would be totally wrong to speak here simply of plagiarism, for Sterne's relation to his source is sufficiently complicated and paradoxical. Burton is a humanist who has faith in culture. For him the *topos* is a venerable, indeed a sacrosanct matter; yet unintentionally his disorderly collector's zeal deprives the commonplace tradition of meaning and reduces it to absurdity. For Sterne, classical education has collapsed; he sees the cultivation of *topoi* exposed as an empty cultural fraud, and the individual *topoi* are to him mere flotsam and jetsam.[19] But this very disillusionment provides him with the freedom necessary to organize the amorphous mass of consolatory *topoi* in accordance with narrative principles by integrating them into an epic context. This is at once made plain by the little anecdote that he inserts by way of anticipation at the beginning of the chapter:

When Tully was bereft of his dear daughter Tullia, at first he laid it to his heart,—he listened to the voice of nature, and modulated his own unto it.—O my Tullia! my daughter! my child!—still, still, still,—'twas O my Tul-

[18] Robert Burton, *The Anatomy of Melancholy* (new ed.; London, 1883), II, 3, 5; pp. 406ff.
[19] It is in character that in one of his sermons, "Job's Expostulation with his Wife," Sterne dismisses Father Shandy's stoical argument that "To die is the great debt and tribute unto nature" as unavailing in the case of a beloved child's death; cf. Maack, *op.cit.*, p. 42.

lia!—my Tullia! Methinks I see my Tullia, I hear my Tullia, I talk with my Tullia.—But as soon as he began to look into the stores of philosophy, and consider how many excellent things might be said upon the occasion —no body upon earth can conceive, says the great orator, how happy, how joyful it made me. (v, 3)

Here Sterne goes beyond the text of his model in one important point. In the chapter of Burton's mentioned above he found only that Cicero (Tully) succeeded in overcoming his grief at his daughter's death by the comfort derived from philosophical maxims. Sterne makes Cicero a prototype of Shandian verbalism, of the pleasures of verbal autointoxication. The great orator is not only consoled but happy and pleased when he discovers how many fine sentiments the occasion of his daughter's death can give rise to. Thus the inorganic stringing together of commonplaces serves Sterne as a primary means of characterization. For, in sharpest contrast to Sterne's own skeptical attitude toward the commonplace, our learned screwball Father Shandy has an extravagant and well-nigh magical faith in the validity and the power of the word and everything sanctioned by linguistic form. This trait Sterne develops with sovereign consistency. An indispensable feature of the consolation *topos* is the lament over all that has perished, whether it be men or things. And so Father Shandy's lament remembers to quote: "Where is Troy and Mycenae, and Thebes and Delos, and Persepolis and Agrigentum. . . . What is become, brother Toby, of Nineveh and Babylon, of Cizicum and Mitylenae? The fairest towns that ever the sun rose upon, are now no more." That is all verbatim Burton, but then Father Shandy adds as his own contribution: "the names only are left, and those (for many of them are wrong spelt) are falling themselves by piece-meals to decay, and in length of time will be forgotten, and involved with every thing in a perpetual night" (v, 3). Improper orthography as a symbol of destruction—that is the form our verbalist's grief over the transitoriness of all things takes! He is so bemused by fine words and high-sounding phrases that in spelling out his rhetorical claptrap he completely forgets what occasioned it: the death of his own son.

In the nature of things this overcharge of idle phraseology must lead to a short circuit with reality, and this is fashioned in such a way as to drive along the epic development. Let us remember that, apart from Toby, it is as yet only Father Shandy who knows of his son's death. It does not occur to him at all to communicate the sad event to his wife. But she happens to be listening at the door, as she so often is, at the very moment when, still in full oratorical swing after ten more chapters, her husband is reciting the valedictory of Socrates:

"I have friends—I have relations,—I have three desolate children,"—says Socrates.—
—Then, cried my mother, opening the door,—you have one more, Mr. Shandy, than I know of.
By heaven! I have one less,—said my father, getting up and walking out of the room. (v, 13)

What a cruel point is given here to the innocent, conventional comedy-motif of the eavesdropper! In the midst of the fun a yawning abyss opens up. Humor somersaults and turns into gruesome grotesquerie. The lack of relation between the quoted passage and the human situation, expressed through Father Shandy's consolation speeches, is paralleled by the no less gruesome lack of relation between husband and wife. The petrified formula barricades the way to mutual understanding. In no other scene has Sterne with such shrill dissonance condensed into a narrative situation the eternal futility of a classical education torn loose from its source. By transposing the mass of quotations into an element of the narrative flow Sterne has not only achieved a masterful integration of their matter; he has trained a searching light on the innermost recesses of the human soul.

This spectacular achievement does not stand alone in kind or quality. It is fully matched by the maledictions against Obadiah. This episode also strikingly illustrates the grotesquely misfit character of the quote as applied to the situation. We find this, to begin with, in the pragmatic nexus of the story. We are still concerned with the phase before Tristram's birth. Father Shandy has sent his servant Obadiah to the house of Doctor Slop in order to fetch his bag of obstetrical instruments. On his way back, Obadiah's excessive caution has made him tie the bag with innumerable knots. When he finally returns, it is high time for Doctor Slop to take a hand in the delivery. One hears the groans of the woman in labor upstairs and the tramping steps of the midwife. In his haste to sever the knots Dr. Slop cuts his thumb to the bone, and he curses Obadiah in strong language. Father Shandy takes offense at the insult to his servant, and he decides upon a sublime revenge. To this end he first expounds his subtle theory of cursing. He sets forth the maxim that the stream of cursing should be sustained until the curser has had his fill: "I swear on, till I find myself easy" (III, 10).

Consistent with this theory, he induces Doctor Slop to read out loud a long list of curses that he keeps handy on the mantle of the chimney. He conceals from the Catholic physician the fact that the document is a copy (the translation of a copy, obviously) of an old formula of excommunication drawn up by Bishop Ernulphus of Rochester at the beginning of the twelfth century. While Uncle Toby is whistling his "lillabullero," Dr. Slop, his wounded thumb wrapped in a handkerchief, recites in a loud voice the document of several pages. So that the reader may not doubt the authenticity of the form, Sterne has the original Latin printed side by side with the translation.[20] The formula of excommunication is beautifully composed. First, it states in the name of what and by what sacred offices and persons the procedure of excommunication is performed; then, where

[20] Sterne's source is the *Textus Roffensis*, ed. Thomas Hearnius (Oxford, 1720), pp. 55-59. In general, Sterne faithfully reproduces the text. His slight deviations represent unintentional slips without any bearing on the narrative technique.

and under what circumstances it takes place; and finally, in hair-raising detail, what parts of the body, from the hair of the head to the soles of the feet, are being cursed. The poor culprit and the reader are spared no detail. This circumstantiality in itself is an element of humoristic incongruity inasmuch as it stretches the already existing break in the continuity of narrative suspense to intolerable limits; for the midwife is still tramping around upstairs with the reader impatiently seconding the tumult. But the husband of the poor woman in labor coolly consumes a sinful amount of time to sip his revenge to the last drop—within the framework of the events a scene of grotesque violence.

The second, at least equally effective aspect of humoristic incongruity consists in the disproportionateness of the curses to the offense. Sterne did not need to change the text in order to achieve this. The few trifling misunderstandings and inaccuracies in the translation are of no account. The disproportionateness consists not only in the quantitative disproportion between the weight of the curse and the trifling offense, but goes deeper. Within the sphere of its origin the solemn religious curse is endowed with magical force. The repeated phrase, "maledictus sit" amounts to a real "maledictus est," barring the contingency of the culprit's repenting and doing penance. Let us recall what a terrible reality still attaches to such cursings in Shakespeare's dramas. But now language has become rationally enfeebled; it has lost the last vestige of magical power. This is also evidenced by the fact that the meaning of the baptismal names has dropped to the status of a whimsical hobby with Father Shandy. In all this, the short circuit of word and meaning, as indicated above, is exemplified. At this late stage the ceremonial religious curse has sunk to the level of a meaningless profanity, to a mere evil wish; and conversely, Dr. Slop's maledictions of Obadiah are no more than an expression of anger. ("I wish all the devils in hell had him for a blockhead," III, 10.) On this "decline of swearing" the digression which follows trains the spotlight. It becomes apparent that Father Shandy, too, fundamen-

tally misunderstands the formulaic curse. He does not see
that it involves a single unified anathema. He regards it
rather as a mere collection of curse words or, in terms of his
own oddball mentality, as a codification of the laws of curs-
ing, analogous to the codification of civil law in the Corpus
Juris Civilis compiled by Emperor Justinian during the de-
cline of the Roman Empire; in his words, "an institute of
swearing, in which ... upon the decline of swearing ...
Ernulphus ... had with great learning and diligence col-
lected together all the laws of it" (III, 12). Father Shandy
thus, more or less despite himself, brings it about by his
act of revenge that the two separate spheres, that of cere-
monial cursing and that of the homespun curse, come to
collide head-on. The disparity is effected by simple means:
through the insertion of Obadiah's name and the reason for
the curse ("for tying these knots") after every phrase, and
also by injecting Father Shandy's dry interpolations and
Uncle Toby's horrified exclamations. "May all the angels
and archangels, principalities and powers, and all the
heavenly armies, curse him. (Our armies swore terribly in
Flanders, cried my uncle Toby,—but nothing to this.—For
my own part, I could not have a heart to curse my dog so.)"
(III, 11). And after the final amen: "I declare, quoth my
uncle Toby, my heart would not let me curse the devil him-
self with so much bitterness" (III, 11). Once again, in this
scene of cursing, the complex of quotation serves to bring
about a semblance of connection between "literature" and
"life," the illusory character of which is at the same time
made evident by all the means employed.

Our point of departure was the knotty relation between
quotation and plagiarism. On one occasion Sterne puts his
finger on that very problem. At the beginning of Book Five
the vision of a breakneck ride in a stagecoach drawn by
fiery steeds is conjured up. In the course of the ride Tris-
tram, in a high state of elation, vows to himself that he will
lock up his study for good and throw the key into a deep
well. As a counterimage there appears a lumbering wagon,
slowly and laboriously drawn up a slope by eight horses.

Why does Tristram forbid himself access to his study? Without doubt, to prevent himself from succumbing to the temptation of plundering other authors. The rapid ride is obviously a symbol for inspired original creative writing, just as, conversely, the lumbering wagon symbolizes barren learning which painfully pieces together its elaborations from borrowed patches. This is followed at once by the eloquent lament on the learned inbreeding in the production of books:

Tell me, ye learned, shall we for ever be adding so much to the *bulk*—so little to the *stock*?

Shall we for ever make new books, as apothecaries make new mixtures, by pouring only out of one vessel into another?

Are we for ever to be twisting, and untwisting the same rope? for ever in the same track—for ever at the same pace?

Shall we be destined to the days of eternity, on holy-days, as well as working-days, to be shewing the *relicks of learning*, as monks do the relicks of their saints—without working one—one single miracle with them?

Who made MAN, with powers which dart him from earth to heaven in a moment—that great, that most excellent, and most noble creature of the world—the *miracle* of nature, as Zoroaster in his book called him—the SHEKINAH of the divine presence, as Chrysostom—the *image* of God, as Moses—the *ray* of divinity, as Plato— the *marvel* of *marvels*, as Aristotle—to go sneaking on at this pityful—pimping—pettifogging rate? (v, 1)

This, the reader feels, is a genuine, deeply experienced lament, although he is somewhat disturbed to find it marshaling in this very passage so great an array of learned allusions. But then we arrive at the amazing discovery, already made by Ferriar, that this diatribe against the piecing together of bits filched from other authors is itself patched together for the greater part out of Burton's assembled borrowings. In his preface, "Democritus to the

Reader," Burton rails against impotent scribblings, which in the seventeenth century no less than in the eighteenth were evidently regarded as a monstrous disfigurement in the world of letters. Paradoxically enough, however, his bitter complaint is studded with learned quotations. And in the jungle of his piled-up words and images we also find the sentences from which Sterne in his turn lifts passages and transplants them into his own diatribe against plagiarism: "As apothecaries we make new mixtures every day, pour out of one vessel into another . . ."; ". . . but we weave the same web still, twist the same rope again and again."[21] The paragraph of Sterne's quoted above is a free rendering of the opening passage of Burton's First Book: "MAN, the most excellent and noble creature of the world, 'the principle and mighty work of God, wonder of nature', as Zoroaster calls him; *audacis naturae miraculum*, 'the marvel of marvels', as Plato . . ." and so forth.[22] Is a vindication of Sterne possible even in this most pointed instance, or does Ferriar's accusation carry the day? The decision in this case is even more difficult than it was in that of his consolatory commonplaces and catalogue of maledictions, because in the instance before us, a digression frankly advertised as such, the lifted passages are not imbedded in any pragmatic narrative context. It must be realized, nevertheless, that Sterne places what he has borrowed into an entirely new ideational frame. He finds it an amusing paradox that it should be a man of Burton's type who rails against literary incest, and with a *salto mortale* of extreme self-irony he adds, as it were, a new dimension to this paradox by using an accumulation of plagiarized passages in Burton's work to pillory plagiarism. In doing so, he had every right to expect that the educated among his readers would recognize

[21] Burton, *op.cit.*, p. 6. The first image was possibly borrowed by Burton from Erasmus, who in his preface to *Enchiridion Militis Christiani* complains of the scholastics who "in their *Summae* mix one thing with another and then mix them again, and who like quacks make and remake old out of new and new out of old, one of many, and many of one." Quoted from W. Schwarz, *Principles and Problems of Biblical Translation* (Cambridge, 1955), pp. 100f.

[22] *Ibid.*, p. 81.

his source and savor the persiflage of his jesting plagiarism.[23] Thus it might be permitted to designate even this bizarre state of things as an integrative use of quotation. If learning as such serves as the butt of Sterne's wit, no less so must the outward trappings in which it invests itself. In the pursuance of his literary game of quoting he has made a specialty of the "learned" footnote. We find it worth our while to dwell on this feature for a moment because this particular device was widely imitated by such German writers as Wieland and Jean Paul. On close view it becomes clear that even these footnotes, for all their appearance of haphazard addenda, contribute more or less to the structural quality of Sterne's narrative art. The least important of such uses is encountered when the footnotes are employed merely for the parody of pedantry, as in the case of source references in unintelligible abbreviations, or in the displaying of nonsensical scraps of knowledge (ii, 19; iv, p. 260)—two forms of literary play that seem to derive from Rabelais. But it also happens upon occasion that the footnote appended to the text has in turn an effect on the text's continuation. In Book i, Chapter 20, this figure is executed in the boldest and most bizarre manner. At the close of the preceding chapter Tristram had briefly alluded to the calamity of his baptism, but he had deferred a more exact explanation because, he reflected, he had not yet told the history of his birth, "and, if it was not necessary I should be born before I was christened, I would this moment give the reader an account of it" (i, 19). The whole chapter that follows is nothing but a capricious digression occasioned by this casually thrown in remark. It begins with an extremely lively interchange between Tristram and the reader, who is addressed as "Madam." He accuses her of having failed to catch his statement "that my mother was not a papist." The reader of the novel is just as nonplussed as "Madam"; even when Tristram once more repeats the point at issue: "It was *necessary* I should be born before I was christen'd." Then, finally, a footnote supplies the expla-

23 Cf. Work's footnote, *op.cit.*, p. 342.

nation. The regulations of the Catholic Church prescribe that a child, in case of danger, be baptized before birth, provided that a part of its body be visible. The doctors of the Sorbonne (compare Rabelais' satirical attacks on the "Sorbonnistes"), however, in a memorandum of April 10, 1733, extended this prescription by making the baptism of the child mandatory even when no part of the child's body was visible, the rite to be performed by insertion of "une petite canulle—*Anglicé* a squirt" (ɪ, 20). Thereupon the complete text of that mandate, which confirms the footnote, is reproduced on several pages, no longer in the form of a footnote but as a continuation of the chapter itself. We leave to the reader the details of that mandate, as well as Sterne's gloss appended with a satyr's leer. What must interest us is the eccentric structure of this passage. The first half of the chapter has no independent justification whatsoever; it is contrived only as a preparation for the point to be made by the footnote, which then reflects back into the text, in that the second half of the text supplies the commentary to the commentary presented by the footnote. This eccentric structure recalls that noteworthy chapter of Rabelais' (ɪ, 38), discussed in an earlier chapter, where a quotation from a psalm determines and interprets all of the preceding text. But this structure is even freer and more playful, and exhibits unmistakable kinship with the extravagant play of line of wildest rococo ornamentation. Measured by the norm of any "normal" narrative method, it is the most crass chaos. Measured by its own inherent norm of humoristic play, it is a peak performance of most ingenious dedication to form.

As is well known, Tristram's method of narration is saturated with reflections about itself. Sometimes he claims that his account is pure improvisation: "I begin with writing the first sentence—and trusting to Almighty God for the second" (vɪɪɪ, 2). Such statements are welcomed by many critics as confirmation of their view that *Tristram Shandy* is a work of absolute formlessness. They completely overlook the fact that such statements are themselves part and parcel of the humoristic narrative manner and cannot be detached from their context and taken literally. They also overlook the fact that assertions to the contrary are not lacking. When Tristram comments at one point on the "texture" of the chapter just completed, he adds a cautionary remark for those that follow: "it is necessary, that . . . a good quantity of heterogeneous matter be inserted, to keep up that just balance betwixt wisdom and folly, without which a book would not hold together a single year" (IX, 12). After all that has been said, it should be clear that these words precisely formulate the significance of the technique of quoting in Sterne's narrative art. Sterne's quotations are "heterogeneous matter" in the most pointed sense of the words. At the same time, thanks to the virtuosity of his literary acrobatics, they are integrated to an astonishingly high degree. The novel "holds together," and indeed, not only for "a single year." Through its most volatile art of the arabesque, it claims its place as a *monumentum aere perennius*.

PART TWO

DEVELOPMENT OF THE ART OF
QUOTING IN GERMANY

CHAPTER V

Christoph Martin Wieland

THE GOLDEN MIRROR
AND
THE TALE OF WISE
DANISCHMEND

WE NOW turn to developments in Germany. Since the middle of the eighteenth century, German fiction had been struggling out of the depths of a more or less provincial backwardness and striving toward European recognition. It is well known that in this process German writers learned much from foreign literature. French and English fiction, especially, influenced it in a fruitful way. It is not our intention to provide a sketch of these often complex influences, nor is it our affair to force together into a causally explicable sequence the phenomena that we seek to clarify. Rather, all that we have treated so far—the humoristic fiction of Rabelais, Cervantes, and Sterne—should be thought of as a literary reality regarded by successive ages as typical in an ideal sense, as a hypothetical space into which German fiction could grow in the course of its upward striving. This process of growth should be illustrated with characteristic examples. Our aim is not for any sort of exhaustiveness. In the selection of the authors as well as of the works, the criterion of representativeness shall be decisive. In the following pages we shall try to retain the same method used in earlier chapters. For the sake of greater concentration we shall focus our view in each case on one novel by the author under consideration; his other works can at most be peripherally illuminated. The first writer who claims our attention is Christoph Martin Wieland.

No one can deny that the literary quotation as such, which consists of the references and allusions of one book to another and of literature to literature, has a rather mediate and derivative character. Only with difficulty can this notion be harmonized with an ideal conception of creative spontaneity and poetic originality. The works treated earlier, to be sure, are far too vigorous to permit the emergence of the slight misgivings implicit in this statement. Matters become different when we leave those literary peaks and seek out the region of moderate height in which Wieland's fiction moves. His works and especially his novels have on the whole a perceptibly cultural or, to borrow an expression of Rilke's, "literature-ish" cast. They are a literature which is nourished more by literature than by "life." For this reason they can be condemned, and critics have often done so, yet one can excuse this state of affairs on the basis of the situation in literary history. Finally, one can try to develop an aesthetic organ for the delicate aroma of this characteristically Wielandesque "literature-ishness." To be sure, it requires a certain measure of effort and selfless surrender not to shrug one's shoulders and reject summarily Wieland's culture-laden playful forms, among which literary allusions and quotations assume an important place. But one should attempt, as we want to do now, to sound them out carefully and test them for their poetic value and their narrative achievement. For reasons that will become clear we shall focus on his novel *The Tale of Wise Danischmend* (*Die Geschichte des weisen Danischmend*); but first let us permit our gaze to range for a moment over other parts of his oeuvre.

In general it might be maintained that for Wieland's narrative style the literary allusion is more characteristic than the actual literal quotation. One example will suffice. In *Agathon* the emotion that the young hero nurtures for the priestess in Delphi is on one occasion described as "resembling that sort of love which (according to an utterance of

Fielding) a well prepared roast of beef inspires in a man who has a good appetite" (VI, 115).[1] Naturally it heightens our delight in this passage in no small measure if Fielding's brilliant digression "Of Love" (*Tom Jones*, VI, 1) resounds in our memory, but even if it does not, the comparison is still comprehensible. The situation is altogether different when the hetaera Danae is at one point whimsically confronted with Molly Seagrim or when Agathon is associated with Saint Preux (VI, 125, 139). The reader is simply expected to know his way in belles lettres (in this case in *Tom Jones* and *La Nouvelle Héloise*) and to understand with no further help this allusion as well as countless others. In the notes to his *The New Amadis* Wieland on one occasion and in complete earnestness impresses on the reader his opinion that "the poet is justified in assuming among his readers a certain knowledge of mythology and history and a certain familiarity with novels, plays and other works of the imagination and wit; and it would hence be unnecessary to supply notes to all such names that are known to everyone who has even the slightest degree of literary education."[2] Let us not dismiss this appeal to the reader's knowledge too hastily as cultural Philistinism. The allusive method that the author here advocates has not merely an aesthetic but also an eminently pedagogical meaning. It stands in the service of aesthetic education. Through its connections with the obligatory ingredients of Western culture, past and present, the horizons of the work are expanded. It is placed in the glittering realm of European belles lettres, and the reader is compelled to keep pace on this road leading ever upward. This educatory impulse may excuse the fact that Wieland's learned allusions here and there turn out to be nevertheless a bit antiquated. This fortunately is balanced by a self-parody of pedantry when he opens a chapter of

---

[1] Unless there is an indication to the contrary, passages from Wieland are cited by volume and page from Wieland, *Gesammelte Schriften* (Akademie-Ausgabe; Berlin, 1909-56), Part I; here: VI, 115.

[2] Wieland, *Werke* (Berlin: Hemple, n.d.), Vol. 17, p. 179.

Agathon, for instance, with the quasi-ceremonious expression: "The source of love (says Zoroaster, or at least he could have said it) is the contemplation of an object that charms our imagination" (VI, 121).

Now does Zoroaster really say this or not? Are we dealing with a genuine or a pseudo-quotation? The reader naturally assumes the latter, but he does not know for sure. He feels that he has been led out onto slippery ice and, at the same time, been amused. We recall that Rabelais and Sterne, in their "learned" notes, occasionally left the reader similarly uncertain about the genuineness of them. Wieland seized upon this play with fictive elements and developed it into a veritable system in the notes to his *The Golden Mirror (Der goldene Spiegel,* 1772) and to his *The Tale of Wise Danischmend* (1775). Though it may be madness, there is method in it. We shall try to reveal the method of this playful form and, even more important, to show that this form of play is not mere caprice but a genuine expression of meaning.

In the *Vorschule der Ästhetik* (paragraph 32) Jean Paul frowns with some justification at the Sterne imitations in Germany—at the "long vapid comet's tail of the then so-named (and now unnamed) humorists, who are nothing but the tattletales of their own gay self-complacency" trailing along behind Sterne. He does not exclude even Wieland from his severe verdict. And he is thinking especially of the "footnote prose" of *Danischmend* and *The New Amadis.* In fact in these works, to which Jean Paul might well have added *The Golden Mirror,* Wieland stands under the spell of Sterne. We know that his admiration for *Tristram Shandy,* with which he became acquainted in 1767, was boundless. "I shall *study* his book as long as I live and still shall not have studied it enough."[3] We shall not consider *The New Amadis.* But with respect to the "footnote prose" of the two novels mentioned, a certain vindication is in order.

[3] Letter of 13 November 1767; cited from Wieland, *Ausgewählte Briefe* (Zürich: Gessner, 1815), Vol. 2, p. 287.

This invention might well have been stimulated by Sterne, though we shall also see that other stimuli were blended with this impulse. In *The Golden Mirror* a rather complicated fictitious editorship underlies the framework. The basic text is claimed to be a book "in Indic language," which is supposed to have served to delight and lull to sleep the sultan Sheik Gebal, a descendant of Sheik Riar of the *Arabian Nights*. The matters reported in this book, however, lie much farther back and are lost in the remote mythical times of the "former" empire of the kings of Scheschian. The basic Indic text, which for its part therefore represents a "late" source, is supposed to have been translated into Chinese, from Chinese into Latin, and finally from Latin into German. This motif is not Wieland's own invention; he appropriated it from the fairy tale "L'Écumoire" of the younger Crébillon (1734), where it is even more richly and colorfully elaborated. In Crébillon the chain of translations extends from an original version in the "langue des Chechianiens"[4] by way of Old Japanese, Chinese, Dutch, Latin, and Venetian to the present French text. One might speak of plagiarism if Wieland had not pointed clearly to his model, by means of a wealth of allusions, in the very first chapter.

But even if this were not so, it would be a case not of simple but of creative plagiarism. Wieland bestows a new and in some measure "serious" meaning upon the whimsical framework device. *The Golden Mirror* is a didactic novel of court intrigue, a *Fürstenspiegel*. Its function is to determine the truth. In his "Dedicatory Epistle," the "Sinaean translator" dwells upon the great difficulty that rulers of the world, in particular, have in recognizing the truth. In order to obtain "practiced eyes" for truth-seeking, "there is no more proven means than to seek out the history of wisdom and folly, of opinions and passions, of truth and deception in the yearbooks of the human race. In these faithful mirrors we see men, customs, and times denuded

[4] De Crébillon Fils, *Oeuvres* (London, 1778), Vol. 2, p. vi.

of all that generally falsifies our judgment when we ourselves are woven into the involved tapestry of the present drama" (IX, 10). The mirrors are called "faithful" because they establish an external and hence also an inner detachment. The farther away the object, the more purely the truth becomes evident in it. For this reason Wieland does not stop with the simple mirror effect that would have been produced if he had merely narrated his Scheschian story without any framework at all. Even then the "Bonzes" of the novel would be the mirror image of the Jesuits, and the empire of "Scheschian" would have been a reflection of the Holy Roman Empire of German nationality. In close fidelity to Crébillon—namely to the tales "Le Sopha" and "Ah Quel Conte!"—he creates a framework by letting the incidents be told to the sultan, Sheik Gebal, by the philosopher Danischmend and the Sultana Nurmahal.[5] The events lie far behind the narrative present, which for its part has already become a gray past as far as we are concerned. By means of this doubling he attains a greater effect of temporal depth. But not only that! The narration in the little circle around the sultan is not merely the reporting of a given content. The very content is gradually produced by the conversation itself. And thus the "truth" revealed by the narrative content is not discovered as an object provided in advance. It is established through the dialectical interplay of question and answer, objection and refutation, opinion and counteropinion. For, in contrast to his model in Crébillon, Sheik Gebal is anything but a muddlehead. By astute interjections he pushes the story along and, with it, the discovery of truth. We are not going too far if, to characterize this method of narration, we cite Goethe's conception of "repeated ethical mirrorings" which "do not merely keep the past alive, but even intensify it to a higher life."[6]

[5] Cf. K. Otto Mayer, "Die Feenmärchen bei Wieland," *Vierteljahresschrift für Literaturgeschichte*, 5 (1892), 374ff., 497ff.

[6] Goethe, *Sämtliche Werke* (Jubiläum-Ausgabe; Stuttgart and Berlin, 1902-07), Vol. 25, pp. 222f.—hereafter cited as JA.

These "repeated mirrorings," now, are continued in the footnote apparatus, which belongs wholly to the fiction and adds to the corpus of the narrative what Jean Paul would call a "colorful border and area of diffusion for strange associations."[7] This invention, too, was obviously inspired by the fictive "textual history" of Crébillon's "L'Écumoire." There the Leipzig scholar Jean-Gaspard Crocovius-Putridus, who translates the Dutch version into Latin, provides the text with "Notes and Commentaries." And his equally learned heirs, Balthazar Onerosus and Melchior Insipidus, "augmenterent encore son livre, le commenterent, éclaircirent les notes, en ajouterent de nouvelles . . ." ("augmented his book even more, wrote commentaries on it, elucidated the notes, and added new ones . . .").[8] But the Venetian translator has discarded all this learned paraphernalia, a fact lamented by the last redactor. Now the French "editor" has only two opportunities to add pseudo-learned notes to his text. (The prologue to *Don Quixote*, as we saw, also ridiculed the learned notes and in similar fashion found a fictive justification for their absence.)

Wieland gratefully seized upon this fiction and developed it further by permitting the various translators to add their comments in a wealth of footnotes accompanying the text. The content of these notes is generally of a critical and restrictive nature, and the restrictive element is even further intensified by the fact that each successive translator repeatedly criticizes the notes of his predecessor. Thus on one occasion the Latin translator, in a testy and subtle bit of reasoning, reveals a "fallacy" in the exposition of the sheik. The German translator, however, exceeds him in subtlety and unmasks this revelation itself as a fallacy (ix, 37). Gradually the reader learns to distinguish between the individual tones of the various commentators. The tone of the Chinese is elegantly ironic. His remarks are to the point, and he turns out many an aphorism of which Lichtenberg or La Rochefoucauld would not need

[7] *Vorschule der Ästhetik*, paragraph 35.
[8] De Crébillon Fils, *op.cit.*, Vol. 2, p. viii.

to be ashamed. The Latin translator, in comparison, is a hairsplitting and verbose pedant, while the German one is a resigned skeptic. And all three love to ornament their language with "genuine" quotations—which increases even more the confusion of this fictional sleight of hand. Thus there descend whole cascades of argumentation which, however, have a tendency finally to disperse futilely. Once, in connection with a quite casual remark, the Chinese gets very excited about the false notion that the Egyptians were a "wise people." The Latin translator, in turn, picks out a wholly irrelevant remark from the words of the latter and contradicts it. Thus the theme is shunted off almost endlessly. The German utters the wise conclusion, which can be nothing but skeptical: "And so we gain this much from the matter: to know that we can know nothing of the affair; and this, in the opinion of the wise Socrates, is always a great deal" (IX, 114). Firm opinions always turn out to be illusory; they are like a stage setting behind which many others can be set up. We recall that device of "maximum deflation" which Jean Paul claims for humor.[9] It is altogether another question whether this dialectical flexibility of humor also implies a "lack of ethical commitment" (*Unverbindlichkeit*), and whether for this reason we ought to second Sengle in his annoyance with the author of *The Golden Mirror*. To be sure we share his admiration for the formal aspects of this work, which he expresses in this way: "It is necessary to go to Thomas Mann's late works in order to find again an equal virtuosity in the play of nuances...."[10]

The technique of repeated mirroring by means of pseudo-learned notes, which proved to be an essential component in the structure of *The Golden Mirror*, is continued in even richer elaboration in *The Tale of Wise Danischmend*. In this novel it becomes even clearer than before that this playful form, though it remains on the periphery, belongs very

---

[9] *Vorschule der Ästhetik*, paragraph 33.
[10] Friedrich Sengle, *Wieland* (1949), p. 266.

much to our theme. First a short recapitulation of the content. The framework plot of *The Golden Mirror* is continued, but here it becomes independent in the form of a main action of a rather simple sort. Wise Danischmend, freed from the imprisonment into which he had been thrust by the intriguing intolerance of the priests, removes himself from the glittering courtly world. In the remote valley of Jemal ("once upon a time") among simple country people he establishes a patriarchal community whose sustaining foundations are family life and good neighbors. The idyllic happiness of this simple world is disturbed only in passing by the machinations of the malicious and cynical "Calenders" (mendicant monks), who have taken it upon themselves to undermine the "good old morals." Danischmend has to flee and ekes out his life as a simple basketmaker, but does not allow this to affect in any way his equanimity and his family happiness. Finally he is summoned back by the inhabitants of the little land, where until the end of his life he acts as a kind of sultan's governor for the well-being of the tiny community.

This "little" world, painted in bright fresco colors, constitutes a clear contrast to the "great" world with its intrigues and vices, envy and lust for power, stupidity and deceit. In *The Golden Mirror* the harsh lights of satire were trained full-glare on this "great" world. The ancient *topos* in which the "cottage" is counterposed against the "palace" is taken up here once again. Both of its components are distributed throughout the two novels in the contrast between civilization, which is satirized, and the Rousseau-like world of innocence. (The terms "cottage" and "palace," even when they refer to real things, have in *Danischmend* primarily the significance of ideological signs.)[11] This juxtaposition probably does not imply that *The Tale of Wise Danischmend* is, as Sengle thinks, a "retraction" of *The Golden Mirror.* Rather, it is its necessary complement.[12] Be that as it may, the novel has a serious ideological concern inas-

[11] See Chaps. 15, 16, and 42 of *Danischmend.*
[12] Sengle, *op.cit.,* p. 280.

much as it hopes to give a valid answer to the question: What are we supposed to think of the "human species"? It does this largely by means of discursive speeches which lend to the presentation an essayistic character. But fortunately, because of the Sterne-like devices of humorous subjectivism, this essayism is sufficiently enlivened to avoid a disproportionately great intellectual pallor.[13]

The long conversation between Danischmend and the old dervish "Calender" (Chapters 13-18) constitutes the ideological heart of the novel. In the thirteenth chapter ("The Calender Tells Danischmend in Confidence What He Thinks of the Human Race") this old sinner develops his coldhearted and cynical philosophy. The world is a madhouse inhabited by dolts and rogues; virtue is merely apparent. Danischmend, no less cleverly than the Calender, opposes to this his warmhearted and mild view of mankind. He supports the natural reality of "virtue," and sees in "enthusiasm" the means through which virtue can be realized despite all suppression. Man is good. Only "sultanship," the usurped despotism exercised by spiritual and mundane oppressors, can wither the inherent goodness of the oppressed. This conviction is genuine but not dogmatic. In contrast to the doctrinaire cynicism of the Calender, Danischmend's theory can be designated as skeptical idealism. When the Calender insists that his view is based on *facta*, we hear the highly characteristic answer: "Facts are anything that you wish to make of them: *from each new point of view* they seem to be something different. And in ten cases to one the ostensible fact on which one confidently based his opinion is nothing but a mere hypothesis" (x, 366; italics mine). Danischmend goes so far as to offer a certain understanding for the Calender's view. It stems from the Calender's unique situation in life. And Danischmend tentatively concludes the conversation with the words: ". . . we cannot and we should not all peer into the

[13] Concerning elements from Sterne in *Danischmend*, see Gerd Matthecka, "Die Romantheorie Wielands und seiner Vorläufer" (Tübingen dissertation, 1956), pp. 200f.

world through one and the same keyhole" (x, 377). The recognition of truth—and this is expressed by the metaphors "point of view" and "keyhole"—is conditioned by perspective. The whole truth can be recognized at best from a multiplicity of perspectives. But this does not mean, as emerges clearly from the context, that each "keyhole" is of equal value. The skepticism promulgated here is not an endless relativism. It is a variation of that idealistic perspectivism which is the sublime product of the intermingling intellectual directions of the Age of Enlightenment.

The footnote apparatus provides an emanation and concretization of the perspectivism which dominates *The Tale of Wise Danischmend*. In comparison with this, the translator's remarks in *The Golden Mirror* seem to be nothing but a rudimentary preform. In the *Danischmend* footnotes, figures from the entire literary and cultural world are introduced who react to what has been presented in the text and thereby illuminate it in their own unique way. On the title page of *Danischmend* stands the notation: *Cum notis variorum*. This statement was common practice in the philological editions of classics in the seventeenth and eighteenth centuries. It meant that the commentator had reprinted the notes of his predecessors in addition to his own, and it was naturally a practice quite familiar to Wieland. No less well known was the playful application that this "Cum notis variorum" had undergone in Pope's parodistic-satirical *Dunciad*. In the heat of the War of Pens that partly instigated this comic epic and partly was instigated by it, Pope planned a continuation of his satire against the "dullness" that had become the idol of the century. Soon after the first appearance of the *Dunciad* (1728), he prepared a new edition with a mighty apparatus of pseudo-learned prefaces, testimonials and annotations, which came out in 1729 as *Dunciad Variorum* (or more precisely: *The Dunciad, in Three Books, with Notes Variorum*). He had exhorted his friends in the literary battle to aid him in the preparation of the footnote apparatus, and he frequently emphasizes the fact that the footnotes stem "from several hands." This, of course, is an exaggeration. Essentially the notes are his own work.[14] The two fictive note-writers appearing most frequently are named "Theobald" and "Scriblerus." The former has a model in reality: Pope's opponent Lewis Theobald, who in his *Shakespeare Restored* (1726) had attacked many imprecisions in Pope's Shakespeare edition. The latter, a fictive figure, is the ostensible author of the *Memoirs of Martinus Scriblerus*, written in 1714 by John Arbuthnot. These "memoirs" appeared in 1741, six years after Arbuthnot's death, in the second volume of Pope's prose writings.[15] Both of these figures are hairsplitting pedants. Thus "Theobald," in a verbose note on the title *Dunciad*, immediately takes a stand for the spelling "Dunceaid" because of its derivation from the root "Dunce"; "Scriblerus" indicates his agreement after weighing and rejecting the spelling "Dunceiade." The very first verse of the *Dunciad* offers Scriblerus an opportunity to propose a series of ludicrous emendations for the beginning of nothing less than Virgil's *Aeneid*! We see that Pope's "Notes Variorum," notwithstanding their fictive nature, still have an authentic reference to life: they serve him as a means of defense in a literary battle. Wieland's "Advertisement of a Dunciad for the Germans" (1755) was also polemical.[16] He promised a jeremiad against all leading "Dunces," among whom he numbered the puffed-up "miserable scribes" of the Gottsched party and above all Gottsched himself.

But the "Notis Variorum" of *Danischmend* lack any polemical instigation or purpose. Wieland uses them purely by artistic preference and raises the parodistic element to the sphere of pure play. By "play" we understand, as before, no kind of irresponsibility. On the contrary, play acquires a certain ethical responsibility because of the fact

[14] *The Dunciad*, ed. James Sutherland; in *The Poems of Alexander Pope*, Vol. 5 (2nd ed.; London and New Haven, 1953), Introduction, p. xxiv, and *passim*.
[15] "Memoirs of Martinus Scriblerus," *The Life and Works of John Arbuthnot*, ed. George A. Aitken (Oxford, 1892), pp. 305-60.
[16] Wieland, *Werke*, Vol. 40, pp. 571-642.

that it helps to give adequate expression to the intended meaning. We have already indicated how well the footnote apparatus is suited to the ideological perspectivism of this novel and how it supports it. Still another possibility inherent in the playful form he selected must have struck Wieland as eminently suited to his nature: the dreamy tenuousness of the boundary between historical authenticity and literary fictivity in the turmoil of voices of the various speakers. It is wholly in the spirit of the Rococo. At the same time it is romantic irony *ante datum* when reality and illusion are allowed to spill over, one into the other. Let us recall the artistic device used so often by interior decorators of the Rococo in Wieland's Swabian homeland. They caused the stucco sculpture to blend into the ceiling paintings so skillfully that the observer asks himself in vain: is the three-dimensionality still genuine or already illusory?

In a similar fashion the reader of *Danischmend* is constantly faced with a scarcely solvable question. Is the content of the footnote authentic or fictive? And even in this form the question is formulated too simply. When we look more closely, it splits up into a series of partial questions because of the multiplicity of transitional forms ranging between those two extremes. At the outermost ends of this scale the reader thinks that he knows the answer. On the one hand, he determines that a few notes supply normal explanations or sources for statements in the text. For instance, when a quotation from Pliny occurs in the text, the footnote gives the source. We cannot imagine what could be fictive here. And if we check on it, it is correct.[17] On the

---

[17] Something else is not accurate: namely the wording of the Pliny quotation itself. Danischmend buys a small estate, "approximately as large as Pliny considers that a learned idler would need"—that is to say, "just as much land as he would need in order to lean his head back against a tree, to regale his nearsighted eyes with a view into the green, to creep back and forth on the same footpath between his cabbage garden and grain field, to know all of his grape vines by heart, and to keep a register of all his little trees" (x, 332). This sounds rather suspicious. What does the source say? "Scholasticis porro dominis, ut hic est, sufficit abunde tantum soli, ut relevare caput, reficere oculos, reptare per limitem unamque semitam terere om-

other hand, if "the typesetter" or even "the indulgent reader" signs a footnote, its illusory nature is immediately evident to the reader. But what about all the gradations lying between these extremes? There is a mass of real authors: Herbelot, Gibbon, Hume, Saint-Évremond, Philodemus, Epictetus, Beccaria, Brantôme, *e tutti quanti*. Are their statements authentic, or are they merely attributed to them? In many cases they clearly bear the stamp of the illusory, but not always. The reader afflicted with exploratory ambitions plunges into the thicket of reference works and old novels. Sometimes he comes across the trace of his quarry. Sometimes he loses its track—and Wieland gazes serenely down upon him from his rococo heaven and rubs his hands in glee at having mobilized and duped a new descendant of the race of Scriblerus and Walter Shandy.

Let us clarify what we have said by a few examples. When Epictetus reacts to a certain "case" mentioned in the text with the words: "I deny absolutely that there could ever be such a case" (x, 340), then the illusory nature of the remark is self-evident. (The specific content is of no concern here.) One can ask at most whether the observation is in keeping with the spirit of Epictetus, whether he *could* have reacted in this way. The possible takes precedence over the real. But when "Santon" appears in the text, it looks quite authentic for this word to be elucidated in a note signed with the name of the famous Orientalist Herbelot: "A kind of Mohammedan monk of strict observance. They devote themselves, in complete isolation from all earthly things, to contemplation; and they believe—or pretend to—that they stand in very close community with the highest being" (x, 328). When we have checked in

---

nesque viticulas suas nosse et numerare arbusculas possint" (Pliny, I, 24, 4). We see that Wieland retains the precise order of the individual statements, but each single part is intensified in color. "Reficere oculos" becomes "to regale his *nearsighted* eyes"; "numerare arbusculos": "to keep a register of all his little trees," and so forth. While Pliny's *eidyllion* itself has a nice quality of vividness, Wieland transforms it by means of his "humoristic sensuousness" into the snug coziness of the Biedermeier period.

Barthélémy d'Herbelot's *Bibliothèque orientale ou Diction-naire universel contenant tout ce qui fait connaître les peu-ples de l'Orient* (Paris, 1697), only to find no rubric that re-sembles "santon" or anything like it, we have reason to be-lieve that we have been made fools of. But further investi-gation reveals that the word "santon" does indeed occur, from the seventeenth century on, in German-French spe-cialized works as the designation for a category of Oriental (mostly Mohammedan) monks of fanatical devotion.[18] In the next note signed "Herbelot," we naturally suspect an-other fiction, but this time we really find the source under the rubric cited, "Schedad Ben A'd." At the same time we note that Wieland has provided the quoted material with embellishments of his own (x, 330). So one can never know for sure. . . .

The situation is different, of course, when it is not the real authors but their fictive creatures who appear as an-notators. In some cases ("Duns," "Tristram Shandy," "Mart. Scriblerus jun.") the reader can identify them. But often he gropes in the dark. The poet's claim that he is justified in assuming among his readers "a certain familiarity with novels, plays and other works of the imagination and wit" turns out to be rather demanding. We should keep in mind, of course, the fact that the educated reader of those days was familiar with many things that have subsequently dis-appeared from the general cultural consciousness. It requires a certain scavenger's luck to recognize in "Didius" that "great church lawyer" who plays an unpleasant subsidiary role in *Tristram Shandy*. Here one can immediately ascer-tain with what mimetic skill Wieland captured the law-yer's malicious and arrogant tone. The same holds true for "Futatorious," who—also in *Tristram Shandy*—plays such a

---

[18] I have gratefully appropriated this information from Jost Schille-meit's review of the German edition of my book in *Göttingische Ge-lehrte Anzeigen*, 216 (1964), 81-100, esp. 97f. I take this occasion to refer to this review, which in fact assumes the proportions of a valu-able contribution, since the author, on his own, develops in a valid and gratifying manner certain lines that are present in my book only in rudimentary form.

miserable role in the burlesque incident with the hot chest-
nut.[19] He too lives up to his role by distinguishing himself
as an authority in the field indicated by his sobriquet
(*futuo* = cohabit or sleep with; x, 341). The commentator
"Pantilius Cimex" is obviously a no less spiteful fellow than
Didius. The reader must recall Horace's incidental remark
against a fictive carper: *"Men' moveat cimex Pantilius?"*
("Should I get all worked up about a louse like Pantilius?"
Sat. i, 10, 78). Wieland, playfully changing the generic
noun to a proper name, makes of the louse Pantilius a Pan-
tilius Louse and causes him to speak in a suitable tone. Es-
pecially successful is the imitation of Arbuthnot's "mock
gravity" in the utterances of "Mart. Scriblerus." The latter
does not content himself with short notes but always de-
clares himself prepared to "develop" the relevant question
more extensively in a thick volume of commentaries. As
a result, "the indulgent reader" once interrupts him in the
middle of a sentence with the words: "God forbid! When
Mr. Scriblerus *develops*, it is exactly as when Mr. Theofilus
Murrzufflus quotes; there is no end of developing and quot-
ing" (x, 354). In accord with the practice of Rabelais and
Sterne, the author had already permitted this Murrzufflus
to contribute a long series of references to Socrates' con-
cept of "Genius"—δαιμόνιον. The references are genuine,
by the way. In general the "mock gravity" is less excessive
here than in Wieland's models. It reaches its high point in
the exclamation concluding the note: "A——h! How my
fingers ache from copying!" (x, 325).

The names of imaginary figures borrowed from existing
writings generally belong to the realm of "learned wit" and
the persiflage of pedantry. They are for the most part
"speaking" sobriquets with an obvious etymology. We may
assume that Wieland also applied this technique inde-
pendently. A number of annotators with comico-learned
names came to life for the first time in his work. This is true,
for instance, of the aforementioned grumpy pedant Murr-

[19] *Tristram Shandy*, Bk. IV, Chaps. 25-29.

zufflus, and it is probably the case with such figures as "M. Pantaleon Onocefalus" (Asshead), "Bucefalus" (Cowhead), and others of the sort. Of course it remains a possibility that sources might turn up for some of these cases.

To catalogue these materials from the viewpoint of whether they are authentic or fictive gives only a provisional and unsatisfactory impression of the ingenious game that is played in the notes. If we want to do justice to the author, we have to recapitulate a few particularly eloquent cases in *Danischmend* more precisely. It is especially the multiple figures brought about by incapsulation or concatenation which arouse our interest. A simple case of incapsulation occurs when "Bekkaria" starts talking in connection with a rape scene. Expressing skepticism, he doubts whether a woman under such circumstances can really complain of force, and suggests that she herself bears part of the blame (x, 398). (The name "Bekkaria" refers to Cesare Bonesano Marchese de Beccaria. A legal scholar famed in the circle of French Enlightenment thinkers, he agitated for the reform of penal law in his *Traité des délits et des peines*, 1764.) To substantiate his opinion, "Bekkaria" refers to a simile that Anne de France once used in order to clarify her point of view in the same matter to her ladies-in-waiting. But he does not reveal the content of the simile, which "in our day cannot well be repeated" before such a good society as our public is! The reader is supposed to look up the story in Brantôme's memoirs. It turns out that the reference is correct.[20] It deals with a rather primitive *topos* from the language of erotic metaphor. We must ask ourselves whether it was really consideration for the prudery of the reader or rather artistic gratification in a new variety of aposiopesis—suppression of the *pointe* by means of the omission of an incapsulated quotation—that was the deciding factor!

The notes to the fifteenth chapter, "A Family Affair," constitute a clear figure of concatenation. Danischmend and

[20] Seigneur de Brantôme, *Oeuvres*, Vol. 1 (Haag, 1740), p. 318.

the Calender, unobserved, witness a touching family scene. This scene is itself a kind of quotation; not a literary one, to be sure, but a literary reproduction of Greuze's famous painting "L'accordée du village." Apart from a few minor changes, the painting is precisely described down to the finest details. The only substantial difference is a switch of right and left, probably because Wieland used a copper-plate engraving that gave a mirror image of the original.[21] This "family affair," now, stands in the middle of the series of chapters that contains the great ideological debate between Danischmend and the Calender, where it fulfills a clear function. It is an illustrative confirmation of the ideal virtue that Danischmend preaches in the neighboring chapters and at the same time offers the Calender an opportunity for cynical glosses. Thus the scene appears in a double intellectual perspective, wholly in keeping with the words of Danischmend that immediately precede: "We cannot and we should not all peer into the world through one and the same keyhole." This perspectivistic illumination is continued in the notes, which somehow reflect the Calender's cynicism. First, "A Collector of Engravings" (!) accuses the narrator of plagiarism: "I would be willing to bet anything that the author stole this scene from Greuze." Thereupon "A Connoisseur" remarks that the author has omitted the jealous sister represented in the painting, and this moves him to insinuate: "Probably he hoped to conceal the theft more readily by such omissions." "Pantilius Cimex," of course, approves of this explanation *ad malam partem*: "Between two possible explanations one must always choose the one most derogatory to the author" (x, 378).

Finally, incapsulation can be combined with concatenation to produce delightful complications. In connection with the phrase "Persian dancer," an annotator known as

---

[21] Mirror image reproduction of paintings was not uncommon at the time. In fact there is a contemporary engraving by Filpart which reproduces "L'accordée du village" in reverse. (This engraving is in the possession of the National Museum in Amsterdam.)

"Mark. d'Argens"[22] refers at one point to a source in his own *Lettres Chinoises* and to the writings of Chardin[23] in order to authenticate the piquant fact that professional dancers in Persia were named "according to the fee by which they sold their nights." "They are not called Fatima or Kanzadeh or Zelika but Ten-Toman, Twenty-Toman, Thirty-Toman. (A toman is a golden coin, about four ducats of our money.)" This information evokes in turn a gloss from "Filodemus" (Philodemos, an Epicurean of the first century B.C.) who exclaims: "They are expensive! ουκ ωνουμαι μυριων δραχμων μεταμελειαν as Demosthenes said" ("I am not going to spend ten thousand ducats for any regrets," x, 338f.). The ostensible quotation, however, can be found neither in Philodemos nor in Demosthenes. It does occur, as Jost Schillemeit has shown, in the *Noctes Atticae* of Aulus Gellius, who in his turn is quoting from a no longer extant work of the Peripatetic Sotion. It turns out to be the punch line of an anecdote, according to which the great orator has secretly visited the famous Corinthian hetaera Lais. When she demanded that sum for the favors of her love, Demosthenes replied with the words cited. The anecdote lifted from Gellius-Sotion is a strikingly appropriate comment on the curious data communicated by the Marquis d'Argens.[24] That Wieland chose Philodemos as his speaker here may stem from the fact that for Philodemos, an Epicurean, remorse has no positive ethical value. It is relevant in this connection to recall his work *De morte* (cols. 32-35), where an innocent man who has been condemned to death is consoled by the fact that his judges will be tormented for the rest of their lives by the remorse awakening in them on his account.[25] Here, of course, the figure

[22] Jean-Baptiste de Boyer, Marquis d'Argens, 1704-71. He lived in Holland as a journalist and was later summoned to Berlin by Frederick the Great and named director of the Academy.

[23] Jean Chardin, 1643-1713, was a famous world traveler who lived many years in Persia. His *Journeys to Persia and India* (10 vols., 1711) was a key source for the Oriental lore of the eighteenth century.

[24] Cf. the persuasive and delightful proof by Jost Schillemeit, *op.cit.*, pp. 99f.

[25] Nestle, *Die Nachsokratiker* (1923), Vol. 1, p. 249.

of concatenation is a mere play of caprice. But as such it succeeds beautifully, producing a graceful rococo curlicue on the lower edge of the page!

A few times, series of notes are rounded off into dainty little closet dramas. As self-contained creations, they illuminate the intellectual situation of the times through the alternation of voices and bear their meaning and value in themselves. Let us conclude by considering two exemplary cases. In the seventh chapter Danischmend is sitting in the last light of evening with his child on his lap, answering the boy's questions "as well as a wise man can answer the questions of a child, which are often subtle by virtue of their sheer simplicity." "But, Papa, said the boy, why is it getting dark? Because the sun has set, my son, answered Papa." At this point "Magister Duns" cuts loose in a note against the notion that any "great wisdom of nature" is contained in such a question. It is rather, he maintains, "a very stupid question. For if the boy had paid attention to why it is bright in daytime—namely, that it gets bright as soon as the sun rises and remains bright as long as the sun is in the sky —then he would have been able to conclude immediately that it must get dark when the sun is gone. The brat should have been mine. I would have taught him to draw conclusions!" What a tenacious life literary fictions have! It is more than half a century since Pope wrote the *Dunciad*. For at least thirty years the figure of "Duns" had been haunting the fields of German literature as a caricature of the rationalism of Wolff and Gottsched—or of Gottsched himself. As early as 1745, Uz, in his poem "Magister Duns," ridiculed the Gottschedians who "depart from the language of the Muse and introduce the language of Wolff into their verses":[26]

> Der Mann bewies, wie sich's gehört,
> Und bat, abstrakt und tiefgelehrt,
> Durch schulgerechte Schlüsse
> Um seiner Chloris Küsse.

[26] Johann Peter Uz, Letter of 27 June 1745 to Gleim; in *Deutsche National-Litteratur*, ed. Joseph Kürschner, Vol. 45, p. 28.

(The man made his proofs, as is fitting,
And, abstractly and learnedly, pleaded
By proper scholastic conclusions
For the kisses of his Chloris.)

Lessing's "Answer to the Question: Who is the great Duns"[27] was directed against Gottsched personally in the very year when Wieland published his "Advertisement of a Dunciad for the Germans" (1755). Gleim and Zachariä also took part in the ridicule of "Duns." Now, a decade after Gottsched's death, his caricature continues to live. In the surly arrogance of the tone, in the insistence upon the almighty "conclusion," one believes that one still hears his voice.

The opposing voice is raised when "David Hume" begins: "If Herr Duns would take the trouble to read my seventh essay attentively he would find that the boy, without having learned logic, has more logic in his brain than he thinks." This is a reference, of course, to the "Inquiry concerning Human Understanding" and specifically to the seventh chapter, "Of the Idea of Necessary Connexion." The fact that Wieland singles out the "seventh essay" indicates that he had in mind the first edition (1748), entitled *Philosophical Essays Concerning Human Understanding*, in which the section subsequently entitled "Seventh Chapter" is still called "Essay VII" and is entitled "Of the Idea of Power or Necessary Connexion." It is this essay that reduced the category of causality to a subjective "idea," based upon "habit" and upon the "belief" growing out of habit. As such it undermined one of the main pillars of dogmatic rationalism. "When we say, therefore, that one object is connected with another, we mean only that they have acquired a connexion in our thought. . . ."[28] It was such sentences as this that also awakened Kant from his "dogmatic slumber." The oft-cited example of the sunrise is found not

[27] Lessing, *Sämtliche Schriften*, ed. Lachmann-Muncker (Stuttgart, 1886-1924), Vol. 1, p. 42.
[28] David Hume, *An Enquiry Concerning Human Understanding*; in Bibliotheca Philosophorum, Vol. 7 (1913), p. 78.

here, but in the note to the sixth essay, "Of Probability," which reduces ostensible certainties to probabilities. "Mr. Locke divides all arguments into demonstrative and probable. In this view, we must say, that it is only probable all men must die, or that the sun will rise to-morrow."[29] It looks very much as though the conception of the controversy between Duns and Hume originated from this source and that it, in turn, had the retroactive effect of inspiring the conversation between Danischmend and his son. The words of "Tristram Shandy," finally, supply the third voice, the humorous subjectivism which supports Hume's skepticism against dogmatic rationalism: "And when a child of four years gets into an exchange of words regarding such things with a highly illustrious doctor, then one can always wager a fool's cap against a doctor's hat that the child is right" (x, 345).

Here we see how typical representatives of the major intellectual powers of the day—rationalism, skepticism, subjectivism—are confronted with one another in a sort of "imagined conversation." To be sure, it is much more abstract than the lovely "Imaginary Conversations" of Paul Ernst, for here it is not imagined that the conversational partners are present physically. Rather, their voices resound through all temporal and spatial separations in the thin air of a purely intellectual realm. In a series of notes to the twelfth chapter, Wieland has built up a conversation of this sort even more fully and with more substance. Characteristically, it is attached to a very incidental remark made by the old Calender as he tells his life story. "All men —perhaps with the exception of a few extraordinary geniuses—become what they are because of *circumstances.*" This materialistic determinism, an important component in the chorus of intellectual opinions of the Enlightenment, suits the old cynic quite well. Yet he does not represent this ideology consistently, but is—witness his parenthetical remark—prepared to concede an exception from time to time. And this limitation now provokes the staunch advo-

[29] *Ibid.*, p. 57.

cate of determinism, "Helvetius," who comments upon it as follows: "The Calender did well to say *perhaps*. For if one looks carefully, it always turns out that even the extraordinary geniuses would not have become what they are without certain special circumstances which gave them precisely this and no other education, interest, and direction" (x, 360). This, as one can easily establish, is an extract from Helvetius' famous materialistic manifesto *De l'Esprit* (1758). It is lifted specifically from the third "Discours," which in the course of its two hundred pages treats the question "Si l'esprit doit être considéré comme un don de la nature, ou comme un effet de l'éducation" ("Whether the spirit ought to be considered as a gift of nature or as an effect of education").[30] The concept *éducation* is defined so broadly that it is practically identical with *circonstances*. The terse result states:

> La conclusion de ce discours, c'est que tous [!] les hommes, communément bien organisés, ont en eux la puissance physique de s'élever aux plus hautes idées; et que la différence d'esprit qu'on remarque entr'eux dépend des diverses circonstances dans lesquelles ils se trouvent placés, et de l'éducation différente qu'ils reçoivent.

> (The conclusion of this discourse is that all men, if they are socially well organized, have in them the physical power to elevate themselves to the loftiest ideas; and that the difference of spirit that one observes among them depends on the diverse circumstances in which they are placed and on the different educations that they receive.)[31]

Helvetius now applies this to *génie*: "C'est que le génie n'est point un don de la nature . . ."; "L'homme de génie n'est donc que le produit des circonstances dans lesquelles cet homme s'est trouvé" ("So genius is by no means a gift

---

[30] Helvetius, *De l'Esprit* (1st ed.; Paris, 1758), p. xiii.
[31] *Ibid.*, p. xix.

of nature . . ."; "The man of genius is thus only the product of the circumstances in which this man is located").[32]

In his stubborn monomania, Helvetius does not see that his view has long since been refuted in advance by the Abbé Dubos in the six introductory chapters to the second book of his *Réflexions critiques sur la Poésie et sur la Peinture* (1719). But Wieland notices it. He also understands the epoch-making value of Dubos' concept of genius, and with a gay hysteron proteron he causes "Dübos" to react to Helvetius' words with circumspect and finely shaded phrases and thought patterns, which he has borrowed from the original with a fine ear. A brilliant adaptation! First Dubos meets his opponent halfway by conceding the reality of "hindering or favoring circumstances":

> But it is also true—and all the inductions and sophistries that Helvetius heaps up against it have no power against a fact confirmed so greatly by general experience—that a person is *born* to be an Alexander, Hannibal, Homer, Lycurgus, Socrates, Phidias, Hippocrates, Archimedes. And spirits of this order are able to break their own way even through the thickest forest of hindrances.

Dubos has explained this very fact—that one must be born to genius—when he illustrated it with reference to the "grands Capitaines." "On n'acquiert point la disposition d'esprit dont je parle; on ne l'a jamais, si on ne l'a point apportée en naissant" ("One does not acquire the disposition of spirit of which I speak; one never has it unless one brought it with him at birth").[33] From the second chapter on he devotes himself especially to the "genius" of artists. The third chapter has a self-explanatory title: "Que l'impulsion du génie détermine à être Peintre ou Poète, ceux qui l'ont apporté en naissant" ("That the Impulse of Genius Determines Those Who Received It at Birth To Be Painter or Poet"). With a wealth of examples from history he shows

[32] *Ibid.*, pp. 470, 473.
[33] Abbé Dubos, *Réflexions critiques sur la Poésie et sur la Peinture*, Vol. 2 (Paris, 1755), p. 8.

how many painters and poets, despite all obstacles, have found the way prescribed by their *génie*. For our purposes it is especially convenient to note that the fourth chapter ("Objection contre la proposition précédente; et réponse à l'objection") precisely anticipates the objection on which for Wieland, the central point of the controversy between Helvetius and Dubos hinges. Dubos uses a simile to refute the objection that genius is determined by social circumstances: ". . . je regarde l'arrangement des conditions diverses qui forment la société, comme une mer. Les génies médiocres sont submergés, mais les génies puissans trouvent enfin le moyen d'aborder au rivage" (". . . I regard the arrangement of the diverse conditions that constitute society as an ocean. Mediocre geniuses are submerged, but the powerful geniuses finally find the means of reaching the shore").[34] In Wieland's text the "ocean" has become "the thickest forest of obstacles."

The beginning of Dubos' fifth chapter summarizes the content of the preceding ones in a lapidary image: "Le génie est donc une plante, qui, pour ainsi dire, pousse d'elle-même . . ." ("Genius thus is a plant which, so to speak, sprouts of its own accord . . .").[35] The image of the growing plant—which was to become so widespread during the Age of Genius—seems too pallid to Wieland in this form. Once again he pulls out all the stops of his "humoristic sensuousness" in order to intensify it. "They [the extraordinary geniuses] resemble a stripling oak which by means of earth, water, air and fire grows up to be an oak, but which becomes an oak tree nonetheless even if blight and termites, rats and moles, goats and cattle unite against it along with all the aforementioned elements." The description turns out to be even more colorful in the following sentence, which reproduces Dubos' second main thesis. There is a fundamental difference between *génies* and *artisans* inasmuch as the latter, through lack of that germinating power that determines character from within, allow themselves to be shaped by external circumstances. By the

[34] *Ibid.*, p. 38.   [35] *Ibid.*, p. 45.

121

term *artisans* Dubos thus understands "ces esprits indéter-minés, qui ne sont propres à tout, que parce qu'ils ne sont propres à rien" ("these undetermined spirits who are suitable for everything only because they are suitable for nothing").[36] In Wieland's drastic recasting this becomes: "Ordinary men, on the other hand, are like a piece of wood, clay or marble in the hand of art. Depending on how one cuts, planes, presses and hews it, it can be made into a stool or a priapus, a bowl or a night pot, an Apollo or a Silenus." Yet even this variegated sensuousness has a learned origin. For Dubos' train of thought has been enlivened by the addition of related but more concretely formulated thoughts from older sources. "A bowl or a night pot" goes back to Paul's Epistle to the Romans (9:21), where God is compared to a potter: "Hath not the potter power over the clay, of the same lump to make one vessel into honour, and another into dishonour?" An even more conspicuous case occurs in the adaptation of the following passage from Horace's *Satires* (i, 8, 1-3):

> Olim truncus eram ficulnus, inutile lignum,
> cum faber, incertus scamnum faceretne Priapum,
> maluit esse deum. Deus inde ego. . . .
>
> (Once I was the trunk of a fig tree,
>   a useless kind of wood.
> The carpenter, unable to decide whether he should
> Make me into a stool or into Priapus,
> Settled on the god. So I'm a god. . . .)[37]

Then Wieland summarizes the main thought once again. "In short, the man of genius is a *work of nature* which bears its form and affective forces within itself. The others are anything that time and circumstances, habit and need, rogues and fools, tyrants and rulers want to make of them." (The word *Bonzen*—"rulers"—leads back to the local color

---

[36] *Ibid.*, p. 62.

[37] I am indebted to Rudolf Hesse for pointing out the borrowings from Horace and from the Epistle to the Romans.

of *Danischmend.*) This is a perfect example of periphrastic quoting, which preserves faithfully the substance of the original and at the same time, by a process of distillation and expansion, creates a new linguistic gem.

An anticlimax follows. Out of the narrow corner of his reactionary churchly orthodoxy "The preacher at ****" expresses his profound lack of understanding for the whole controversy. "I think nothing of all these philosophies and of this distinction between geniuses and ordinary men. There is not a word about it in my *Quenstädt*."[38] The popular homiletic tone is reproduced delightfully: "We are all poor sinners, and if we do not turn back and become like unto little children, then in the end Master Hangman will come and fetch the geniuses as well as the common people." This voice from the Lutheran parsonage is then confirmed, with an authoritarian ring, by "J.C.H.":[39] "In this matter the Reverend is right." Once again, here is a totally empty statement which accurately attests to the humorist's fondness for "maximum deflation." At the same time, like a firm pedal note, the statement rounds off this conversation constructed of climax and anticlimax.

The dreamlike melee of genuine quotations, half-quotations, and pseudo-quotations in the "Notis Variorum" of *Danischmend* takes its place in a tradition which by then was already centuries old: the ridicule of quasi-scientific pedantry. Although this element of persiflage is evident at

[38] Johannes Andreas Quenstädt, 1617-88, Lutheran theologian, professor in Wittenberg. Of his many writings (Jöcher's *Allgemeines Gelehrten-Lexikon*, VI [1819], catalogues seventy-one of them), probably the following is meant: *Theologia didacticopolemica, sive systema Theologica* (Wittenberg, 1685 and 1696).

[39] The initials J.C.H. possibly conceal the theologian Johann Christoph Harenberg, famous around the middle of the century, who—a Pastor Goetze *ante datum*—in 1747 and 1748 attacked the deist Edelmann in a two-volume polemic (*Die gerettete Religion, oder gründliche Widerlegung des Glaubensbekenntnisses Johann Christian Edelmanns*). In his reply Edelmann lampooned him as "St. Harenberg." As late as 1765, Harenberg launched a polemic against the Freemasons, to whom of course Lessing also belonged. Cf. Jöcher's *Allgemeines Gelehrten-Lexikon*, II (1787); and Hermann Hettner, *Geschichte der deutschen Literatur im achtzehnten Jahrhundert* (1862-70), *passim*.

every step, it recedes somewhat behind the deeper concern, which is to allow the perspectivistic art of illumination to cast its many colors over and beyond the border of the novel's text.[40] This art of illumination seeks its meaning and finds its justification in a basic conviction that Wieland shares with Sterne. It is expressed incomparably in the motto of *Tristram Shandy*: "Not facts in themselves move men, but their opinions regarding these facts."[41]

[40] The concept of perspectivism as it is developed here corresponds closely to the elucidations of Kayser, *Entstehung und Krise des modernen Romans*, pp. 13-20.

[41] The artistic treatment of footnotes in the two novels that we have investigated reveals an essential characteristic of Wieland's general intellectual manner; this is confirmed by Goethe's statement as noted by Falk on the day of Wieland's burial: ". . . es war Wieland in allen Stücken weniger um einen festen Standpunkt als um eine geistreiche Debatte zu tun. Zuweilen berichtigt er den Text in einer Note, würde es aber auch nicht übelnehmen, wenn jemand aufträte und wieder durch eine neue Note seine Note berichtigte. Übrigens muss man Wieland deswegen nicht gram werden; denn gerade diese Unentschiedenheit ist es, welche den Scherz zulässig macht, indes der Ernst immer nur eine Seite umfasst und an dieser mit Ausschliessung aller heitern Nebenbeziehungen festhält." Goethe, *Gedenkausgabe der Werke* (Zürich: Artemis-Verlag, 1948-*ca.* 54), Vol. 22, p. 670.

CHAPTER VI

E. T. A. Hoffmann

LIFE AND OPINIONS OF
TOMCAT MURR

THE basic experience underlying E.T.A. Hoffmann's entire work is a radical dualism of ideal and real. He sees life as an irreconcilable conflict between the common world of every day and the high-pitched human spirit that wishes to transcend mundane reality and storm the heavens of the ideal. This dualism found its purest expression and its most adequate narrative form in *Life and Opinions of Tomcat Murr* (*Lebensansichten des Katers Murr*). The complete title reads: *Life and Opinions/ of the/ Tomcat Murr/ along with/ a fragmentary Biography/ of the/ Conductor Johannes Kreisler/ in/ random Waste-sheets/ edited by/ E.T.A. Hoffmann.* The amusing pretense of the narrative is that through an oversight of the typographer, the "waste-sheets" (fragments of Kreisler's biography) were inserted at random into the biography of Tomcat Murr. It has long been known that this device goes back to certain hints in Jean Paul. We do not need to go into the historical connection here. As far as we are concerned, the only important fact is that such a fiction makes possible and justifies an alternation of two almost unrelated imaginary worlds, which are held together only by a very slender pragmatic thread. But through the fiction of the oversight they are constantly brought together in radical confrontation.

This duality of structure palpably reflects the ideological dualism of the novel. On the one hand there is the world of the Philistine Tomcat—on the other, that of the musician Kreisler. Naturally the figure of Kreisler, which—in view of its development throughout Hoffmann's work—has not un-justly been called the poet's "alter ego," is an incomparably deeper conception than the literary cat. Similarly, the Kreis-ler section of the novel is unmistakably the primary and more substantial part, while the Murr part is derivative and determined by its contrastive function within the novel. As far as external form is concerned, however, the relationship is just the opposite: Murr's autobiography is presented as the "actual" novel, and the Kreisler fragments appear only as a haphazard appendage. This very reversal conceals an ironic meaning. The unessential and banal has a firm, broad base in life and glorifies itself in a continuous self-por-trayal. The essential human destiny is inconstant and fleet-ing; it is forced to the edge, and only through the accident of a comical oversight do we obtain fragmentary knowl-edge of it.

One might assume that these two worlds, linked by their very opposition, would be realized linguistically by clear differentiation and contrast between their stylistic levels as is the case, for instance, in *Don Quixote* or in Jean Paul's *Years of Indiscretion (Flegeljahre)*. This assumption holds true, however, only to an astonishingly slight degree. This may be conditioned to a certain extent by the strongly formulaic character of Hoffmann's writing, which is typical of his style and which deserves to be investigated thor-oughly.[1] Thus, the frequent and only slightly differentiated *fortissimi* in the expression of poignancy as well as of pathos and horror are characteristic for the *entire* novel, whether they occur in the Murr section or in the Kreisler section. To express the inner turmoil of Kreisler, Master Abraham, or Julia, Hoffmann uses—in a sense of genuine pathos—such expressions as: "an ineffably sweet woe agi-tated his soul," "gripped by the deepest horror," "deep ter-

---

[1] A valuable model for any investigation of this sort is supplied by Werner Kohlschmidt's study, "Die symbolische Formelhaftigkeit von Eichendorffs Prosastil. Zum Problem der Formel in der Romantik," *Form und Innerlichkeit* (1955).

ror thrilled through me," "agitated by inner terrors."[2] And how does the enamoured Murr express himself when he hears his darling Miesmies sneeze? "Oh, the sound penetrated my soul with sweet tremors, my pulses pounded— my blood coursed boiling through all veins—my heart was about to burst—all ineffably painful delight that crazed me streamed forth in the extended *meow* that I uttered" (pp. 162ff.). Obviously such expressions are ready-made stock bits which, according to the context, can be used with a "genuine" or "false" meaning, in a serious or parodistic sense. It is not the wording itself, which after all remains constant, but only the context that is decisive for the intended meaning. The same holds true also for many key ideological phrases. Kreisler: "I cannot express the agonies of my condition when . . . everything suddenly seems to me to be miserable, futile, drab, dead, and I felt myself transposed *into a disconsolate wilderness*" (p. 77). Murr: "For must I not perceive everywhere that I stand alone as though *in the deepest wilderness* since I do not belong to the present age, no, to a future age of higher culture, since there is not a single soul alive who is able to admire me properly?" (p. 161; italics here and above are mine). What in one area is genuine language of the soul is talked to pieces by shallow vanity in the other. Examples for such interchangeability of words and expressions could be cited almost ad infinitum.

From this observation we gain access to the understanding of Hoffmann's art of quoting. On the basis of the fundamental dissimilarity of the two parts, one might at first assume that the quotations occurring in the Murr section would have to stem from different *sources* than those in the Kreisler part. But the opposite is true. One gets the impression that Hoffmann has at his disposal an abundant supply

---

[2] *Kater Murr*, pp. 149, 150, 154, 177. I quote here and elsewhere from E.T.A. Hoffmann, *Werke*, ed. Georg Ellinger (Berlin, 1927), Vol. 9. Let me call attention at this point to Ellinger's copious and, for our purposes, revealing commentary in Vol. 16.

of ready quotations which can be used equally well in both parts. But one might well ask whether the two parts differ specifically in the manner in which the ethical and aesthetic implications of the quotations are used, just as we have seen was the case in the use of formulaic expressions.

At first glance, to be sure, this does not seem very probable. Hoffmann generally employs his quotations with a certain carefree boldness and negligence. He strews them about just us they occur to him and completely lacks that somewhat hairsplitting cautiousness with which, for instance, Wieland weaves his quotations and allusions into delicate shapes. The contrast between Wieland and Hoffmann is illuminating in more than one respect. In comparison with Wieland's epicurean selectivity, Hoffmann's use of quotations has a certain robustly common touch. This difference stems, of course, from their different artistic individualities. But beyond that, it is conditioned by a factor that transcends the individual: by the deep-reaching change, from the standpoint of literary sociology, that has taken place in the meantime. The arsenal from which Wieland drew consisted by and large of classical literature and of the foreign belles lettres of his century. His quotations provided a gourmet dish for literary connoisseurs. And so it probably had to be. For where did there exist a widely recognized German literature which had penetrated the general consciousness of the reading public, and upon which he could draw in his quoting? This literature was just in the process of being developed by Wieland and his contemporaries. Hoffmann, on the other hand, stood at the end of the great golden age of German literature. An abundant reservoir of national works had been accumulated and, in the consciousness of the educated literary public, had achieved canonic validity. Its sayings and formulaic expressions had taken root in the memory of an obviously rather broad audience. Hoffmann was able to draw from this supply as freely as he wished. His quotations are not select and farfetched, but consist for the most part of current poetic expressions of the sort that go from mouth to mouth in the process of becoming *geflügelte Worte* ("winged words"). (Reversing causality and chronology, one could almost believe that Hoffmann had plundered Büchmann!)[3] Characteristically, poetic expressions disseminated orally by means of song, drama, and opera libretto make up the majority of Hoffmann's quotations. Indeed, a foreign writer stands at the top of the list: Shakespeare. But it is the Shakespeare of the Schlegel-Tieck translation which, through book and stage, had become the common property of educated Germans. He is followed by Goethe, Schiller, Lessing, Jean Paul, Tieck; by such representatives of the literature of popular consumption as Knigge and Lafontaine; by operas and operettas, especially Mozart; and by errant tidbits from the German philosophers. In addition, of course, there are always foreign writers and those of antiquity: Rousseau, Cervantes and Tasso, Ovid and Virgil. But these too crop up for the most part in allusions taken from the supply of general culture. The broad scope of *Tomcat Murr* reflects the extent to which literary education had spread by the end of the age of Goethe. But we should not forget the other side of the coin. For it is especially the problematic secondary phenomena which accompany general literary education that force themselves upon us in any study of Hoffmann's use of quotations.

When the poet quotes on his own and at his own expense —this is the case only in the Kreisler section, because Murr's first-person narrative offers no natural opportunity for the interjection of the writer—he usually does so in an attitude of ironic detachment from the pragmatic narrative content. Prince Hector, whose wickedness the narrator implies dimly from the very beginning, receives a portrait of Princess Hedwiga, to whom he will perhaps become engaged.

When the Prince saw the portrait, he was aroused to almost the same state of ecstasy as his princely colleague in

---

[3] Translator's note: Georg Büchmann's *Geflügelte Worte* (the German equivalent of Bartlett's *Familiar Quotations*) has been the most popular collection of quotations in Germany since its first appearance in 1864.

The Magic Flute. Like Tamino, he would almost have cried if not sung: "This picture is enchantingly beautiful." And then further: "Can this sensation be love? Yes, yes, it is nothing but love!"—Among princes it is normally not love alone that causes them to strive for the most beautiful girl. But Prince Hector at this moment was not thinking of other connections when he sat down and wrote to Prince Irenäus, asking whether he might be permitted to woo for the heart and hand of Princess Hedwiga. (pp. 168ff.)

We see that as a point of reference outside the here and now of the plot, the quotation offers possibilities for ironic illumination and interpretation. Precisely because the two young men are not even remotely comparable to one another, a glaring light is supposed to be cast on the degeneracy of the prince by contrast with the noble youth Tamino, who through virtue and benevolence becomes worthy of the honor of being accepted into the sanctuary. The target of the irony is naturally Prince Hector, not Tamino; but it is unmistakable that even the latter ("his princely colleague") is more or less implicated in the irony. This double edge of Hoffmann's irony will concern us further.

Prince Hector . . . went into service for the French and was uncommonly brave. But one day, when a zither girl bawled at him: "Do you know the land where the lemons glow," he immediately departed for the land where lemons of that sort actually do glow, that is to Naples, and put on in place of his French uniform a Neapolitan one. (p. 167)

Again the irony is supposed to strike primarily at the wicked prince, surrounding him with a pallid aura of banality and inferiority. But it cannot be denied that the expression of this irony ("bawled," "lemons of that sort") simultaneously constitutes a terrible banalization of the song sung by Goethe's Mignon. And unfortunately it is questionable whether Hoffmann was entirely aware of this effect or even of the bowdlerization of the text (*glühen*, "glow" instead of *blühen*, "blossom"!). Liberties in quoting by no means always have a poetic intention in his works. They are often caused by haste and an uncertain memory.

When Kreisler and his paternal friend Master Abraham spice their speeches with quotations or literary allusions, it is done in a similar spirit of disengaging irony. The literary reminiscences constitute a potent means by which they gain distance from the pressures and dangers of their own existence. When Kreisler has barely survived an attempt on his life, his amusing epistolary report to Master Abraham begins with the words:

> "La fin couronne les oeuvres!" I could have cried like Lord Clifford in Shakespeare's *Henry VI* when the very noble Duke of York had struck him a death-dealing blow. For by God, my hat plunged, grievously wounded, into the bushes and I directly behind it, backwards like a man of whom one is accustomed to say in battle: "He's falling, or he has fallen."—Such people however rarely get up again, but your Johannes, my dear Master, did so, and right on the spot. (p. 218)

The same free sovereignty with regard to his own situation is implicit in Master Abraham's words when, with reference to his role as magician at the court of Sieghartsweil, he compares himself to the imp Droll in *Midsummer Night's Dream* or to Prospero in *The Tempest* (p. 38). In general, references to Shakespeare play a big role in the Kreisler sphere. Hamlet supplies half of the Shakespeare quotations. It has been pointed out, and rightfully so, that a hidden parallel obtains between Kreisler and the Danish prince.[4] Hemmed in by intrigues and suspected crimes, Kreisler finds protection behind a mask of farce, as does Hamlet behind a mask of affected insanity. In conversation with the abbot, who wants to talk him into a life dedicated to the

---

[4] Cf. Jean F. A. Ricci, *E.T.A. Hoffmann, l'homme et l'oeuvre* (Paris, 1947), p. 460.

church, Kreisler rightfully suspects improper motives. He cannot contain his annoyance: "Estimable people, have you never heard Prince Hamlet, even on the most rickety stage, say to an honest man named Guildenstern: 'though you can fret me, yet you cannot play upon me.'—Confound it!— That's precisely my situation!—Why do you listen to the harmless Kreisler when the harmony of love that is locked in his breast only screeches in your ears?" (p. 250). The quotation originates in a similar situation. For Hamlet, too, understands that Guildenstern is spying on him under the mask of polite good-naturedness and that the latter—much like the abbot with the wife of Counselor Benson—is tied up with the opposing party. And he adds: "Why do you circle about me to get my scent as though you wanted to drive me into a net?"; and shortly thereafter (Act III, Scene 2): "Call me what instrument you will though you can fret me, yet you cannot play upon me." The comparison with Hamlet, despite all its ironic detachment, serves the purpose of fortifying Kreisler's self-clarification. Borrowings from contemporary romantic writing, especially from Tieck, also have sometimes a similar function of illuminating Kreisler's own existence (pp. 73, 77).

At one point a quotation of this sort penetrates directly to the heart of Kreisler's existence and serves as a springboard for his most authentic and substantial confession. Princess Hedwiga has told him the gruesome story of the unhappy painter Leonhardt Ettlinger, who was inflamed by love for her mother and went mad for this reason. She thinks that she recognizes Ettlinger's features in Kreisler and she fears for his future destiny. Whatever the case may be with regard to the genealogical relationship between Kreisler and Ettlinger, and with regard to Kreisler's knowledge of these things, Kreisler is deeply stirred by the words of the princess and feels himself threatened more strongly than ever by insanity. His answer is to make the most fervent attempt to obtain clarification concerning the problem that oppresses him: To what extent is love possible for an artist? He hopes by this effort to oppose the threat of madness.

> "When . . . I once heard a rogue of a servant, in a highly amusing play, address the players with the sweet words: 'You good people and bad musicians,' I quickly divided, like the supreme judge, all humankind into two different heaps. The one consisted of the good people who are bad musicians or rather no musicians at all. But the other consisted of musicians proper. Yet no one was supposed to be damned, but all were supposed to be redeemed, though in different ways." (p. 144)

In ever bolder and ever more inspired words he depicts the difference between bourgeois love, which lands in the safe and desolate port of marriage, and the longing *eros* of the artist, which flames up "in a pure heavenly fire, that only lights and warms without destroying its object with ruinous flames" (p. 144). In Brentano's comedy *Ponce de Leon*—for it is the "highly amusing play"—Valerio gives his instructions to the village schoolmaster, who is supposed to assemble a band of musicians: "These bad musicians and good people, then, will assemble under your guidance in the forest, where they shall keep themselves, if possible, as quiet as possible. . . ."[5] The words appropriated by Hoffmann are here spoken only in passing and have scarcely any further significance. Hoffmann in his reproduction radically changes the pragmatic situation: his hero addresses the players directly instead of mentioning them in the third person. But this means very little and is probably based merely on an inexact recollection. What is important and meaningful is the transposition of the quoted words (though it too is probably unconscious). The first vocative is the subject, while the second supplies the predicate of the judgment that is concealed behind Hoffmann's formulation "You good people and bad musicians." The "good

[5] Clemens Brentano, *Gesammelte Werke*, ed. Heinz Amelung and Karl Viëtor (1923), Vol. 4, p. 475.

people," who are immediately identified with the sober middle-class citizens, are for Hoffmann by definition and of necessity "bad musicians." Conversely, true musicians cannot be "good people." A radical dualism of bourgeois and artist: that is the weighty meaning with which Brentano's casually uttered expression is loaded here. It is like an isolated grain that reaches its growth only through Hoffmann's creative appropriation.[6]

For such free spirits as Kreisler and Master Abraham, literary education is a genuine foundation for life precisely because they are able to exploit literature in a sovereign fashion. The literary Tomcat, on the other hand, who proudly appropriates the honorary title of *homme de lettres* (p. 27), is wholly the slave of his own "education." Kreisler quotes rarely and moderately; Murr's language bristles with quotations and quotation-like literary expressions—one could even say that it is a kind of literary warehouse, a single and continuous process of quoting in the broadest sense of the word. There is no reason why we should not call Murr a Philistine or, by preference, even a cultural Philistine *ante datum*.[7] But we must keep in mind that cultural Philistinism here does not merely imply dry

[6] According to Büchmann's *Geflügelte Worte* (25th ed., rev. by Bogdan Krieger; 1912), the expression "good people and bad musicians" gained currency through Heine. "I consider it advisable to cite all obscure authors along with their house number. These 'good people and bad musicians'—thus the orchestra is addressed in *Ponce de Leon*—these obscure authors always still own a copy of their long lost booklet, and in order to dig it up one must therefore know their house number" (Heine, *Ideen. Das Buch Le Grand*, Chap. 13). Hoffmann is mentioned here without any precise statement regarding his share in the popularization of the expression. On the basis both of the transposition of "musicians" and "people" and of the change in situation (address to the players), however, it is more than probable that the quotation reached Heine by way of Hoffmann. Hoffmann had also quoted Brentano's expression in the "Remarkable Sorrows of a Theater Director"—there with reference to *Ponce de Leon* and with the same transposition as in *Tomcat Murr*. Be that as it may, it is clear that not Heine but Hoffmann gave the expression its deeper implications.

[7] Cf. my essay "Nietzsches Bildungsphilister und der Philister der Goethezeit," in *Verzamelde Opstellen*, Festschrift für J. H. Scholte (Amsterdam, 1947).

rationalism, but is rather of a very composite nature. Murr is a rationalist through and through and at the same time an exuberant sentimentalist. Especially the latter component determines the characteristic tone of his language, which issues from a continually inflated chest. It drips with such expressions as "beautiful soul," "sympathetic hearts," "genius," "striving youth," "cultural impulse," and "proclivity for higher culture." This little stylistic sampling alone, which could be augmented at will, shows that not only phrases of sentimentalism have suffered. Even the lofty contents of the philosophical idealism of the era between Kant and Hegel have been trivialized into slogans. The sentimentalism is bound up with pseudo-philosophical rapture that exceeds itself in pompous utterances concerning "the spiritual power, the unknown force, or however else one might name the principle that rules over us" (p. 29) and similar expressions. The "principle that rules over us" has so enchanted Murr that he can designate the saleswoman from whom he has stolen a sausage as "the sausage principle thirsting for revenge" (p. 114). The inexhaustible and sometimes rather shallow comedy of such expressions stems from the incongruity between the sublime expression and the intended object, which is laid on with a heavy hand. The exalted feeling expends itself wholly on banal objects—tasty sausages, fried fish, or sides of bacon. In the cat Minna, Murr recognizes his "mama" and learns that she is living in needy circumstances. He pulls himself together and decides to offer her a herring head. But: "Who can measure the fickleness of the hearts of those who wander under the light of the moon!" Naturally he himself gobbles up the herring head. This disloyalty to the praiseworthy intention is introduced by the following outpouring:

Why did fate not close our breasts to the wild play of accursed passions!—Why must we, a thin vacillating reed, bend before the storm of life?—Hostile destiny!—O appetite, thy name is Tomcat!—With the herring head in my mouth, I climbed, a Pius Aeneas, onto the roof—I wanted

to go in through an attic window! Then I got into a state
that, alienating my ego from my ego in a remarkable
manner, still seemed to be my proper ego.—I believe that
I have expressed myself comprehensibly and cogently,
so that from this depiction of my remarkable state any-
one will be able to recognize spiritual depths. (p. 58)

It must be assumed that contemporary readers had no
trouble recognizing in the last sentences various tags bor-
rowed from the professional jargon of a Fichtean philosoph-
ical idealism. Parody always presupposes a certain familiar-
ity with what is being parodied. Our passage is one proof
among many for the fact that the language of the phi-
losophers at that time was banalized and talked to pieces
by its popularization. (As an analogy, consider the spread
and superficialization of existentialist jargon in our own
day.) More than two decades earlier Schiller, instigated by
the spread of Kant's terminology, had written in a letter
from Jena: "Here on every street one hears resonances of
form and matter. . . ."[8] Obviously the same thing was hap-
pening to the language of transcendental idealism.[9] Kant
himself fares no better. When the poodle Ponto is chatting
with Murr about rational morality, he reduces his belief to
the formula "throw a sprat to catch a herring." This re-
minds the Tomcat that he "had read somewhere that every-
one must act in such a way that his manner of behavior
could hold true as a general principle, or in the way that
he might wish that all might act toward him" (pp. 116ff.).
It is clear that Kant's categorical imperative is meant here:
"Act in such a way that the maxim of your will at
every time might hold true simultaneously as the principle
of a universal law." But it is equally clear that the banal and
utilitarian supplement "or in the way that he might wish

---

[8] Schiller, letter of 11 February 1793 to Bartholomäus Fischenich;
in *Schillers Briefe*, ed. Fritz Jonas (Stuttgart, 1892-96), Vol. 3, p. 252.
  [9] Murr's spiritual conflict has a parallel in Kleist's *Amphitryon*
(II, 1, verses 727-46), where Sosias' confusion regarding his other
"I," which has beat him half to death, is expressed linguistically in
witty imitation of Fichtean terminology.

that all might act toward him" wholly undermines the
Kantian precept. Similarly, the thoughtful metaphysical
hypothesis from Leibniz' *Theodicy*—that God created the
world as the best of all possible worlds—has degenerated
to an empty slogan of shallow optimism expressed in Murr's
conviction "that the world with its joys, including fried
fish, chicken bones, milk porridge, et cetera, is the best."
And he (namely the Tomcat) is the very best thing in this
world since its joys were created only for him and for his
sake (p. 233).

Thus parody and banalization go hand in hand. This holds
true, even more than in the case of philosophical theorems,
for the more fragile poetic phrases that are vulnerable be-
cause of their very linguistic form. Even here the border-
line between consciously parodistic deformation and un-
conscious bowdlerization cannot always be precisely as-
certained. When Murr cries out, in the already quoted her-
ring head passage, "O appetite, thy name is Tomcat!" and,
on another occasion, "O frailty, thy name is cat!" (p. 285),
in both cases the parody of Hamlet's "Frailty, thy name is
woman!" (Act I, Scene 2) is immediately evident. Here
absolutely no relation obtains, as it did in Kreisler's *Hamlet*
quotation, between the original meaning of the quoted ma-
terial and its new context of meaning. The parodistic
comedy consists in the fact that the quoted material has
been totally emptied of meaning. The situation is different
when Murr relates how he has conquered the heart of the
housemaid and gotten quite used to the hand which
"Wochtags ihren Besen führt und Sonntags dann am
besten karessiert" ("on weekdays pushes its broom and
then on Sundays gives its best caresses," p. 276). Here, of
course, the parodistic intent in the use of the *Faust* quota-
tion—"Die Hand, die Samstags ihren Besen führt,/Wird
Sonntags dich am besten karessieren" ("The hand that
wields the broom on Saturday/ Will, comes the Sunday,
give the best caresses")[10]—is clear enough in the new "catty"

---

[10] Goethe, *Faust I*, verses 844f.

context. But on the other hand one must entertain the suspicion that the extensive linguistic distortion happened without the poet's conscious awareness. The rhyme between *führt* and *karessiert*, which is not present in Goethe, and no less the new pentameter "and then on Sundays gives its best caresses," seem to suggest that the distortion was activated by Hoffmann's mistaken recollection.

The same thing happens to Goethe's poem "Jägers Abendlied":

> Im Felde schleich' ich still und wild,
> Gespannt mein Feuerrohr,
> Da schwebt so licht dein liebes Bild,
> Dein süsses Bild mir vor.
>
> (I prowl in the field, still and wild,
> My rifle cocked;
> Then your dear image, so brightly,
> Your sweet image, hovers forth before me.)

The enamoured Murr tries to rid himself of his love torments by mouse hunting: "Therefore I betook myself, as soon as it had gotten dark, into the cellar and wandered through the gloomy corridors singing: 'Im Walde schlich ich still und wild, gespannt mein Feuerrohr'" (p. 165). Here, too, we see the automatic response to fleeting memory: the replacement of the monosyllabic abbreviated present tense (*schleich'*) by the imperfect (*schlich*) and of the word "field" by "forest," which strikes the German mind as being more poetic. The epic assimilation of the following verses succeeds nicely as Murr continues his report: "Ha!—instead of the prey that I sought to hunt, I actually saw her *lovely image*; out of the depths it actually *stepped forth* everywhere." The word "lovely" (*hold*) that is always on the tip of the Tomcat's tongue replaces the word "dear" (*lieb*), which to his mind is less poetic; and the delicate "hovers forth" is normalized to "stepped forth." Nothing is left of Goethe's verbal coloration. The assimilation is continued when the borrowed poetic phrase catalyzes Murr's own "poetic" powers. His speech becomes rhymed and immediately thereafter turns into proper verses:

And the bitter grief of love [Liebes*schmerz*] cut my all too easily vulnerable heart [*Herz*]! And I spoke:

> 'Cast on me your lovely gazes,
> Morning light so virginal,
> And as bride and bridegroom blissful
> Murr and Miesmies wander home.
> Thus I spoke, enraptured Tomcat,
> hoping now for vict'ry's prize.
> Wretched! With her eyes veiled over
> Roofwards, timid cat, she fled!"

(The italics and the arrangement as verse are my addition.) Here we find the Spanish trochees that were so popular during the Romantic period, and in the German text even the assonance of the line ends has not been forgotten.

To this same category of the direct parody of fashionable poetic forms belongs the episode where Murr tries his hand at the difficult form of the sonnet (p. 82) and at the possibly even more exacting form of the *Glosse* (p. 83). Here it is especially striking that Murr—even in his "gloss," where the precise wording of the basic text matters greatly—grievously bowdlerizes the latter. In Goethe's "Claudine von Villa Bella" the love-lament of the heroine closes with the words:

> Liebe schwärmt auf allen Wegen;
> Treue wohnt für sich allein.
> Liebe kommt euch rasch entgegen;
> Aufgesucht will Treue sein.

> (Love runs about on every path;
> Fidelity dwells alone.
> Love advances rapidly towards you;
> Fidelity demands to be sought out.)[11]

But in Murr's version the glossed quatrain runs:

[11] JA, Vol. 8, p. 208.

Liebe schwärmt auf allen Wegen,
Freundschaft bleibt für sich allein,
Liebe kommt uns rasch entgegen,
Aufgesucht will Freundschaft sein.

Through the linguistic trivialization—*bleiben* ("remains")
instead of *wohnen* ("dwells")—the strophe loses much of
its mellow delicacy, just as it is deprived of its ardent
meaning by the change of *Treue* ("fidelity") into *Freund-
schaft* ("friendship"). It is true only to a very limited ex-
tent that the new antithesis of love and friendship better
suits the new context into which Murr's gloss is taken; for
the two concepts "love" and "fidelity" would have achieved
the same effect. Rather, one has the impression here again
that Hoffmann, carefree and unhesitating, wrote down
whatever happened to be resounding in his ear, probably
from some performance of the operetta.

This Goethe quotation, like many of the others, is not
explicitly indicated as such. So one could accuse Murr of
plagiarism—which would well suit the satirical image of a
shallow *homme de lettres* that Hoffmann has sketched in
the figure of his Tomcat. Naturally the writer calculates
that at least some of his readers will recognize the quota-
tion and thereby understand the joke. But the borrowing
can also be less easily recognizable, as for instance in
Murr's love dialogue with Miesmies: "'Dearest,' I began
softly, 'be mine!'—'Bold Tomcat,' she replied, confusedly,
'bold Tomcat, who are you? Do you know me? If you are
honest like me and true, then speak and swear to me that
you really love me'" (p. 164). Here the acuity of a shrewd
philologist is needed[12] in order to discover the source of

---

[12] Ellinger supplied the proof for this Jean Paul parody, as well
as the proof for the allusion to Jean Paul's "Biographische Belustigun-
gen unter der Hirnschale einer Riesin" in Murr's expression "my bio-
graphical entertainments on the roof" (p. 44). Hoffmann's relation
to Jean Paul is remarkably intricate. Several passages that are striking
for their poetic beauty reveal in their imaginative flight and in their
exuberant imagery the unmistakable mark of Jean Paul's coloring. At
the same time they deviate to such an extent from Hoffmann's normal
style that they strike us almost as a conscious Jean Paul imitation.

this passage in Jean Paul's novel *Titan*, where the amorous conversation between Albano and Linda runs as follows: " 'Bold man,' she said confusedly, 'who are you?—Do you know me?—If you are like me, then swear and tell me whether you have always been true!' "[13] Here the writer takes a secret pleasure in the plagiarism of his hero. It belongs to the same conception of jovial mystification when the "editor" occasionally interrupts in a marginal comment and accuses the Tomcat of literary thievery—once from *As You Like It* and another time from Chamisso's *Peter Schlemihl* (pp. 234, 285). Basically the same playful image occurs when Hoffmann appropriates for his narrative, with only slight modifications, a partial motif from *The Marriage of Figaro*: Cherubino's leap from the window and the lament of the drunken gardener over his devastated flower bed. Prince Irenäus, to whom the relevant incident is reported by his own huntsman, thinks that he has caught this wholly unliterary soul in a literary plagiarism: " 'Lebrecht,' the prince interrupted the huntsman, 'Lebrecht, that seems to be an imitation because the very same thing occurs in the opera of Herr Mozart, called the *Marriage of Figaro*, which I saw in Prague. Remain faithful to the truth, huntsman!'— 'Not even,' Lebrecht continued, 'not even a syllable do I speak that I cannot affirm with a bodily oath' " (p. 319). Sterne's play with the concept of "plagiarism" in *Tristram*

This is true above all of the words that Kreisler speaks to Julia on their first encounter: ". . . when you sang, all longing grief of love, all the delight of sweet dreams, hope, desire surged through the forest and precipitated itself, like refreshing dew in the fragrant chalices, into the breasts of listening nightingales!" (p. 65). Is this perhaps a hidden quotation similar to the one that Ellinger discovered? In any case it is remarkable that the "biographer," who belongs to the framework fiction, comes back to this passage and once again copies out the "rambling excursus" expressly in order to represent Kreisler "as an extravagant man who, especially as far as musical inspiration is concerned, often seems to the calm observer to be almost like a madman" (p. 125). By this means the gently parodistic element is intensified even if the author cannot be equated with the fictive figure of the "biographer," who has a rather Philistine streak.

[13] *Titan*, Part IV, Cycle 110.

Shandy is much more subtle, to be sure, but Hoffmann's variation is amusing enough.

Parodistic quoting succeeds best when the joke that Hoffmann is making by means of the pedantic Tomcat with his literary education is epically integrated. A few examples of this have already been encountered. The story of Murr's infatuation constitutes a splendid example in this connection. In order to make sure that it is love stirring in his soul, he studies Ovid's *Ars amatoria* and Manso's *Art of Loving* through and through—"but none of the signs of a man in love as cited in these works seemed properly to suite me. Finally it flashed through my mind that I had read in some play that an indifferent mind and a neglected beard were sure signs of a man in love!—I looked in the mirror. Heavens, my beard was unruly!—Heavens, my mind was indifferent!" (p. 163). (The two characteristics are taken from the long list of symptoms of infatuation enumerated in *As You Like It*, Act II, Scene 2, where Rosalind has the teasing intention of proving to Orlando that he is *not* in love.) Now Murr "knows" that he is really in love and similarly, after the first disappointment to which Miesmies subjects him, he studies Ovid's *Remedia amoris* in order to get rid of his love by strict observance of the advice given there. "Venus otia amat. Qui finem quaeris amoris,/ cedit amor rebus, res age, tutus eris!" (*"Venus loves leisure. You who seek an end of love,/ Since love gives way to action, act, and you will be secure!"*).[14] So Murr dutifully sets out on a mouse hunt, for it is possible "that mouse hunting might also be included among the *res*" (p. 165). Since this method is of no avail, he tries his luck with a second rule of conduct: "Exige, quod cantet, si qua est sine voce puella,/ non didicit chordas tangere, posce lyram" (*"Demand that she sing, if the girl has no voice;/ Demand the lyre if she has not learned to strike chords"*).[15] "Ha, I shall find her again, my sweet Grace, there where I saw her the first time, but she shall sing, yes, sing, and if she produces

[14] *Remedia amoris*, verses 143f.
[15] *Ibid.*, verses 333, 336.

even a single false note, then it is all over, then I shall be healed, saved" (p. 165). And only when the beloved has victoriously passed this trial—with supreme elegance she sings an aria from Rossini's *Tancred*—Murr surrenders without reservations to the joys of love. Even in his loftiest exaltations he remains an *homme de lettres*, taking the last word in its most literal sense. The tyranny of the letter over the spirit, of the book over life, could not be more adequately represented and transformed into narrative.[16]

The letter kills. For a spirit like Murr literature is a Greek gift, more of a curse than a blessing—this serious meaning shimmers through the jovial jokes at every point. Murr, conversely, is the representative of a type which has done a disservice to literature. His figure reveals the terrible banalization of poetic language, the shallow talking-to-death of the lofty meanings of German literature, at the very moment of its greatest blossoming. The worm gnaws at the fruit which still ornaments the tree. As a first diagnosis of the imminent decline of German culture, *Tomcat Murr* transcends all satire that is literary and hence partial to assume proportions of cultural criticism, a true *mene tekel*. It is particularly this evidence of cultural criticism that makes this novel, and the art of quoting applied in it, so inestimably valuable for us today. This will be borne out by what follows.

The contribution of quotations to the structure of the *Life and Opinions of Tomcat Murr* is in general very slight. All the more notable is the importance of the two quotations that stand, respectively, at the beginnings of the Murr and of the Kreisler sections. They determine the tenor of what follows and embody in their underlying relatedness the whole dualism of those two worlds. The beginning of the novel—that is, of the first chapter of Murr's autobiography—reads: "There is something beautiful, splendid, sub-

---

[16] On this theme cf. Sigmund von Lempicki, "Bücherwelt und wirkliche Welt. Ein Beitrag zur Wesenserfassung der Romantik," *Deutsche Vierteljahrsschrift für Literaturwissenschaft und Geistesgeschichte*, 3 (1925), pp. 339ff.

lime about life!—'O you sweet habit of existence!' exclaims
that Netherlandic hero in the tragedy. And I too! But not
like the hero in the painful moment when he must
part from it—no!—in the very moment when I am pene-
trated by the full bliss of the thought that I have now ar-
rived fully in that sweet habit and have no intention of ever
getting out of it again" (p. 29). The paraphrase employing
the word "that," instead of naming Egmont directly, paro-
dies the quasi-elegant complacency of the man of letters.[17]
Again we must ask: What has remained of Egmont's
words? Only the empty shell, and even it has been cracked.
Compare the glaring superficiality of Murr's exclamation
with the fervently restrained tone of Egmont's speech.
These words are the first that he speaks when he has be-
come certain that there is no rescue for him, and they intro-
duce the magnificent dialogue in which he struggles
through to a manly composure and to the affirmation of his
destiny. "Sweet life! Lovely, friendly habit of existence and
action—how shall I part from you?"[18] The praise of life as
the lovely and friendly "habit of existence and action" in
which Egmont's daemonic vitalism is affirmed has made
way for the apologia of a surfeited enjoyment of life, for
the praise of "habit" as all that is banal and commonplace.
It is the very verbal agreement that makes the intellectual
short circuit all the more painfully evident. The debase-
ment of a precious bit of cultural property by Philistine
exploitation: by virtue of this implication the opening quo-
tation of *Tomcat Murr* becomes a symbol disclosing the
meaning of the whole.

The Goethe quotation placed at the beginning of the

---

[17] Even clearer is the parodistic function of the word "that" in the
following sentence: "I felt with that poet the sweet idyllic joys in the
little house on the bank of a murmuring brook shaded by thickly
foliaged birches and weeping willows, and I stayed, giving way to
my dreams, under the stove" (p. 67). Despite the implication that
a specific poet is meant, we are obviously dealing with a concatenation
of commonplace idyllic clichés of a completely anonymous sort. The
implied association turns out to be purely illusory and is intended
to be understood as such by the reader.

[18] Goethe, JA, Vol. 11, p. 332.

Murr section is deprived of its power of meaning. By contrast, the opening quotation of the Kreisler fragments is charged with a tension that it does not possess of its own self, and it anticipates the dangerous tensions that prevail in Kreisler's world. The narrative insertion of this quotation is highly complicated. The first "waste-sheet" is located chronologically not at the beginning of the Kreisler plot, but at its absolute end. Cast in the form of a conversation between Master Abraham and Kreisler, it reports retrospectively and from a rather remote temporal perspective on the birthday celebration of the prince which is imminent at the end of the novel. Moreover, this conversation takes place at the very point of time at which the Murr plot, which chronologically follows the Kreisler plot, breaks off at the end of the second book. In a temporal framework as involved as this, this first waste-sheet holds a unique key position. The innocent reader naturally still knows nothing of all this, and he suspects nothing of the tragic complications which will come to a head at that very celebration. Even afterwards it remains a puzzle to the reader exactly what has happened. We know that the celebration was supposed to play an important role in the fateful development leading up to the double wedding of the notorious Prince Hector with Hedwiga and of the stupid Ignatius with Julia. We are aware that Master Abraham was working against this destiny when the celebration degenerated into wild panic by virtue of his magical arts. It is also implied that Master Abraham's undertaking failed. But we are left in the dark concerning the denouement.

The first Kreisler fragment transposes the reader *in medias res* with a triple intensification. First, true to its function as a "waste-sheet," it begins in the middle of a sentence. Secondly, the unprepared reader does not know who is speaking to whom. And even less does he understand that here a conversation is incapsulated in still another conversation. Master Abraham is speaking to Kreisler, but his words do not belong to the narrative present. In the form of direct speech, they recapitulate a conversation with

145

Prince Irenäus at an earlier level of time, namely immediately after the aforementioned birthday celebration. And into this incapsulated conversation, in turn, the anecdote is inserted concerning the three soldiers who, on a stormy night on the Pont Neuf in Paris, rob a poor barrister of his hat, his cloak, and his Spanish cane, crying out each time: "A strong wind is blowing, sir!" (p. 33). The whole anecdote is a quotation—ostensibly from Rabelais, but in reality from the fifty-ninth chapter of Sterne's *Sentimental Journey*. Hoffmann's recapitulation is a free retelling. Sterne's *pointe* ("'Tis an ill wind which blows nobody any good") is lost, but the author compensates by giving the anecdote a wholly new meaning. The three soldiers (the number three is original with Hoffmann) attribute the guilt, which in reality they bear themselves, to the powers of nature. Because of this the anecdote stands in a secretly ironic contrast to the further content of the conversation. For Master Abraham protests his innocence to the prince: "'Most merciful lord,' I replied, bowing humbly, 'what was responsible for all misfortune but the storm—the ghastly bad weather that erupted when everything was going so smoothly. Can I control the elements?'" (p. 34). In reality, the conjuror very definitely did "summon up the elements" (p. 35)! And at the same time he tells the prince the anecdote that reveals his own protestation of innocence to be nothing but an empty evasion. But the rascal, counting with justification on the stupidity of his royal partner in conversation, can afford to permit himself this disclosure.

Yet the achievement of the Sterne quotation is not exhausted in this hidden irony. "A strong wind is blowing, sir!" One can scarcely imagine a more suggestive upbeat to the eerily grotesque scene, painted by a satanic Breughel, in which the garden party degenerates through mystifications and natural powers into wild panic. And in this visionary scene—the high point and conclusion of the whole novel, which has been arbitrarily pushed to the beginning —not only does the artful intrigue culminate. The meaning of the Kreisler narrative is compressed into its mood of magical twilight. Externally and internally, Kreisler stands in a raging storm. He is exposed to dangerous powers and threatens to perish in them. The "strong wind" is a valid symbol for the existence of the artist, as is the "sweet habit of existence" for Murr's Philistine life. In their reciprocal interrelation the two quotations reveal the basic antithetical pattern of the novel's fabric of meaning at its very threshold. The writer who was able to make these two quotation-themes resound contrapuntally in one another was a true "musician"!

CHAPTER VII

Karl Leberecht Immermann

MÜNCHHAUSEN

IN APRIL 1830, while working on his first major novel, Karl Leberecht Immermann wrote to his brother: "It has now gotten a name, 'The Epigones,' and treats, as you perhaps surmise from the title, the advantages and misfortunes of being born too late. Our age, which stands on the shoulders of the labors and diligence of our ancestors, suffers from a certain spiritual superfluity. The fruit of their achievement lies ready for us to inherit; in this sense we are epigones. Out of this situation a very unique debility has arisen, and I consider it the task of my work to portray it in all its manifestations" (III, 7ff.).[1]

The word "epigones," with which Immermann characterizes his own generation, became a common slogan through his novel. This does not mean, of course, that the phenomenon it signified came first and only to his attention. The literary-cultural situation to which Hoffmann refers in *Tomcat Murr* could be designated as epigonal, and our analysis may have made it clear that this aspect of the age—which, to be sure, had not yet been christened with a specific name—was implicit in his parodistic use of quotations, reverberating there as a clearly audible sound. The concept of the epigone may not yet have been around as early as the 1820's, but the feeling certainly was.[2] In this

---

[1] I quote in this chapter from the five-volume edition of Immermann's *Werke*, ed. Harry Maync (Leipzig: Bibliographisches Institut, 1906). *Münchhausen* is contained in Vols. I and II, *Die Epigonen* in Vols. III and IV. Maync's copious notes were often valuable for our study.

[2] Incisive information on the complicated history of the concept can now be found in Manfred Windfuhr, "Der Epigone. Begriff,

connection it is interesting to consider that the narrative time of Immermann's *The Epigones* (*Die Epigonen*) explicitly covers the "last eight or nine years before the July Revolution" (IV, 112). At the beginning of the novel's action, around 1822 or so, he has one of his characters utter the well-known words which correspond to the passage just quoted from the letter and which he wrote down shortly before that letter: "We are—to state the entire misery in *one* word—epigones. And we labor under the burden that customarily adheres to every inheritance and to the fact of being born too late" (III, 136). This is precisely the time in which Hoffmann's *Tomcat Murr* was being written and published. The July Revolution made a deep caesura in Immermann's historical consciousness. Around the middle of the 1830's, which witnessed the main work on *The Epigones* and its completion, he views that period before the revolution lying behind him "already almost as a mythic past" (IV, 112). (In a similar manner Thomas Mann, in the foreword of *The Magic Mountain*, calls the story of Hans Castorp "far older than its years"; its "exaggerated pastness" stems from the fact that it takes place *before* the "epoch when a certain crisis shattered its way through life and consciousness"—the crisis of the First World War.) From all of this we must probably conclude that in Immermann's consciously historical thinking the "epigonal" had been at least as much an element of the recent past as it was of the post-revolutionary present.

Nevertheless, and even despite the fact that in the following pages we shall be discussing not *The Epigones* but *Münchhausen*, our theme gives us a compelling reason to begin with the concept of the epigonal. For in the light of both novels it must be said that it is one thing to diagnose the illness of an age, and quite another thing really to shake off this illness from oneself. Immermann achieved the former; whether he succeeded in the latter is questionable. As a symptom of the epigonal situation he notes a "very unique

Phänomen und Bewusstsein," *Archiv für Begriffsgeschichte*, 4 (1959), 182-209.

debility" or, as he formulates it more precisely in the novel, "a very unique corruption of language" (III, 136). He is alluding here to the paradoxical phenomenon that the German language, which during the great golden age of the spirit had been cultivated to such a high point and enriched with cultural contents of worldwide scope, had lost its innocence, as it were, through this very process of breeding, becoming for those born later an encumbered language that they can use only in an unoriginal, derivative, and cliché-ridden manner. Did Immermann know how to control this decay? At the risk of playing the devil's advocate we must conclude that the very words he uses in the letter above to depict and lament the state of the epigones suffer from the corruption of language. Let us listen once again to his lament: "Our age, which stands on the shoulders of the labors and diligence of our ancestors, suffers from a certain spiritual superfluity." The image used here, whether the author was aware of it or not, goes back to an old *topos* stemming from the High Middle Ages: We are dwarfs who sit on the shoulders of giants. For Bernard of Chartres, the probable originator of the *topos*, it specifies the relationship of his contemporary present to the authors of classical antiquity, and expresses his veneration of the spiritual ancestors as well as a certain modestly proud self-esteem. The dwarfs see more and farther than the giants— not by their own power, but because they support themselves on the former. Another representative of twelfth-century humanism uses the image to refute those who reproach him with being nothing but a compiler; still another man enlivens the image with the well-known fable of the eagle and the wren.[3] This proud meaning is missing in Immermann's words, in which the configuration of dwarf and

---

[3] See J. de Ghellinck, S.J., "Nani et Gigantes," *Archivum Latinitatis Medii Aevi*, XVIII (1945), 25ff.; there (p. 26), the words of Bernard of Chartres as transmitted by John of Salisbury: "Dicebat Bernardus Carnotensis nos esse quasi nanos gigantium humeris insidentes, ut possimus plura eis et remotiora videre, non utique proprii visus acumine aut eminentia corporis, sed quia in altum subvehimur et extollimur magnitudine gigantea."

giant is implied.[4] It has actually been reversed. It is not so much in this distortion of meaning that we recognize the corruption of language, as in the formal obscuring and mutilation of the image. One can raise oneself, to be sure, on the shoulders of one's ancestors, but not on the shoulders of their labors and diligence, because labor and diligence have no shoulders. The obscurity is even further intensified by the fact that the abstract expression "our age" (and not, for instance, "contemporary man") is made the subject of the sentence. Such inexactnesses betray the loss of original vision and of the ability to prevent what has been handed down from degenerating into cliché. And unfortunately it must be conceded that our example is just as symptomatic of the uncertainty of language with which Immermann has to struggle at every step, as it is of the situation of the epigone in general.

Let us first briefly adumbrate from a typological standpoint the area of form and genre in which quotations occur in *Münchhausen*. Whether this is really a humoristic novel and even one of the great humorous novels, as people often like to assert, is beside the point. But it is certain that it is indebted to the tradition of the humorous novel for a great many of its elements. The motifs and formal traits that are borrowed from *Don Quixote* or *Tristram Shandy*, or that would be unthinkable without the stimulation of those works, are plainly apparent. The same might be said for *Gargantua and Pantagruel*, which Immermann once set out to adapt and which he took up again during the composition of *Münchhausen*.[5] The impact of Jean Paul's novels is

---

[4] Here it must be kept in mind that Immermann, half a year earlier in his comic epic *Tulifäntchen*, had used the contrast of giant and dwarf in a very similar sense. Tulifäntchen, a dwarfish noble offspring with a giant's plans in his heart, is a parodistic personification of the degenerate nobility and, at the same time, of the prevailing Gothic romances. But his Tom Thumb figure is also characteristic of the times in a more general sense. "This is the age of small men!" is the thrice-repeated leitmotif.

[5] Cf. Manfred Windfuhr, *Immermanns erzählerisches Werk. Zur Situation des Romans in der Restaurationszeit*, Beiträge zur deutschen Philologie (Giessen: Schmitz, 1957) Vol. 14, pp. 117-21.

no less obvious, while the form of the double novel is obviously directly dependent on *Tomcat Murr*. These are all familiar facts and it suffices merely to mention them. Immermann alludes to this whole pedigree when he gives his novel the typological subtitle "A story in Arabesques," and he repeats this designation on various occasions in the text of his novel (I, 181; II, 222). But precisely this ostensibly arabesque-like element in *Münchhausen* reveals to us its epigonal nature and helps us to determine more precisely what is meant by "epigonal." The word "arabesque" (originally the designation for a decorative form consisting of interwoven vegetative and animal elements) had become, during the period of Romanticism, and in a transferred significance, the catchword for a positive poetic ideal. In his ardent efforts toward a new "mythology" that would be valid for art, Friedrich Schlegel goes so far as to see in the arabesque "the oldest and original form of human fantasy." The spirit of the arabesque is implied in the words that he applies to Shakespeare and Cervantes: "Yes, this artfully ordered confusion, this delightful symmetry of contradictions, this wonderful eternal alternation of rapture and irony which lives even in the most minute parts of the whole, seem to me to be a unique and new kind of mythology of wit."[6] In this lofty and ultimately devout conception the artful confusion of form, which appears in so many works of the Romantic poets and most brilliantly in Brentano's novel *Godwi* (with the subtitle "A Novel Run Wild"), had found its final justification.

On the surface, Immermann participates in this "confusion." The wanton inversion of the sequence of chapters, the incapsulated epistolary exchange with the bookbinder, the fact that the author makes a physical appearance in the novel, and many other elements attest to it. But he no longer

---

[6] Friedrich Schlegel, "Gespräch über die Poesie," in the section "Rede über die Mythologie." Quoted according to the revised version in Schlegel, *Sämtliche Werke* (1822-25), Vol. 5, p. 271. See also the thorough study by Karl Konrad Polheim, *Die Arabeske, Ansichten und Ideen aus Friedrich Schlegels Poetik* (Paderborn, 1966).

believes in the arabesque as a genuine art form, much less as the nucleus and source of a binding aesthetic ideal. Rather, the formlessness of *Münchhausen* is an aggressive parody of formlessness as an empty and banal modishness. Nothing shows this so clearly as the intentionally trivial words with which the bookbinder instructs the author:

> Sir, the proper manner of writing is out of fashion. Any author who wants to accomplish anything must take recourse to the improper style, and then a tension arises that keeps the reader out of breath and chases him *perforce* all the way to the last page. So just stuff and shove everything wildly topsy-turvy like the floes in an ice drift; deny heaven and earth; and hatch events that run around without characters like dogs who have lost their master. In one word: confusion! confusion!—Believe me, sir, without confusion you cannot accomplish anything nowadays. (ɪ, 68f.)

The spirit of the arabesque has vanished, along with faith in the arabesque. Immermann carries out his confusion with a kind of pedantic thoroughness, and the reader cannot rid himself of the feeling that these ostensible arabesques have been constructed with compasses and a square.

In the figure of the title-hero this novel hopes to capture and denounce the "spirit of the time" (*Zeitgeist*).[7] Because of this fact alone, *Münchhausen* is actually not so much a humorous as a pragmatic satiric work—a regular mirror of fools. The objects against which the satire is directed almost all have a generally literary character, and even more: they belong primarily and expressly to the realm of books and their production. Now this does not necessarily have to mean that the satire itself therefore has a bookish and wooden character; one can hardly claim, as Maync does, that satire always ages quickly and dies along with its

[7] Regarding the theme "criticism of the times," see Benno von Wiese, "Karl Immermann als Kritiker seiner Zeit," *Der Mensch in der Dichtung* (1958).

victim.[8] The crown witnesses that Maync cites to support this claim—Aristophanes, Rabelais, and Swift—prove rather the contrary. Is the force and vigorous effect of their satire impaired by the fact that we are no longer acquainted with the objects of it? Is, for instance, Rabelais' Judge Bridlegoose a less lively figure for us if we are not acquainted with his extraliterary model? The satire here attains such a degree of fictional independence that it leaves its object far behind. Immermann's satire, in general, is far removed from any such autonomy. Despite his efforts to transcend bookishness by parodying it, he remains bound to books. He keeps getting entangled in the nets that he wants to rip apart. To be sure, this holds true in varying degrees. Such figures as the old baron and his daughter Emerentia have, despite all, acquired a kind of fictional integrity.

The matter is more questionable as far as the figure of the title-hero, which suffers from a certain disunity, is concerned. At times Münchhausen is the object of satire inasmuch as he represents the concentrated embodiment of those negative tendencies that Immermann lampoons as abortions of the *Zeitgeist*. On other occasions, for great stretches, he is the mouthpiece through which the writer expresses his criticism of the very same phenomena. In this scintillating capacity he cannot free himself from the bookish realm in which he originated and against which he is directed. He is supposed to be a unified symbol, and remains a variegated allegory. He is supposed to wing his way up into the realm of aesthetic semblance, but he remains all too expressly tied down to extra-aesthetic reality. The same holds true even more strongly of the many and often rather shapeless figures who crop up in Münchhausen's innumerable tales. They are frequently aesthetically untrue because, as intrusions of extra-fictional factuality into the world of fiction, they are all too "real." One representative example: Münchhausen relates how he had been a kitchen boy in the house of a prelate who "pro-

---

[8] Harry Maync, *Immermann. Der Mann und sein Werk im Rahmen der Zeit- und Literaturgeschichte* (1921), p. 526.

cured" a new kitchen maid every half-year. With these cooks the boy progresses through a six-stage school of love. On the first level he learns sensuousness. "At that time old Wally was serving in the kitchen—a natural daughter, it was said, of Lucinde Schlegel. Among the servant staff she was nicknamed 'the skeptic' because in view of her ugliness and flaccidity she was extremely sceptical of ever getting a man. If one heard her talk one might have believed that she had led a rather free life, for her utterances sounded insolent and indecent enough" (I, 140f.). With this cook as well as the following ones we have a splendid opportunity to practice a bit of German literary history—the relation of Gutzkow's *Wally the Skeptic* to Friedrich Schlegel's *Lucinde*, of Bettina to Goethe, of Pückler-Muskau to Henriette Sontag, and so forth—but it would be better if we could simply laugh at them. However, the humorous effect does not come off so well. The relations between the satire and its objects are so crudely direct and at the same time so calculatedly correct that no sudden surprise and no liberating laughter are produced. We calculate soberly along with the author, our critical sense remains alert, and in this state of mind we find the individual references rather trivial and forced. *Münchhausen* literally teems with such calculated and oversubtle relations, and they clearly reveal a basic structural element of Immermann's humoristic procedure.

At the same time it can by no means be claimed that this writer lacks a genuine comic spirit. Immermann is a master in the invention of tangible, clearly outlined, and memorable comic situations and configurations whose origin in comedy is evident and whose effect is scarcely lessened by their often excessively constructed character. He succeeds best in such comedy when he stays farthest away from "literature." But pure comedy never satisfies him. He has higher goals in mind. He is pursuing—in *Münchhausen* no less than in *The Epigones*—a "universal tendency." In order to do justice to it, he always carries around the whole burden of his by no means slight literary education, trying on every occasion to work it in somehow. The claims of universality that have been almost automatically imposed on the novel ever since *Wilhelm Meister* constitute, in fact, the "burden" that adheres to Immermann's "heritage and legacy."

In a book so excessively impregnated by bookishness, the literary quotation—as one might expect—plays a great and characteristic role, and it is clear that important insights regarding its inner construction can be gained by an analysis of this role. Since certain main characteristics that were established in the previous chapter for *Tomcat Murr* return here in slight or more radical variation, we choose as our starting point a quotation which the learned Tomcat shares with the Liar Baron and which has already been discussed extensively because of its key position in *Tomcat Murr*, namely the words of Egmont: "Sweet life! Lovely, friendly habit of existence and action—how shall I part from you?" Münchhausen weaves it into his cryptic report on his love affair with Emerentia in the following way: "I gave her my heart, which was worth more than a million, and received from her a few louis d'or. Lovely, friendly cardgame of life, in which both gamble to lose by winning!" (i, 147). If we compare Hoffmann's and Immermann's use of this quotation, the common denominator is instantly apparent: the clear and crass banalization of the Goethe passage. Immermann's parody, however, makes us more uncomfortable than Hoffmann's. This is not so much because Immermann quotes more freely and distorts the words almost beyond the point of recognition, but because we sense that here the quotation is dragged in much more at random and that, very much in contrast to Hoffmann, it accomplishes little or nothing functionally. Because of this, the banality forces itself even more strongly upon us. Of course we cannot generalize this observation and this discomfort prematurely. But even so, when we consider the artistic quality of Immermann's quotations the problem of banality thrusts itself upon us again and again —and almost consistently to an alarming degree. We intentionally said "the problem" and not merely "the phenomenon of banality." For the ambivalence into which our judgment is forced corresponds to and originates in the highly problematic and hybrid character of Immermann's quoting procedure itself.

To make this clear, let us begin once again with that key passage in *The Epigones*, where the epigonal is defined as "a very unique corruption of language." The passage goes on: "One has taken this palladium of humanity, this birth certificate of our divine origin, and made a lie of it, despoiling its virginity" (III, 136). So the corruption of language refers to truth and falsehood; the problem of the epigonal is thus no less an ethical than an aesthetic one. This obviously leads directly to the figure of the Liar Baron, to the "Arch-Windbag" for whom "a certain theoretical untruthfulness . . . has become second nature" (I, 203). Where would the corruption of language reveal itself more clearly than in the manner in which a validly formulated expression, the transmitted words of a poet, is employed? Thus, the shallow and banal quoting is tantamount to a sharp criticism of the times. The writer is trying to say: Look, this is the way the shallow, mendacious *Zeitgeist* expresses itself, and its embodiment is Münchhausen. This is true, but it is only one side of the truth. The other side is this: As a satirist Münchhausen also speaks in the name of the author and the author speaks through him. It is therefore ultimately the author who makes himself guilty of these banalities. So for our investigation it makes little difference whether he puts the quotations into the mouth of Münchhausen and other figures of the novel or whether he weaves them into his own speech. The painful paradox lies in the fact that he hopes to head off this corruption by representing it satirically, and thereby becomes the accomplice of this very corruption.

This problem has already made itself felt in the case of Hoffmann; but here it is incomparably more urgent and more alarming. In part, this is probably related to the fact that Hoffmann's genuine and irresistible comic spirit outtrumps banality and even justifies it to a certain extent; whereas in Immermann's works this opposing force is developed much less fully, simply because he has it much less at his command. His literary arsenal overlaps extensively with that of Hoffmann. He employs primarily quotations that were current among the educated classes and well on their way to becoming common sayings. They stem in large measure from the better-known dramas of Shakespeare, Goethe, and Schiller—which does not surprise us if we consider that dramatic texts must have been especially familiar to Immermann because of his activity as director of the Düsseldorf Theater. But the figures that he creates with this material are far more rudimentary than Hoffmann's. Very often the wit is of a somewhat brittle and stiff correctness. For instance, when Münchhausen is explaining a wondrous natural phenomenon—that the cows belonging to a certain Indian tribe with an unpronounceable name do not produce sweet milk but sour, curdled milk—he begins with the words: "Pindar says: 'The finest is water'; but I say: the primordial is sour" (I, 19). Or when he reveals to the baron that he is a father: " 'I have a daughter—' 'You?' 'I. I have her because she is mine, I might say with Polonius if I wanted to jest; but I do not want to jest about this daughter' " (II, 213). The quotation from *Hamlet* is inserted smoothly and correctly; it "fits." But it accomplishes just as little as the Pindar quotation.

This merely witty quoting succeeds best when the situation itself is already charged with latent comic power and thus provides the contrasting background—which does not happen too rarely. Thus Münchhausen and the old baron, out of pure friendship, shout the coarsest sincerities into each other's ears and finally fall into each other's arms with great emotion, sealing their pact with the words of Schiller's Marquis Posa:[9] " 'Your brother!' whispered the guest— 'And in the boldest meaning of the word!' " (I, 277). A similar effect is achieved by Emerentia's words, which also

[9] *Don Carlos*, verse 993.

158

parody *Don Carlos*,[10] in the farcical love scene with the ostensible "prince," Karl Buttervogel: "I have no need to become more closely acquainted with your toilette. Depart, to bring back peace to my days and slumber to my nights!" (II, 167f.). In order to enrich this simple procedure Immermann devises the trick of linking two quotation fragments of different origin, if possible in a single sentence. "Arm in arm with you, I feel an army in my fist!" exclaims Münchhausen when he thinks that he has won a rich heiress (I, 146). It is a prerequisite for the comic effect of such quotation linking, naturally, that the reader knows the original text of the two quotations pretty much by heart and hence recognizes their distortion. This presupposition of knowledge surely applies for the two famous closing speeches of Schiller, the first from *Don Carlos*: "Arm in arm with you,/ I challenge my century to battle"; and the second from *The Robbers*: "I feel an army in my fist—death or freedom! At least they shall not capture anyone alive!"[11] A further example of such quotation linking, again from two dramas by Schiller, is Münchhausen's speech to the Englishman who saves his life in the story "I" and then coldly leaves him in a lurch: "Go, false hypocritical Briton, we are even! Arm yourself with the whole pride of your England—I, a German youth, reject you!" (I, 340).[12] A similar reduplicating figure of speech occurs when the quotation is magnified to the second power and, at the same time, undergoes a variation: "I am the Caesar of Lies. I can say of myself, like 'the hook-nosed fellow of Rome': 'I came, saw, and—lied!' " (II, 212). Here not only is Caesar's famous phrase cited, but at the same time the quotation that Falstaff had already borrowed from the "hook-nosed fellow of Rome."[13] It seems to me to be characteristic of the nature of Immermann's witty ingenuity that greater fullness (or apparent fullness) is bestowed upon the basically rather

[10] *Ibid.*, verses 3919f.
[11] *Ibid.*, verses 1013f.; *Die Räuber*, Act 2, Scene 3 (near the end).
[12] Freely adapted from Schiller's *Maria Stuart*, verse 1632, and his *Kabale und Liebe*, end of the first act.
[13] Shakespeare, *Henry IV*, Part 2, Act IV, Scene 3.

thin joke by a mechanical principle of construction: addi-
tive linking and intensification.

The quotations examined so far are derived mostly from
Schiller. Apparently his full, sonorous language is particu-
larly inviting for parody. At the same time one has the feel-
ing that the parody, in the last analysis, can do very little
damage to Schiller's tremendously sturdy poetic vigor. The
case is quite different with Goethe's incomparably softer
and more delicate poetic language. On one occasion
Iphigenie's simple and touching words, spoken to introduce
the Song of the Parcae—"Before my ears resounds the old
refrain"[14]—are ripped out of context, in somewhat distorted
form, and made to usher in the idiotic verses that gambol
through the confused head of the hysterical old maid
Emerentia: "Before my ears hums an old refrain: 'Once you
loved the nutcracker, after the nutcracker you loved me ...'"
(I, 293). On another occasion Münchhausen parodies the
conversation between Orestes and Pylades in which the
horrible crime of Clytemnestra is delicately touched upon
and then shrouded in silence:

> Orestes: The day came—
> Pylades: O, let spirits out of Hell
>   Tell one another nightly of that hour![15]

In Münchhausen's reproduction, this passage takes the fol-
lowing form:

> "The day came—
>   O let spirits out of Hell
> Tell one another nightly of it!
> —The day came on which eerie figures entered my life,
> threatening powers enveloped me with a ghostly net and
> ordered the horrible separation." (I, 147)

This refers to Münchhausen's discovery that the ostensibly
rich heiress whom he is courting is as poor as a church
mouse. The reader feels embarrassed. He feels the parody

[14] *Iphigenie*, verse 1718.
[15] *Ibid.*, verses 628f.

to be tasteless and even somewhat plebeian. Even if he scrutinizes his feeling critically, he cannot say that it is mistaken. Probably it can scarcely be argued objectively that certain poetic phrases are too sacrosanct to be exposed to parodistic exploitation. But certainly we have the right to ask whether the parodist has any conception of the quality of what he is parodying. Here the answer obviously seems to be no. Immermann's utterances regarding Goethe's poetry give evidence of a crass lack of intuition and hence are not lacking in a certain involuntary humor. Thus he thinks that he can designate Goethe's nature as "after all only the subjectivity of the eighteenth century carried to the extreme" (v, 240). He detects in such works as *Hermann and Dorothea* and *The Elective Affinities* "a total lack of understanding regarding form, a breakdown of form" (v, 376). In his striving for "organic objective forms of life" and for "eschewal of the egoistic and individual,"[16] he is engaged in a "life and death struggle"[17] with the subjectivist Goethe. We involuntarily think of Tulifäntchen the giant-killer!

It is not only in connection with Goethe that Immermann is guilty of ravishing the "virginity" of language that he himself so bitterly laments. The case is similar with his Biblical quotations. In an interminable and hence rather soporific tirade against the stage author Raupach, who here bears the name Hirzewenzel, Immermann makes the latter exclaim:

"Verily, verily, I say unto you, a pestilence will come across our continent, called cholera . . . Woe unto thee, Jerusalem of the Sands, thou that doth favor the Jews and constantly crucify the prophets; thou shalt receive cholera twice because thou shalt have performed my play *Gentian* so often!" (i, 45)

At the beginning stand the words which, as a set formula,

16 Letter of 29 June 1836; cited from Windfuhr, *Immermanns erzählerisches Werk*, p. 84.
17 Diary entry for 3 August 1831; *ibid.*, p. 85.

so often enforce the speeches of Christ in the Gospel of John. The exclamation of woe imitates Matthew 23:37 and refers to the cholera epidemic that, a few years earlier (1831), had raged in Germany and with particular virulence in Berlin ("Jerusalem of the Sands"), at which time Hegel met his death. The words "who dost favor the Jews" are a free addition of our author. Again it strikes us as lacking in taste that Immermann makes a national catastrophe, at that time still so close, into the object of his joke. And it is also perhaps not merely exaggerated prudery if we feel the satire against Hegel, who is mystically identified with the windbag Münchhausen, to be rather vulgar.

"O if only I could name him abstractly enough! The pure concept, cept, ept, pt; seemingly deceased on the 14th of December 1831 as a result of cholera, seemingly buried in the cemetery beyond the gate where, in the coffin in his stead, lies that Nothingness which again is Something, existing in the deed, sniffing snuff and playing whist, hence not merely comprehended with the subjective feeling, thinking, and believing, but really and hence rationally—in a word: the great, immortal, eternal Hegel, who is the Paraclete, that is to say, the Spirit, promised fulfillment of the Ages, with whom the millennium begins, in which the Hegelians shall rule." (II, 181)

One easily recognizes the tags strewn here from Hegel's terminology, which has degenerated to empty hocus-pocus. The phrase "really and hence rationally" is almost a quotation and obviously alludes to the sentence of Hegel that has become a slogan: "What is rational is real, and what is real is rational."[18] We recall that Sterne, Wieland, and Hoffmann had capitalized similarly on the philosophical jargon current in their day. The Hegel persiflage clearly stands in a sort of tradition. The comparison with these predecessors makes us realize what a nadir this tradition reaches with the parodistic quoting in *Münchhausen*.

[18] From the introduction to Hegel's *Grundlinien der Philosophie des Rechtes*.

The "castle in the sky of Münchhausen's nihilism," according to a statement of the author, is supposed to be "counterbalanced" by the "realism and positivism" of the interpolated episode "High Farm" (*"Oberhof"*).[19] "All men now feel a need for generally valid foundations of existence, for organic and objective forms of life," Immermann wrote at least a year before beginning work on *Münchhausen*.[20] In the "High Farm" section the "terrestrial" element of the peasant world, as opposed to the "mercurial" aspect of the Münchhausen world, is supposed to find narrative form as a perfect example of such organic and objective forms of life. Whereas the Münchhausen sections of the double novel are literally larded with quotations and other kinds of literary fragments, the quotation has only a slight and unessential part in the formation of the "High Farm" story. The writer's serious aim consists in integrating, in a narrative fashion, the ideological meaning indicated in the letters above; and the manner and degree to which this succeeds makes this part of the novel just as interesting as it is respectable. But quotations contribute nothing significant to this accomplishment; rather they constitute, in general, looser passages in the narrative structure. Their occurrence generally signifies a shift from feeling to sentimentality, from pathos to bombast. We can limit ourselves to one example. A chapter devoted to the love idyll of Oswald and Lisbeth, which at best teeters close to the edge, finally plunges into the abyss of *kitsch* when the poet, in conclusion, exclaims: "Those were the days of which it is written: 'They blossom once and not again!'" (II, 34). This chapter ending probably strikes us as shallow and saccharine because here the quotation from Schiller's poem "Resignation" ("The May of life blooms once and not again") is an all too cheap substitute for a creative formulation by the author himself. We feel that here the hack writer has won out over the poet.

[19] Letter of May 1838 to Amalia von Sybel; cited from Windfuhr, *Immermanns erzählerisches Werk*, pp. 192f.
[20] Letter of 29 June 1836 to Dr. Deycks; *ibid.*, p. 84.

Closely related to the hack writer, however, is the ideologist, and the poet in Immermann struggles to assert himself in spite of these two elements of his own being. We experience this battle in its ups and downs, in its victories and defeats. In conclusion, a passage characteristic of this captivating drama can illustrate this. One of the most splendid chapters of the book, convincing in its mighty power of composition, bears the title "A Tragedy on the High Farm." It depicts how the old farmer spends a night searching his whole farm for a lost sword—the sword of Charlemagne, as he believes, and the symbol of the power and dignity of the ostensibly ancient popular tribunal (*Fehmgericht*) over which he presides—and almost loses his reason in the course of the futile search. The narrative report begins in the third paragraph, and the chapter might well have begun with this paragraph. As is often the case, however, the writer gives way to an inner compulsion to heighten the dignity of what is being represented by a general introductory observation. And these generalities, just as we might expect from everything that has been said earlier, have a pronounced didactic and bookish character. The literary intensification of represented reality, which is so characteristic of Immermann's "poetic" realism, is introduced by the word "Tragedy" in the title. But this word is full of implications from literary history that demand to be uttered explicitly. "Melpomene has two daggers. The one is bright, and honed to a razor-sharp edge, cuts quickly and inflicts clean wounds that bleed purely. The other, rusty and full of nicks, tears wretched destruction into the flesh. With the one she approaches kings and heroes; with the other she frequently is accustomed to sneak in among peasants and average citizens" (ii, 299).

This introductory passage is a play on a principle of classical poetics which prevailed from Aristotle down to the eighteenth century and which is best known to cultivated Germans through Opitz' formulation: namely, that tragedy is supposed to represent only heroic objects, and not "persons of lowly state and simple things."²¹ This dogma is denied here, of course, but it glimmers through in the distinction between two kinds of daggers and even more strongly in the value distinction in the connecting sentence: "The one strikes for great and undeniable possessions, for crown, for kingdom, for life—the other torments for trivialities, for a sound, for the echo of a sound." This value distinction is remarkably ambivalent: Melpomene torments peasants and bourgeois only for trivialities! And it is then relativized again immediately and almost retracted by the following sentence: "For men are tormented not by things, but by opinions about things." This, as the attentive reader has noted, is with slight variations the well-known saying of Epictetus which Sterne had already used in completely different form as the motto of *Tristram Shandy*.²² The quotation is skillfully chosen and stands in a double relationship: on the one hand it fits smoothly into the general sequence of thoughts, and on the other refers strikingly to the specific content of the chapter, the grief for the alleged sword of Charlemagne.

At this point the narrator could get down to the matter at hand and thus to a report of the action. But still unable to leave the firm path of ideological typology, he adds: "The palace is not the only scene of tragedy." Once again we detect a fixed literary model that glimmers through the formulation like the old writing of a palimpsest. Is not the farm owner a peasant, and does not the peasant—not in reality to be sure, but according to the typological and schematic conception of the seventeenth, eighteenth, and partially also the nineteenth, centuries—live in a "cottage"? And is not the contrast of "cottage" and "palace" firmly engraved on the literary and cultural consciousness of the West? From Horace's "Pallida mors aequo pulsat pede pauperum tabernas/regumque turres" ("Pallid death pounds with

---

²¹ Martin Opitz, *Buch von der deutschen Poeterey*, ed. W. Braune (1876), Chap. 5, p. 22.
²² The motto to *Tristram Shandy* reads: Ταράσσει τοὺς Ἀνθρώπους οὐ τὰ Πράγματα, Ἀλλὰ τὰ περὶ τῶν Πραγμάτων Δόγματα.

the same foot against the hovels of the poor/And the fortresses of kings")[23] there had developed, in the seventeenth and eighteenth centuries, the widespread *topos* which plays off the innocence of the cottage against the corruptness of the palace.[24] It was still capable of being politically activated in the motto of Büchner's journal *Hessischer Landbote*: "Peace to the cottages! War to the palaces!" Büchner means real cottages, the cottages of the poor. But how do matters stand with regard to the wealthy High Farm, especially in view of a notion which is turned to impressively good account in the narrative: that the wealthy peasants in Westphalia, and above all the local peasant magistrates, constitute by nature a kind of noble caste? Is not therefore the concept "cottage" ridiculously inadequate and is not the presumed *topos* nothing but imagination on our part? But if we look in the paralipomena of *Münchhausen*, we can find a confirmation. The notes for our chapter read: "Night. Tragedy not only in palaces but in cottages" (II, 429). It is no accident, of course, that the word "cottage" is missing from the text of the novel; the writer suppressed it consciously. It would have been highly inappropriate for the contrast between "rich man" (the peasant magistrate) and "beggar" (the minstrel who eavesdrops on him maliciously) which is actualized in this very chapter. But by this imperfect state itself, by its simultaneous believing and suppressing, this chapter opening makes evident how greatly the traditional literary ideology is by its nature at odds with the realism that Immermann strived for in his writing. If we keep in mind this hostile constellation, then our admiration can be all the more genuine for the reconciliation that is nevertheless attained, to a certain degree, between these inimical elements.

[23] *Carmina* I, 4, 11-13f.

[24] In this connection, see my essay "Hütte und Palast in der Dichtung des 18. Jahrhunderts," *Formenwandel*, Festschrift für Paul Böckmann (Hamburg, 1964), pp. 138-55. I am presently preparing a more comprehensive study of this theme.

Immermann sometimes regarded himself rather critically. "More character than talent," we read in the description of the "well-known Immermann" who enters the field of fictional action in the sixth book of *Münchhausen* (II, 151). In the same place Baron Münchhausen even says directly to his creator's face: "You are no genius— . . . you are at most a talent. Yet you are not even that, but only an imitator" (II, 161). Even if we deduct the romantic irony that proclaims itself in this narrative disguise, an ample amount of sharp self-criticism is still left. Even a person who has an eye open for the weak and problematic aspects of Immermann's writings probably will not push his criticism as far as the writer himself does here. He will prefer to say: still more character than talent; or even: still more talent than genius. Yet everyone who concerns himself with Immermann involuntarily succumbs to an ambivalence of feeling and judgment regarding his person and the qualities of his work. We esteem and like him from the point of view of character and intellect; we admire his honesty and high principles, his bright mind, the substance of his personality, and the breadth of his cultural criticism. We recognize his poetic potential, and out of pure admiration and love we are unwilling to let pass unchallenged the conclusion that his work—not only its uncertain and derivative beginnings, but also the "mature" work, the two big novels—is artistically so uneven and ambivalent. From the special point of view of our study these artistic weaknesses inevitably appear in a sharp light. If we compare Immermann's art of quoting with that of the writers treated earlier, then the difference in rank becomes painfully obvious; it is pointless to try to escape this conclusion. The capacity to make of the quotation an adhesive power capable of bearing meaning, and to integrate it into the total structure of the work, has visibly subsided. Because of this Immermann's work strikes us sometimes as strained, at times as cool and tame.

To be sure, we soon perceive that these weaknesses do not indicate merely an individual shortcoming; they stem in large measure from the literary and cultural situation of the times. This is not supposed to be an extenuating circumstance, but only a description of the state of affairs. One could scarcely find another writer in whom excellence as well as weakness are so clearly conditioned by the contemporary situation as in Immermann, and it attests to a sufficient degree of self-understanding that he himself recognized and formulated this state of affairs. For his conception of the epigonal must be understood not only as objective cultural criticism but as self-criticism. Immermann is a writer in an impoverished age, and this makes him in certain respects an impoverished writer. He belongs to the "dwarfs" who sit on the shoulders of "giants." And because his self-criticism is less corruptible than that of many other writers, he does not feel at all comfortable in this position. Specifically with a view to his art of quoting, we cannot miss the painfully self-critical tone that resounds in his often-quoted words on the misfortunes of the epigonal state: "With borrowed ideas it is the same as it is with borrowed money: he who manages frivolously with someone else's goods becomes ever more destitute" (III, 136).

CHAPTER VIII

Theodor Fontane

L'ADULTERA

AND

STECHLIN

IN THE sixth chapter of Theodor Fontane's novel of manners *Cécile*, the heroine and her somewhat older husband, St. Arnaud, are taking a walk accompanied by young Herr von Gordon, with whom they have just struck up an acquaintance. Their arrival at the Hotel zur Rosstrappe is observed by two jovial gentlemen from Berlin, whose saucy conversation the reader has already had a fleeting chance to overhear. Being in the finest dinner mood, which has been heightened by the influence of a few coffee-cognacs, they do not restrain their commentary.

"There they are again," said the older man, pointing at the St. Arnaud couple and Gordon, who was following directly behind them. "Just look, he already has her shawl over his arm. He doesn't shilly-shally around very long. That thou doest, do quickly. I am just surprised that the old fellow. . . ." (I, 4, 255)[1]

This brief scrap of conversation strikes us as immensely realistic. That is precisely the fresh and insolent tone of a *bon vivant* from Berlin. And wholly absorbed into this tone is the Biblical quotation: the words that Jesus speaks to Judas at the Last Supper.[2] We sense what an irreverent, even impious spirit is expressed in this application of the

---

[1] I quote Fontane's *Gesammelte Werke* (Berlin, 1905-11)—hereafter cited as GW—by series, volume, and page.

[2] John 13:27.

stirring Biblical words to the advances of a young ladies' man. But it would be ridiculous, of course, to attribute this attitude to the narrator. Rather we admire the incorruptible accuracy with which he reproduces this conversation in order to illuminate in a brilliant flash a bit of reality—and here a reality of the coarsest kind. The narrator takes no sort of stand with regard to the words spoken by his character. To be sure, we will not go astray if we infer from this passage a pensively serious criticism of civilization, but it is not expressly uttered. What actually lies before us is simply the objective fact of the spoken words.

"What is a novel supposed to do?" Fontane once asked in a book review, and the key sentences of his answer go as follows: The novel is supposed to "tell us a story in which we believe"; it is supposed to "cause a world of fiction, for moments, to appear as a world of reality" (II, 9, 238f.). From a long series of documents, mainly letters, it emerges clearly that Fontane is, to be sure, thinking partly of the narrated content with respect to this credibility; but primarily his attention is focused on the form of representation or—what in his eyes is almost identical with this form— the specific manner in which his characters speak. He sums up his attitude in a nutshell: "All my attention is devoted to letting the people speak as they really speak" (II, 7, 22f.). It is easy to see that we are dealing here with a kind of vicious circle. The "real" speech of a figure in a novel is, after all, no more predetermined than the figure itself. Rather, it is the manner in which the author causes his characters to speak that determines what kind of characters they are. But it is not especially useful to strain Fontane's credo on the rack of logic in this manner. If we are willing to stretch the point a bit—and Fontane would be the last to object— then it must be said that Fontane's credo holds true. For his novels constitute in their totality an imposing evidence of his success in causing his people to talk "as they speak in reality."[3] This sounds so simple, yet actually we are dealing

[3] See in this connection Mary E. Gilbert, *"Das Gespräch in Fontanes Gesellschaftsromanen,"* Palaestra, Vol. 174 (1930).

here not with anything simple, but with a very subtle and scarcely penetrable miracle of narrative technique. The following study should help to make this miracle somewhat comprehensible.

Fontane's fictional conversations strike us as wholly genuine. The reader gets the impression that they flowed from the author's pen just as easily as they spill from the lips of his characters. But that is an illusion. On the contrary, Fontane was a highly conscientious and even—if we can believe his own words—a ponderous worker. The rapidity and effortlessness with which he sketched the outlines of his novels was matched by the time-consuming effort of the polishing, the *Pularbeit* that he constantly talks about. "God be my witness. But this slowness results only from a feeling for style, from 'filing.' What I have written down does not satisfy me. And the tinkering that is now required takes three times as long as the first draft and twenty times longer than the first outline" (II, 9, 289). On the alert, we are astonished when he writes immediately thereafter: "But this external rapidity of my power of creative imagination is paired up with an infinitely weak power of expression. I cannot find the right word." Subjectively the statement is certainly honest, but nevertheless an "infinitely weak power of expression" is almost the last thing we would be willing to attribute to Fontane. The true state of affairs is probably this: his particularly fine sense for the accuracy of words intensified the demands that the work placed upon him for the expression that must be found in each case.

In the case of such a conscious and circumspect manner of working it can be important to cast a glance into the workshop in order to try to understand the nature of the works from their origin. In this way we can also gain an insight into the nature and role of the quotation in Fontane's novels. Especially revealing in this connection is the material that Julius Petersen published in his study of "Fontane's First Berlin Novel of Manners" and the textual samples abundantly supplied there.[4] This study deals with the

[4] Julius Petersen, "Fontanes erster Berliner Gesellschaftsroman,"

171

plan and the voluminous preliminary sketches for a novel on which Fontane was working in the years 1877-79 and which was supposed to have the title *All Sorts of Happiness* (*Allerlei Glück*). These preliminary sketches—and it does not matter here why the novel was never completed—represent, according to Petersen's felicitous formulation, the "quarry" from which the building stones for a series of new works were taken, and they contained an arsenal of motifs that were exploited in almost all of the following narrative works. Of essential significance for us is Petersen's claim, which is supported by a wealth of material, that the conception of the characters in many cases originates primarily from their manner of speaking. This becomes especially clear for one of the projected main characters: Bertha Pappenheim, who, coming from the petty bourgeoisie, rises to become a celebrated actress. First of all, the specific manner of speech is captured on a sheet of paper, but the speaker is still unspecified; even the question of whether it is a man or a woman is still undecided.

A person (gentleman or lady) speaking in Berlin dialect, but a higher and cultivated Berlinisch, that is to say High German larded with Berlin expressions: "Lotterig. Verbiestert. Oh Jerum jerum Löffelstiel. Unter der Kanone. Fauler Zauber. Nicht ein Schimmer. Er ist mit einer Tante behaftet. Mann kann nicht vorsichtig genug in der Wahl seiner Eltern sein."[5]

There follows a long series of similar Berolinisms. Appended to this is a second sheet that is already headed "Bertha Pappenheim." The manner of speech has precipitated itself, as it were, into a figure. On this second sheet the popular expressions are mixed with quotations from classical poetry. The following excerpt contains an example of this: " 'Der Mensch ist frei und wär er in Köthen

Sitzungsberichte der Preussischen Akademie der Wissenschaften, Philosophisch-Historische Klasse (1929), pp. 480-562.
[5] *Ibid.*, p. 504.

geboren.' All of her humorous quotations, in addition to her really elevated quotations, must be in *this* style."[6]

Here and in many other cases Fontane's procedure becomes wholly apparent. As a preliminary, a "warrant" is issued which precisely describes the manner of speech of the person in question. In this description the quotes to be used and the types of quotation play a conspicuously important role. It is striking that the quotation is of interest not primarily because of its content; it is taken from the very start as a symptom of the individual manner of speaking and therefore as a means for the characterization of the novelistic figure. The expression of these characterizing quotations is conditioned, however, by the social level to which the fictional figure belongs. This holds true for the major characters and even more so for the secondary figures, for whom essentially the same "wanted notice" procedure is followed. Bertha's father is taken to a bowling club.

Six, seven persons, *mainly bourgeois*, belong to it. [My italics.] A gentleman in his mid-fifties is the liveliest; he constantly quotes. Because of this the Registrar is reminded of his daughter Bertha. But all the quotations are adapted to bowling. "If the cloak falls then the Duke falls, too." "The bullet passes by." "Greet my Lotte for me." "Four elements rule the world." "The last four of the tenth regiment." "These seven surrounded the ruler of the world." "Six hit and seven mock." "For three makes one and four makes none, that is the witches' one-times-one." "You have got to say it twice."[7]

The series extends even further and amounts to a total of twenty quotations. It is not clear in every case how the narrator intended to adapt them to bowling, but that is his worry, not ours. However, it is our affair to recognize that

---

[6] The verse quoted—"Man is free even if he were born in Koethen"—is a pun on the famous lines from Schiller's poem "Die Worte des Glaubens": "Der Mensch ist frei geschaffen, ist frei,/ Und würd' er in Ketten geboren" ("Man is created free, is free/ Even if he were born in chains"), after Rousseau's *Social Contract*.

[7] Petersen, *op.cit.*, pp. 536f.

the quotation here serves to express not merely an individual character, but also the spirit of a certain social fact, namely the middle-class bowling club. Parodistic quoting is a characteristic and integrating element of the social-cultural reality that Fontane wants to represent. It stands in the service of his effort to let the people speak just as they do in reality.

What this means is the following: the quotation in Fontane's novels of manners is essentially a conversational quotation. It has its place in the conversations of the characters. (The few cases in which the narrator cites quotations on his own are so inconsiderable that we can easily ignore them.) This resolute restriction of quotations to conversation involves a drastic limitation of the area in which the quotation can unfold its efficacy. We realize this if we recall what rich designs were shaped by the quotations of the narrator himself, particularly in the works of Rabelais, Sterne, and Wieland. In Raabe we will encounter a similar state of affairs once more. The wealth of Fontane's art of quoting is of a different kind. It consists in a subtle nuancing within the limits of a reduced area. What is astonishing and admirable, however, is the fact that the inner wealth is not lessened by this reduction. Actually, in order to prove this we would have to consider all of Fontane's novels of manners. To choose any single novel, as has been our practice up to now, would seem here to be somewhat arbitrary. For these novels—which in this respect are not unlike Balzac's *Comédie Humaine*—are effective above all through their imposing totality. Under these circumstances the most suitable procedure might consist in a compromise. We will pay particular attention to the start and the finish of this series of novels: that is, to the first novel, *L'Adultera*, and to *Stechlin*, which concludes the series. By drawing a line in this way from one cornerstone to the other, we hope to arrive at results that will be valid for the whole series of Fontane's novels of manners.

Generally speaking, literary criticism has not treated *L'Adultera* very kindly, and it would be difficult to say

that the critics have been unfair in every respect. Toward
the end, for the last third or quarter, the novel declines;
particularly the conclusion is weak and not very convinc-
ing. This is quite obviously related to the fact that the
figure who actually brings the work to life and carries it has
disappeared from the field of vision. For it is not the main
figure and titular heroine Melanie van der Straaten who is
the immortal figure of this novel, but her husband. Coun-
cillor van der Straaten, Fontane's first "classic Berlin type,"[8]
is a fully rounded character, and this character is unique.
If one tries to enumerate his individual "characteristics,"
one comes up with a conglomeration that makes a rather
uneven impression: wit and sentimentality, energetic activ-
ity and dull fatalism, dogmatic complacency and self-
irony, good-naturedness and spiteful suspiciousness, culture
and coarseness. In their narrative shaping these appar-
ently disparate elements constitute, however, a highly con-
vincing unity; and it should be observed that this shaping
is carried out wholly by the reproduction of a manner of
speech. To be sure, Fontane anticipates this linguistic char-
acterization in the first chapter with a kind of psychological
portrait in the form of direct description. But it is highly
typical that the characterization of Van der Straaten's man-
ner of speech constitutes a large part even of this portrait.
Here the reader is informed in advance of Van der
Straaten's "preference for drastic proverbs and local say-
ings of the blunter sort," of his "favorite phrases," his
"Berolinisms," "bonmots," and "jesting repartees" (i, 3, 3f.).
The first quotation of the novel is also imbedded in this de-
scription. Van der Straaten likes to say that he has no desire
to impose any restraints upon himself. "And when he had
spoken in this way, he looked around with a feeling of satis-
faction and concluded contentedly and cultivatedly: 'O
touch it, touch it not,' for he loved to intersperse lyrical pas-
sages, and especially those that gave expression to his char-
acteristically Berlin-like proclivity for the comfortably sen-

[8] Conrad Wandrey, *Theodor Fontane* (1919), p. 177.

timental. It is self-evident that he also, in turn, cast an ironic eye on this very propensity" (1, 3, 4). Just as in the preliminary sketches to *All Sorts of Happiness,* the quotation is cited and commented upon explicitly as an element of an entire manner of speaking and as an expression of character. At the same time, the realm from which the quotation is borrowed has a characterizing significance. Conversely, the councillor's proclivity for the comfortably sentimental is not a bad indirect characterization of Emanuel Geibel's poem, which begins with the words: "Where a still heart glows full of love,/ O touch it, touch it not."[9] The fact that his passion for quoting is called "cultivated" is an important element to which we shall return.

By its very nature the use of the quotation as an element of conversation occurs most frequently in those favorite situations of Fontane's where the conversation unfolds most abundantly as a social phenomenon, namely at dinner and during excursions to the country. Both situations are fully developed in *L'Adultera,* and Fontane's art of shaping conversations entirely as *tranches de vie* here celebrates triumphs that are not surpassed by the later novels. We can do justice to this art of quoting only if we observe carefully how the quotations are absorbed into the whole disjointed and zigzagging flow of the conversation. Let us first consider a fragment of conversation from the dinner chapter, where the exuberant joviality moves constantly on the border of irritability and annoyance. At one point Van der Straaten, in his imperturbability, almost lets matters come to a head between him and his brother-in-law, Major Gryczinski. The latter attempts to allay the storm, and he is aided by the fact that just at that moment the cork pops out of one of the champagne bottles standing ready. He breaks off in the middle of a sentence and says merely, while he fills the councillor's glass: "May peace be thy first peal!" An overworked and obvious quotation, to be sure— it is the last line of Schiller's famous poem "Das Lied von

---

[9] Emanuel Geibel, *Werke,* ed. R. Schacht (Leipzig, n.d.), p. 140: "Rühret nicht daran."

der Glocke"—and wholly in accord with the nature of the correct and somewhat trite major, but it is effective.

Van der Straaten was the last man to resist a challenge like that. "My dear Gryczinski," he began in a tone of suddenly awakened sentimentality, "we understand each other, we have always understood each other. Give me your hand. Lacrimae Christi, Friedrich. Quickly. The best part of it, of course, is its name. But that's the name it has. To each his own—one man this, the other that."

"To be sure," laughed Gabler.

"Ach, Arnold, you overestimate it. Believe me, the blessed fellow was right. Gold is only a chimera. And Elimar would confirm it if it weren't a sentence from an opera which is passé. Unfortunately passé, I must say. For I love nuns that dance. But here comes the bottle. Just leave the dust and the cobwebs. It must remain in its entire pristine holiness. Lacrimae Christi, how that sounds! (1, 3, 37f.)

The rapid shift in mood and the blow-by-blow of statement and answer in the short time interval while the servant fetches the bottle of Lacrimae Christi—champagne is not good enough for the reconciliation—is wonderful. The sentimentality suddenly switches into irony, in the form of the ironic commentary on name and expression that is so characteristic of Fontane's linguistically aware characters. Immediately following comes the equally typical (for Fontane, that is) generalizing statement—"To each his own . . ."—which sounds like a quotation and is perhaps a loose variation on the old expression "Suum cuique," which was already widespread in antiquity. (It is worth mentioning, in our context, that Frederick I of Prussia chose these words as the motto of the Order of the Black Eagle, which was founded in 1701, and that it has been the official device of Prussia ever since.[10] But what does the painter Arnold Gabler mean with his laughingly uttered "To be sure" and

---

[10] I am indebted to Dr. G. N. Knauer for pointing out this fact.

THEODOR FONTANE

what does the rapid answer—" . . . you overestimate it"
—imply? If the conversation had stopped here, we could at
most guess the solution of this riddle. The same would hold
true for the observation that "the blessed fellow was right."
We gather only through the use of the familiar quotation
from his opera *Robert the Devil* that Giacomo Meyerbeer is
meant by this designation.[11] And only now can we conclude
in retrospect that the "To be sure" was based on a witty
double-entendre: Gabler relates the statement "To each his
own" not to the wine bottle, but to Van der Straaten's bulg-
ing purse. But Van der Straaten obviously understands this
instantly; his ready comprehension is no less rapid than his
gift for gab. In the pyrotechnic display of the conversation
the statements do not follow in logical sequence. What is to
come casts its shadow in advance, and there arises thereby
a rebus-like hysteron proteron in which only the quotation
supplies the reader with the key that he needs to decipher
the rebus. Despite their rapidity, moreover, Van der
Straaten's words are almost excessively rich in meaningful
secondary implications. His "you overestimate it" parodies,
in passing, the constant complaint of the eternally carping
table companion Duquede that something is "overesti-
mated." And the designation "the blessed fellow" has a
double meaning: Meyerbeer is "blessed," first, as one who
is deceased; but blessed also in contrast to the unblessed
"sorcerer" of Bayreuth, the "Tannhäuser and Venus Moun-
tain Man" Richard Wagner, against whose "rotten charm"
Van der Straaten had just been railing immoderately
(I, 3, 35). We see that even in the narrowed realm of "real-
istic" dialogue, genuine play is possible.

The quotation acquires an additional functional dimen-
sion when it occurs at a turning point of the plot and helps
to determine its course. Van der Straaten's eternal mockery
and jibes against the morality of married women belong

[11] The designation "blessed" (*der Selige*), namely, fits neither the
eponymous hero nor his devilish friend Bertram, both of whom use
the expression "Gold is nothing but a chimera" (*Robert der Teufel*,
Act I), and it thus can probably refer only to Meyerbeer.

among those elements which motivate Melanie's turn away
from her husband and her adultery. He helps by anticipa-
tion, so to speak, to bring about the act of adultery. These
taunts reach their apex on a boating party in the country,
during the interlude in the coffee house. He permits himself
some rather bold jokes at the expense of the proprietor's
buxom wife. Her white apron supplies him with the rather
farfetched cue for a rhymed couplet spoken "in an inten-
tionally sarcastic singsong manner"(I, 3, 73):

> Aber sei weiss wie Schnee und weisser noch:
> Ach, die Verleumdung trifft dich doch.

> (Be she white as snow and even whiter:
> Gossip and slander will nonetheless smite her.)

Where did he get these silly verses? It seems quite likely
Van der Straaten has in mind the cruelly cold words that
Hamlet speaks to Ophelia (Act III, Scene 2): "be thou as
chaste as ice, as pure as snow, thou shalt not escape
calumny." He remodels this quotation in a popular and
childish tone. It is in keeping with this tone that he is able,
by changing "pure as snow" into "white as snow," to awaken
associations with a phrase that comes from a rather simple-
minded children's verse by Friedrich Justin Bertuch,[12] and
that was current in those days as a popular saying: "Little
lamb, white as snow" ("Lämmchen, weiss wie Schnee").
(This phrase returns later, as we shall see, at a fateful
point.) The singsong crudely fashioned in this way from
two unrelated quotations has a very portentous effect.
Melanie sees Rubehn turn aside angrily. "Her husband's

---

[12] The source for the quotation "Lämmchen, weiss wie Schnee" can
be found as early as the eighth edition of Büchmann's *Geflügelte Worte*
(1874). I am indebted to Dr. K. H. Hahn of the Goethe- und Schil-
ler-Archiv in Weimar for finding the now forgotten (and hardly avail-
able) poem "Das Lämmgen," in Friedrich Justin Bertuch's *Wiegen-
liederchen* (Altenburg, 1772), pp. 30f. The first strophe goes:

> Ein junges Lämmgen, weiss wie Schnee,
> Gieng einst mit auf der Weyde,
> Und sprung muthwillig in dem Klee
> Mit ausgelassner Freude.

behavior and manner of speaking through all these years had embarrassed her hundreds of times, had even caused her the bitterest embarrassment; but it had had no more serious consequences. Today for the first time she was ashamed of him" (I, 3, 72).

What now immediately follows is calculated to intensify her shame and indignation considerably. Van der Straaten continues to comment on the physical characteristics of the innkeeper's wife:

> "We have here, if I have observed properly or, let us say, if I have guessed properly, a wedding of modern and antique: Venus Spreavensis and Venus Callipygos. A bold claim, I concede. But in Greek and in music one can say everything. Isn't that so, Anastasia? Isn't that so, Elimar? Moreover, I recall, in justification of myself, a marvelous Callipygos epigram . . . No, not an epigram . . . What do you call a couplet that does not rhyme. . . ."
>
> "A distich."
>
> "Right. So, I recall a distich . . . baah, I have forgotten it. . . . Melanie, how did it go? You quoted it so well that time and laughed so heartily. And now you have forgotten it, too. Or are you simply *pretending* to have forgotten it? . . . Please . . . I hate that. . . . Try to think of it. It had something to do with peach fuzz, and I said that one could practically feel it. And you thought so, too, and agreed with me. . . . But the glasses are empty. . . ."
> (I, 3, 73)

The distich to which Fontane lets Van der Straaten allude here really exists, but the old rascal has carefully destroyed the trail by which the reader could identify it without much trouble. My search would probably also have been in vain if the manuscript had not finally given me a hint. An early sketch of the passage, pasted to Leaf 26r of the manuscript, goes as follows:

> Venus Callipygos. Do you know the epigram by

Heyse? No, not an epigram. Damn . . . What do you call
a couplet that doesn't ryme.
A distich.
 Right, distich . . . But now I have forgotten it. (He
then quotes only the second line about the peaches.)
Wonderful . . . peach . . . the fuzz. You can practically
feel it.[13]

So it is Paul Heyse. But even with the help of this refer-
ence the source cannot be ascertained so easily. As far as
I can see, the distich is to be found only in the volume
Verse aus Italien. Skizzen, Briefe und Tagebuchblätter
(1880), in the series of poems "Kunst und Künstler." When
he later assembled the comprehensive collection of his
poems, *Gedichte*,[14] Heyse edited this cycle anew and in do-
ing so suppressed the very couplet that interests us here.
It goes:

> Göttliches Weib!—"O pfui, die Hetäre!"
> —Warum so entrüstet?
> Hast du doch selbst wohl schon
> "göttliche Pfirsch!" gesagt.

> (Heavenly woman!—"O pfui, that hetaera!"
> —And why so indignant?
> Haven't you sometimes yourself
> spoken of "heavenly peach"?)[15]

It is open to debate whether Van der Straaten's "interpreta-
tion" of the distich, which relates the "heavenly peach" so
closely to the notion "Callipygos," is the "correct" one, just
as it is problematic why Heyse finally left it out of his col-

---

[13] The manuscript is located in the Märkisches Museum in Berlin. I
am deeply indebted to Dr. Hans Werner Seiffert of the Deutsche
Akademie der Wissenschaften for a copy of this passage and the fol-
lowing ones.

[14] I consulted the fifth edition (1893).

[15] Paul Heyse, *Verse aus Italien. Skizzen, Briefe und Tagebuch-
blätter* (1880), p. 35. Regarding the question Venus or hetaera, cf.
Pauly-Wissowa, *Real-Encyclopädie der classischen Altertumswissen-
schaft*, Vol. 10 (1917), p. 1668: "Die Kallipygos genannte Statue in
Neapel wird jetzt allgemein als eine Hetäre erklärt."

lected poems. From the point of view of literary sociology the latter question is surely of a certain interest. More important in our connection, however, is the insight that the sketch affords us with regard to Fontane's prowess at integration. In the above sketch, the mention and interpretation of the distich is attributed exclusively to Van der Straaten; it belongs only to the narrative present. In the final version the motif is transferred to the narrative past and is rooted firmly in a situation involving several persons. Van der Straaten, in a highly indelicate manner, appeals to an earlier intimate conversation with his wife and thus involves her as an accomplice in his present bad behavior. At that point her heart turns away from him completely, and on the trip back in the boat, confused and deeply moved, she lends a willing ear to Rubehn's veiled declaration of love.

Despite all questionable elements, the reader feels that Van der Straaten has a certain "presence" as a character. And this is confirmed completely in his last nocturnal conversation with Melanie in the chapter "Farewell." It is one of the finest dialogues that Fontane ever created. No mere polite conversation, it is an open and honest exchange between two people at the height of their mutual crisis in life. He knows about her adultery and the child that she is expecting. And with this knowledge he proposes an attitude of kindness; a position which actually attests to his own basic kindness and magnanimity. There are no high-flown words about sin and forgiveness, no trace of idealistically inflated tones. On the contrary, the words with which he introduces his proposal are rather prosaically blunt and evince a relativistic, almost nihilistic skepticism:

> "Bah, the afternoon preachers of world history make too much of it, and we are dumb enough to repeat what they say. And we always forget our own unique glory, and we always forget how things were, and are, and will be. Or was it better in the days of my godfather Ezekiel? Or when Adam delved and Eve span? Isn't the whole Old Testament a thriller novel? The six-fold secrets of Paris!

182

And I tell you, Lannie, in comparison with all that, we are like pure little lambs, white as snow. Orphan children. So listen to me. Nobody is going to know about it, and I'll keep it as though it were my own. It's yours, after all, and that's the main thing. And as long as you don't mind, I love you and want to keep you. Stay! There won't be any trouble. There *won't*. But stay." (I, 3, 118ff.)

These are deeply serious words, and the form in which this seriousness is expressed is unprecedentedly genuine. Van der Straaten simply cannot be faithless to his own manner of speaking; even when it is a question of all or nothing he plays with phrases and literary allusions like a virtuoso. The old saying "When Adam delved and Eve span,/Who was then the gentleman?" resounds, and in rapid association the Old Testament is cited to outtrump Eugene Sue's thriller *Les Mystères de Paris*. A strong appeal is made to our sympathy, and yet the writer wants us to understand that Melanie must be repelled by this tone. "Everything that he said came from a heart filled with goodness and consideration, but the form in which this consideration was clothed continued to injure. He treated what had happened—all his sincere emotion notwithstanding—cursorily as a bagatelle and with a pronounced touch of cynical humor" (I, 3, 119). It is certain that Fontane intentionally aids our comprehension by causing Van der Straaten to work in again the phrase "Little lamb, white as snow" from the Bertuch children's verse, whose use in a radically different context had aroused Melanie's shamed indignation during the boating party. And we scarcely need to doubt that the author intended her to be reminded of that embarrassing scene by these very words. The repetition of the quotation thus amounts to a further motivation, but it is almost cryptic because only the very attentive reader will recognize the quotation, be aware of its repetition, and understand its significance for Melanie's behavior.

Fontane often borrowed his materials from real life. We know that the material for *L'Adultera* was supplied by a society scandal in the realm of high finance in Berlin only a few years earlier. Van der Straaten's "model"—very much with a grain of salt!—was the industrialist Privy Councillor Louis Ravené, whose wife Theresa von Kusserow had fled in 1874 with the banker Gustav Simon and, two years later, contracted a happy marriage with him.[16] At an important turning point in Fontane's story we can see what a remarkable symbiosis is achieved by reality and literature acting as reciprocal stimuli. The scene of the act of adultery is Van der Straaten's luxurious greenhouse, and we know that a newspaper account of the plant auction in Ravené's greenhouse after the death of the owner supplied the inspiration for this. The newspaper clipping pasted to Page 29r of the manuscript reveals precisely how Fontane allowed specific details of reality ("palms," "ferns," "Dracaena") to come to the aid of his imagination. But the title of the chapter, "Under Palms," is actually a quotation—a circumstance which initially remains cryptic until it is brought to light toward the end of the chapter. When Melanie and Rubehn leave the greenhouse, they find their friend Anastasia waiting outside for them.

"Where in the world have you been?" Melanie asked disconcertedly. "I was worried for your sake and mine. Yes, it's true. Just ask. And now I have got a headache."

Anastasia, laughing, took her friend by the arm, saying only: "And you are surprised about your headache! You can't walk under palms without suffering the consequences." (I, 3, 97)

One may at least surmise that the associative connection between the actual greenhouse, located somewhere in Moabit, and the well-known quotation from Goethe's *The Elective Affinities*, which even then was already circulating as a commonplace ("No one wanders under palms without suffering the consequences"),[17] supplied the germinal

[16] Theodor Fontane, *Briefe an Georg Friedländer*, ed. Kurt Schreinert (1954), p. 351.
[17] *The Elective Affinities*, Bk. II, Chap. 7: "Aus Ottiliens Tage-

source for the conception of this chapter or at least for its setting. And Fontane capitalized on this association. This becomes clear if we compare, again, the final version with the preliminary sketch. The latter goes as follows:

Under Palms.

The portrayal of a greenhouse. The palms, the ferns, the dracaena—among them the orchids. The soft hothouse atmosphere; the fragrance of the flowers; a fountain; irrigation; then the cupola with somewhat fresher air. Here and in the corridors the love scene. When they left the greenhouse she said: "You can't walk . . ." But he kissed her and closed her mouth. And so they parted.[18]

At this point Fontane still had the intention of putting the quotation in Melanie's mouth. That is simple, but also rather banal. By attributing it to the friend Anastasia, Fontane achieves a much more sophisticated and at the same time more definite play. In the first place, the quotation now fits precisely into the tightly closed nexus of motivation. It is suggested by and refers to Melanie's headache, which in turn is caused by the "intoxicating fragrance" of the orchids, by the "soft hothouse atmosphere" that plays such an important role in the complex motivation of the adultery.

But the accomplishment of the quotation is not exhausted in this careful motivation. It gets its real pungency in the final version by the ironic double perspective in which it appears. Anastasia's tone is slightly ironic in itself, but her remark is nevertheless harmless and naive. Her ignorance is contrasted with the insight of the reader, who must give to her words a different and heavier content because he is aware of the real state of affairs. Thus the subjective irony of the speaker is overlaid by the objective irony of the situation. The effect of this ironic ambivalence is supported by the fact that a basically identical stylistic figure constitutes

---

buch"; JA, Vol. 21, p. 212. The expression appears as a *geflügeltes Wort* in the eighth edition of Büchmann (1874).

[18] Leaf 28r of the manuscript described above.

the last note of the chapter and thus acts as a response to Anastasia's "palm" quotation. Van der Straaten comes home from a visit to the minister. Overjoyed by his appointment to a certain government commission, he gives an ironic twist to his feeling of happiness by stylizing it in literary bombast: "From this day on a new era of the House of Van der Straaten will be dated" (I, 3, 97). It is no quotation, to be sure, but it looks as though the sentence is modeled after Goethe's statement following the cannonade of Valmy, well known to every schoolchild: "From here and from today there goes forth a new epoch of world history. . . ."[19] And it might be that its ironic pungency arises from the incongruous disproportion between world history and the House of Van der Straaten. The speaker does not understand, but the reader surely does, how matters really stand with regard to this "new era"!

The actual achievement of Fontane's art of quoting—thus might we sum up our conclusions up to this point—is based upon their realistic accuracy. His art of quoting is above all a self-subordinating element of his narrative ability to express almost tangibly what is individually and socially characteristic and, as it were, physiognomic. In addition the quotation has the much less clearly defined function of constituting bridges that lead beyond its own local effect and thus contribute to the architectonic coherence of the narrative. We had a chance to observe coherence of this sort in the chapter "Under Palms," where the relationship between the title and the Goethe quotation appearing at the end effects a "rounder rounding" of the sort that Fontane promised himself with the title of the novel *L'Adultera*.[20] This effect is even more intense when the quotation is raised to the power of a proper leitmotif. The effect of such leitmotifs is less "accurate" than it is poetical and lyrical, and this corresponds to the fact that it is an effect borrowed predominantly from the realm of the romantic song. During the evening boat trip in the chapter "Whither Are

[19] *Campagne in Frankreich*; JA, Vol. 28, p. 60.
[20] Letter of 11 September 1881 to S. Schottländer; GW, II, 11, 56.

We Drifting?"—a title also picked up again later as a leit-motif—Melanie and Rubehn hear songs echoing over from the other boat, and these songs constitute a clearly escalating series with hidden reference to their situation: "Long, Long Ago," Mendelssohn's "O säh ich auf der Heide dort," and finally "Schön Rohtraut." The refrain of Mörike's song "Lovely Rohtraut" catalyzes a very veiled confession of love. " 'Be still my heart,' repeated Rubehn and said quietly: 'Should it?' Melanie did not answer" (i, 3, 79). In the chapter "Under Palms" a reference to this same refrain acts upon the motivation. Rubehn reminds Melanie of those songs during the boat trip, and when she then softly utters the word "Rohtraut" (Fontane, incidentally, writes "Roth-traut"), the love which has hitherto been left unexpressed comes to an open avowal (i, 3, 96). Much later, when she is already married to Rubehn and has become the mother of his child, Melanie finds in the words "Be still my heart" the fortitude for smiling renunciation when she discovers that her narrow-minded relatives are "not at home" for her (i, 3, 139). At home her new husband consoles her with the second line of the Mendelssohn song, which has also reverberated in her heart ever since the evening of the boat trip: "With my cloak I protect you from the storm, I protect you" (i, 3, 141). It does not seem to be quite justified to speak in these and similar cases of "misuse of the leit-motif."[21] But it must be conceded that Fontane's greatest power does not rest on this poetically lyrical side. In his later novels this rather rudimentary constructive element recedes more and more into the background. The conversational quotation gains monopoly.

The rhetorical embellishment of the quotation and of the literary reference is a general element of conversational style in the social milieu of our novel. To be sure, the other figures of the novel cannot match Van der Straaten's virtuoso gift of phraseology, but in this case too it could be shown how greatly their use of quotation varies according to character. If we disregard this differentiation, there re-

[21] Wandrey, *op.cit.*, p. 176.

mains a common denominator that has a certain bearing on the sociology of literature. As an integrating element, quoting belongs to the "cultured" form of conversation in the casual society of the prosperous bourgeoisie depicted here. And we do not need to doubt that Fontane captured a genuine element of the social-cultural reality surrounding him. This element, of course, happens to suit his personal predilection—note the frequent play with quotations in his letters and theater critiques! But on the other hand it can be observed that he holds this phenomenon at an objective distance for the purpose of cultural criticism. Particularly in this respect the figure of Councillor van der Straaten is of value as a symptom. We recall that in the first chapter his quoting of a verse by Geibel is designated as "cultivated," and similarly that his taste for popular quotations is explicitly mentioned there. These two facts are intimately related. The culture of this particular bourgeois is a culture of current quotations, and as such it has almost typological significance for the society of the times.

The publication of Georg Büchmann's collection *Geflügelte Worte*[22] in 1864 and the vast popularization of this repeatedly reprinted book—*L'Adultera* appeared in 1882, simultaneously with the thirteenth edition of Büchmann—are eminently symptomatic of the level and nature of "cultivated" education among the German bourgeoisie in the last third of the century. The level is high, but its nature is nevertheless questionable. Culture is no longer taken, as it still was in the age of Goethe, to be the dynamic process through which the personality organically unfolds. It is regarded rather as a permanent condition or, more precisely, as a ready supply from which one can draw at will. (If one takes the not inconsiderable trouble to check how many of the quotations used in *L'Adultera* occur in an old edition of Büchmann—I used for this purpose the eighth edition, 1874—the proportion turns out to be astonishingly high.)

---

[22] The term *geflügelte Worte* (originally Voss's translation of Homer's phrase Ἔπεα πτερόεντα) as a designation for common quotations was a neologism coined by Büchmann; it then became itself a "winged word."

From evidence in his letters it emerges clearly that Fontane was deeply alarmed at the problematic nature of contemporary culture, which had rigidified into conformity and at the same time had become fragmented and of little ethical authority. As early as 1878 he uses the word "culture" within ironic quotation marks:

> Masses are always kept in order only by fear or religion, by secular or religious regimentation, and any attempt to do so without these great provosts of the world must be regarded as futile. It was thought that a substitute had been found in "culture." "Compulsory education" and "compulsory military training" were glorified. Now we have a nice mess on our hands. . . . Compulsory education has taught everybody how to read and has buried the last remnant of authority with the arrogance of semi-culture. . . . Rousseau turns out to have been right when he wrote as early as 1750: "Arts and Sciences cannot constrain it."[23]

We recall in this connection the ghastly irreverence implicit in the Biblical quotation cited by the Berlin snob in *Cécile*.

Even Van der Straaten's culture, as considerable as it may seem to us, turns out to be a conceited and irreverent semi-culture when examined closely; innumerable little elements prove that this was also Fontane's conception. We recall especially Melanie's bitter words: "But he does not know any secrets, because nothing strikes him as being worthy of secrecy. Because nothing is sacred in his eyes" (I, 3, 78). The questionable artistic taste of this enthusiastic picture collector also belongs to semi-culture, according to Fontane's notion. The fact that he has a Tintoretto copied—the "L'Adultera" picture—might well strike us as a positive sign of his good taste. But it is a conspicuous fact that Fontane, in the letters written during his short trip to Italy in 1874, expressed himself more critically, and at the same time more extensively, about Tintoretto than about any

[23] Letter of 3 June 1878 to his wife; GW, II, 6, 249.

other Italian painter. A bust of Christ by Albrecht Dürer "represents in my eyes more true art than all Tintorettos together." The colossal painting of paradise in the Great Council Hall in the Palace of the Doges is "a salad of angels' legs." Then there is his judgment on the Crucifixion in the Scuola San Rocco: "the lack of human warmth is actually alarming."[24] Fontane also has no high esteem for the "Murillo-manner" (II, 10, 341). Van der Straaten's praise of the Murillo Madonnas attests to a low understanding of art that is all wrapped up in the sensual and balances on the edge of the risqué (I, 3, 35). As much as Fontane's artistic judgments may surprise us, it must be clear that Van der Straaten's preference for Tintoretto and Murillo, according to the author's intention, lies on the same level as his enthusiasm for Piloty and for Meyerbeer's thriller opera (I, 3, 72).

In Fontane's last years his cultural criticism became even more radical; in any case it is expressed much more sharply. The solid old Franconian way of life in Mecklenburg is played against Prussianism, "this lowest form of culture that ever was."[25] "The people in Mecklenburg are . . . less 'cultured,' but also less 'mal-cultured!' This can be seen in the fact that scarcely any other part of Germany has produced so many talents. In Berlin, because of the eternal studying and examining the people are least talented—a bureaucratic drill machine."[26] The crassest and most impressive testimony, however, states: "I have almost reached the principle: 'Culture is a misfortune for the world.' Man must be intelligent, but not cultured. But since culture, like catarrh when there is an east wind, can scarcely be avoided, one must constantly be on guard lest a minor infection become a case of galloping consumption."[27] In this connection Fontane quotes Nietzsche's phrase about "herd cattle." As

[24] Letter of 10 October 1874 to Karl and Emilie Zöllner; GW, II, 10, 339f.
[25] Letter of 6 June 1897 to Wilhelm Hertz; GW, II, 11, 424.
[26] Letter of 13 July 1897 to James Morris; GW, II, 11, 426.
[27] Letter of 9 August 1895 to Meta; GW, II, 7, 311.

a matter of fact, a certain similarity to Nietzsche's cultural criticism is unmistakable—not so much in an ideological sense, but as far as the situation and the climate are concerned. All of Fontane's objections to "culture" could rather fittingly be epitomized with Nietzsche's expression "cultured Philistinism"![28]

THE last-mentioned documents lead us directly into Fontane's final period of composition. Indeed, his cultural criticism affords an apt transition from his first to his last novel of manners. To understand the human world that appears in *Stechlin*, it is proper to ask in what sense these people are cultivated and what attitude toward the phenomenon of culture is revealed in their speech and action. In the first place it should be pointed out that here essentially a single social milieu is represented: the milieu of the old nobility of Prussian aristocracy, those who were present "even before the Hohenzollern." Whether these people are at home in the country or in the city, whether they are impoverished like the Stechlins or prosperous like the Barbys—these differences play an unimportant role in view of the common background of the social climate. This common element of the aristocracy differs radically from the spiritual atmosphere and style of life among the rich bourgeoisie that we get to know in *L'Adultera* and in *Frau Jenny Treibel*. In the tone of mutual understanding that transcends all differences and brings about a strong atmosphere of coherence and roundness, a very unique and characteristic sort of culture expresses itself. The genuine spiritual culture of these nobles (whether we are supposed to take their representation to be one of unflinching realism or rather of an idealizing realism is a question in itself) displays itself indolently; it does not posture at all and it encounters stubborn cultural pride with a smiling skepticism. Naturally there are borderline cases. Assessor Rex is certainly not free of a trace of cultural vanity, even if he is able to

---

[28] Cf. my essay "Nietzsches Bildungsphilister und der Philister der Goethezeit," in *Verzamelde Opstellen*, Festschrift für J. H. Scholte.

keep it tactfully subdued. Once when he plays off "the loftier"—i.e., the higher—culture of the North Germans against the South Germans, Captain Czako answers: "God forbid. Nothing that is related to grammar and examinations is ever lofty. Were the patriarchs examined, or Moses, or Christ? The Pharisees were examined" (i, 10, 275f.).

It is considered good breeding, rather, to give ironic emphasis to one's own cultural deficiencies. With winning self-irony Czako speaks of his "waxworks culture" (i, 10, 139), and in the same attitude Woldemar von Stechlin willingly concedes his confusion of two painters who have almost the same name. That has a finer and at the same time more cultivated effect than the pedantic earnestness with which the professor of art Cujacius instructs him regarding the difference between Millais and Millet (i, 10, 318, 322). A certain boredom with academic knowledge belongs to the general intellectual atmosphere, and it is good form to make jokes about it. In a rather intricate bit of conversation Czako says: "Of course, Melusine is more. Everything that comes out of the water is more. Venus came out of the water, Hero too . . . No, no, excuse me, it was Leander." Woldemar replies: "It does not matter. Leave it as it is. Such a garbled Schiller passage always does you some good" (i, 10, 285f.). He is the real son of his father, who also never misses a chance to make adverse comments on school culture. But it would be quite mistaken to read this skepticism as a nihilistic hostility toward culture. These aristocrats refer cultural values to their personal situation in life and adapt them to their own intellectual *niveau*, regarding whose relatively modest level they have no illusions. Even if this in itself constitutes a reduction of the lofty cultural values that pervade classical German idealism, still there is a genuine human kernel in this adaptation. The cultural values that have been leveled in this way are, for them, genuine possessions with which one can live. As a reaction against cultural conformity, the values are relaxed subjectively. Woldemar's trip to England is undertaken under the motto: ". . . things in themselves don't matter.

What one experiences gains its importance through the person who experiences it" (I, 10, 228). The manner of the experience becomes more important than the experienced cultural elements themselves.

Roughly the same holds true generally of the conversations—and our novel consists almost wholly of dialogue. The manner of speaking interests the conversing partners just as much as, and often even more than, the factual content of the conversations. It is basically this conspicuous element that bestows upon the dialogues their convincing character as real conversations. Everything depends on the undertones. These people are almost without exception highly conscious of language. They listen attentively to the expressive value of their words and comment upon the nuances in short subordinate clauses and parentheses that refer to the accuracy, but even more to the stylistic value, the cultural atmosphere, of the words. And they are keenly aware of their own subjective attitude toward certain words. There are innumerable parenthetical remarks of this sort that interrupt a factual statement: "If I didn't hate the damned word," "if that's the right word," "for I am not afraid of such a word," "as, I believe, is now said," "unfortunately I must take recourse to this Berolinism," and so forth. And they are colored in an incredibly subtle manner to suit the individual speaker.

The real master of this kind of commentary is old Dubslav Stechlin. His linguistic considerations generally come about when he weighs two competing expressions, one against the other. Once when he uses the expression "second breakfast," he adds: "an oldfashioned designation which nevertheless still sounds better to me than 'lunch.' 'Second breakfast' has something distinctly cozy about it and clearly implies that one has already had a first. . ." (I, 10, 68). No less accurate and entertaining are his reflections on the varying emotional value of two words for dropsy (*Hydropsie* and *Wassersucht*), the words for thriller and novel (*Schmöker* and *Roman*), and for tuxedo and dinner jacket (*Schniepel* and *Frack*). His elucidations of

193

the cultural and historical atmosphere can also, on occasion, deal with a quotation or common saying. "I personally prefer to stick to coffee, 'black as the devil, sweet as sin, hot as hell,' as Talleyrand is supposed to have said. But pardon me for bothering you with anything like that. Even my father used to say, 'Yes, we country folk, we still repeat the old jokes from the Congress of Vienna.' And that's already a generation ago" (I, 10, 64). It is clear that the writer Fontane is here imparting an essential element of his own critical awareness of language to his figures, especially to his favorite figure Dubslav Stechlin. We shall see that this sensitivity to the manner of speaking and this dominance of "how" over "what" are also of determining significance for the use of quotations.

In *Stechlin*, quotations and quotation-like expressions do not appear in such thick concentration as in *L'Adultera*. And qualitatively a difference is perceptible as well, but not necessarily in favor of the earlier novel. Here one searches in vain for such a rich—but also somewhat forced —virtuosity in quoting as that of Councillor van der Straaten. The mature art of our author (or, if you like, the greater virtuosity) now consists expressly in toning down the virtuosity and, by way of compensation, working out more subtly the individual nuances. The most important bearer of quotations is without a doubt Dubslav Stechlin, and even his use of quotations remains within moderate limits. We shall focus our attention primarily, if not exclusively, upon him. During the first dinner conversation at Schloss Stechlin, Czako tosses out a question intended solely as a spur to conversation. How would the carps in Lake Stechlin behave if the lake were stirred up by great world events and a conflagration should rise from it? Dubslav responds in an equally lighthearted spirit. "My dear Herr von Czako, the answer to your question poses certain difficulties even for an inhabitant of Stechlin. No created spirit can penetrate into the inner recesses of nature. And the carp is numbered among the most inward and reserved creatures; namely, it is very dumb" (I, 10, 31). What we have here is actually a quotation magnified to the second power. The maxim stems originally from the didactic poem "Die Falschheit menschlicher Tugenden" ("The Falseness of Human Virtues") by Albrecht von Haller, where it occurs in the form of a correctly alternating Alexandrine line: "Ins Innre der Natur dringt kein erschaffner Geist."[29] The line owes its familiarity in the nineteenth century to Goethe, who quotes it in his oracular poem "Allerdings," in the cycle of philosophical poems "Gott und Welt," in order to take issue with it polemically—or more precisely, to take issue with those who repeated Haller's statement thoughtlessly. The beginning of the poem goes:

> *"Ins Innre der Natur"*—
> O du Philister!—
> *"Dringt kein erschaffner Geist."*
> Mich und Geschwister
> Mögt ihr an solches Wort
> Nur nicht erinnern!
> Wir denken: Ort für Ort
> Sind wir im Innern.

> (*"Into the inner recesses of nature"*—
> O Philistine!—
> *"No created spirit can penetrate."*
> You have no need to remind
> Me and my kin
> Of such a saying!
> We think: Wherever we may be
> We are within.)[30]

The fact that this quotation has been raised to the second power is not of central importance in our connection because it is not to be assumed that Dubslav (or perhaps even Fontane) is aware of this circumstance. Also it is immediately clear that the objective substance of the maxim, in being used as conversational spice, has largely evaporated. Even its form has been adapted to conversational

[29] Albrecht von Haller, *Gedichte*, ed. L. Hirzel (1882), p. 74.
[30] JA, Vol. 2, p. 259.

prose by the avoidance of the rigid Alexandrine meter. But what a narrative masterpiece of subjectifying adaptation to the intellectual nature of the speaker! This gliding scale of concepts: "inner recesses" (*das Innere*); "inward" (*innerlich*); "reserved" (*verschlossen*); "dumb" (*dumm*), and the values implied by it express figuratively the nature of this born *causeur*, who shortly before had brilliantly formulated his preference for a humanity directed outwards: "Silence does not become everybody, and then too we are supposed to distinguish ourselves from animals by speech. So he who talks the most is the purest human being" (I, 10, 24). In the same chatty style Dubslav turns against Bismarck's opinion that red wine is "the natural beverage of the North German" and expresses his own preference for Main wine in a squat bottle: "You see, gentlemen, all long necks are anathema to me; but this one, that's what I call a pleasing shape. Isn't it said somewhere: 'Let me see fat people,' or something like that. I agree with that; fat bottles, they are for me" (I, 10, 83ff.). Naturally, Fontane could easily have reproduced the exact words of Shakespeare's Julius Caesar (Act I, Scene 2): "Let me have men about me that are fat." The emphasized impreciseness ("or something like that"), however, suggests the indolent ease of the dinner-table conversation. Dubslav makes no attempt to conceal the fact that the exact wording eludes him. Through this very deviation from the text the quotation becomes a conversational element taken from real life.

In earlier chapters—for instance, in connection with E.T.A. Hoffmann and Immermann—we were sometimes unable to win any positive meaning from imprecision in quoting, and we were forced to conclude that this imprecision was based only on the carelessness of the writer. With Fontane the case is different. The deviations from the wording of the text are shaded so functionally, and at the same time, so subtly, that we can conclude with assurance that a conscious sense of gradation of meaning is at play. But only if we listen very attentively can we guess the psychological and stylistic reasons for these deviations from one

case to the next. The following bit of dialogue constitutes a
little masterpiece of integration. Dubslav has inquired dis-
creetly about Woldemar's possible plans to get engaged,
but the latter still does not wish to mention a name because
he is not sure enough of his affairs and because he does
not want to "talk away" his happiness. His father supports
this attitude:

> "Good, good. I approve of that. That's the way it is. We
> are always surrounded by envious and malicious crea-
> tures with foxtails and batwings, and if we boast or act
> assured, they laugh. And as soon as they laugh, we are
> as good as lost. Nothing can be done with our own pow-
> er. I'm not even sure of the blade of grass that I pluck
> here. Humility, humility. . . . And yet I come to you with
> the naive question (for one constantly contradicts one-
> self), is it something elegant, something really fine?"
> (I, 10, 63)

These are completely mundane reflections on an equally
mundane theme: marriage and social acceptability. But
here and there the language has a certain archaic patina,
and with a little attention we detect the proximity of
Luther's use of the German language and, more specifically,
reminiscences of Luther's hymn "A Mighty Fortress."
"Nothing can be done with our own power" ("Mit unsrer
eignen Kraft ist nichts getan") is obviously a free rendition
of the first line of the second strophe of the hymn: "Mit
unser Macht ist nichts getan." But with what virtuosity the
atmosphere for this quotation has been built up! The
"malicious creatures with foxtails and batwings" represent
only a humorous embodiment of human social envy. The
imagery, however, belongs to the realm of late medieval
and Reformation lore concerning the Devil; the reader au-
tomatically thinks of Grünewald's Isenheim Altar and
Luther's inkpot. In Dubslav's soul, consciously or uncon-
sciously, there also resounds the beginning of the third
strophe of the Reformation song: "And did the world with
devils swarm,/ All gaping to devour us." There is still

not a trace of actual quoting here but, in the course of talk-
ing, Dubslav becomes more and more wrapped in Luther's
aura, so that the conclusion of the following sentence, " . . .
as good as lost," picks up verbatim the conclusion of the
second verse of the second strophe: "Wir sind gar bald ver-
loren." At this point, in a light modification, the whole first
line of the second strophe follows.

The way leads, therefore, from an associative reminis-
cence via an isolated fragment of a quotation to a proper
quotation; and in the process the sequence of the passages
borrowed from the song is exactly reversed. At the
same time the fusion with the momentum of the conversa-
tion is so complete that one could easily fail to see
how deeply Dubslav's words are involved with quotations.
But here this fusion strikes us as highly realistic. One of the
notes in the manuscript goes as follows: "Dubslav. In his
political views completely Junker, monarchy, Lutheranism,
nobility, army. But his views are nevertheless shaken. . . ."[31]
His orthodoxy is not in the best possible shape; he is a skep-
tic and an honest admirer of Old Fritz. But "Lutheranism"
is in his flesh and blood, and colors his thoughts and words.
We can be sure that he would be able to quote the verse
"Mit unser Macht ist nichts getan" word for word. But we
also understand why he does not do so. A literal quotation
would be too obtrusive here and too solemn. Because it
really is part and parcel of his personal intellectual prop-
erty, he can play freely with the quotation. He can adapt it
to the flow of his talk and his gentle irony; he can reduce it
and translate it into mundane terms without giving the least
impression of parody. With his ironic but also modest un-
derstatement we shall compare the dull earnestness with
which Katzler, in his election speech, exploits the verse
"And did the world with devils swarm" for political pur-
poses, and the manner in which the dogmatic Professor
Cujacius arrogates Luther's "Here I Stand" (i, 10, 222, 320)
for his own purposes.

[31] See Julius Petersen, "Fontanes Altersroman," *Euphorion*, 29
(1928), 55.

Dubslav is not a "Here I Stand" man, but his skepticism is also not absolute and complacent. His ponderings about theological doctrine in the days of his last illness and in his presentiment of death attest to an honest striving for valid insights. In this context the following little interior monologue functions as a priceless mood-setting chord. Dubslav looks up at the clock, which is ornamented with a figure of death bearing a scythe, and counts the chimes. "Twelve," he said, "and at twelve o'clock everything is finished and then the new day begins. Of course there are two twelves, and the twelve that is striking up there now, that is the noonday twelve. But noon! . . . Where are you, Sun?" (ɪ, 10, 440). The reader understands the basic contrast of noon and midnight and the symbolic union of life and death although all this, in the hazy outlines of these reflections, is not stated explicitly. But the symbolic union belongs to common Christian thought, firmly implanted in the consciousness of the faithful. The sentence with which the little monologue ends shows how much all of this reverberates here. The second strophe of Paul Gerhardt's "Evening Song" begins:

Wo bist du, Sonne, blieben?
Die Nacht hat dich vertrieben,
Die Nacht, des Tages Feind.

(Where, Sun, have you remained?
Night has driven you away,
Night, the enemy of day.)

Nowhere in literature is the transition from nonfigurative to figurative use of day and night so artfully carried out as in this hymn. Again Dubslav quotes with such restraint that one almost reads past the quotation. And again there is a good reason for the deviation, which here is minimal. The addition of the single first syllable ("Wo bist du, Sonne, *ge*blieben?") destroys the metrical pattern, makes prose out of the verse, and thereby assimilates it wholly to the thinking of the old man and the prose of his interior monologue.

In an essay about *Stechlin* Julius Petersen sees the characteristic mark of Fontane's late style as the fact "that most figures meet more or less . . . in the manner of speaking that is characteristic of their author himself; it is the unifying background against which the subtler shadings define themselves. . . . What Fontane calls the 'casual or witty speech of the Berlin salon' has become the almost unified form of expression in his novels of manners—an instrument that produces no great intervals, but infinitely fine modulations."[32] Petersen's illustrations for this, to be sure, stress the common basic tone more than the individual modulations. The accuracy of his observation on the latter, however, can be shown extremely well by the use of quotations in *Stechlin*. Again and again, in the main figures and also in the secondary figures, we note admiringly how precisely the quotation and the manner of its use are tailored to their minds and the manner of their speech. Professor Cujacius, the Peter Cornelius enthusiast, lets himself go in invectives against modern painting. "The train . . . is now lying beside the tracks huffing and puffing. It is only a pity that its firemen did not perish there with it. That is the curse of evil deeds . . . I don't wish to quote the rest of the passage in the presence of ladies" (I, 10, 319). The wholly useless interruption of the quotation from *Wallenstein*,[33] which is known to every German and completely decent, has the effect of ridiculous prudery and yet implies a certain dashing elegance which is characteristic of the professor's whole way of speaking. When, through his fault, an argument arises with the no-less-dogmatic music teacher Wrschowitz, the latter answers the allusion to his nationality with the telling words: "I am Czech. But know that there is German proverb: 'The German lies when he is polite,'" (I, 10, 407). The distortion of the words of the Baccalaureus in *Faust*

[32] *Ibid.*, pp. 68f.
[33] Schiller, *Wallenstein*, "Die Piccolomini," Act V, Scene 1: "Das eben ist der Fluch der bösen Tat,/ Dass sie fortzeugend immer Böses muss gebären" ("That is the curse of an evil deed,/ That it must continually give birth to evil").

("Im Deutschen lügt man, wenn man höflich ist": "In German, one lies when one is polite")[34] is again precisely measured and characterizes both the agitated conversational situation and the foreigner who is less at home in German literature.

We could go on for a long time, ascertaining individual modulations of this sort. There would also turn out to be a slight distinction between the respective milieux of the Stechlins and the Barbys, between the country and city atmosphere. Certainly the common element is stronger than the differences. Yet the formulation "casual or witty speech" is more apt for Melusine and her circle than for Dubslav and those around him. Let us restrict ourselves to one last example. In one conversation (I, 10, 323) Melusine reproduces the sarcastic words of a critical colleague of Professor Cujacius' regarding the latter's stereotyped representations of Christ and his pious business acumen: "For forty-five years he has been painting the same Christ over and over again and traveling around the provinces assigned to him. But he is such an art fanatic—one is even tempted to say, such a church fanatic—that one might almost say of him: 'it seems that his Christ preaches everywhere, but has become for all that no lovelier'" ("Es predigt sein Christus allerorten,/ Ist aber drum nicht schöner geworden"). This witty bit of backbiting presupposes a very fine ear on the part of the listener. We ask ourselves what it reminds us of until we recall, rather laboriously, the words of Mephistopheles in the scene with the traveling scholar: "That is what all the students believe,/ But they have never learned to weave" ("Das preisen die Schüler aller Orten,/ Sind aber keine Weber geworden").[35] Retained, in addition to the syntactical structure, are the rhyme and the doggerel, but because the rhyme is impure and the rhythm so close to prose, the sentence reads like normal prose. The actual content of the quotation has completely disappeared, and we are probably supposed to assume that the socially ac-

34 Goethe, *Faust II*, verse 6771.
35 Goethe, *Faust I*, verses 1934f.

ceptable delicateness of the parodistic variation consists precisely in this depletion of meaning. The example seems to me to be particularly suited to illustrate the nature of Fontane's modulation of speech. Despite the general similarity, this oversubtle wittiness would be simply inconceivable for, say, Dubslav Stechlin.

In an even more exclusive sense than in Fontane's earliest novel of manners, the significance of the quotation spends itself in his last novel wholly in the quotation's function as an element of dialogue. The leitmotific function of the quotation, which was rudimentary even in *L'Adultera*, has been given up completely in *Stechlin*. It was one narrative means among others to "let the figures speak as they really speak." We may now return to this formula, for our analysis has shown that it is not to be taken as the proclamation of a naive and unflinching realism. The fact that Fontane lets his people talk as they really talk does not prevent them from speaking an eminently Fontanesque language. Thomas Mann was right when he applied to Fontane himself a phrase that Fontane coined for Gottfried Keller, judging—in a thoroughly laudatory sense—that Fontane had "made God's whole wide world speak in his own Fontanetone."[36] And we may also feel free to assume that Fontane would have been quite satisfied with this verdict. Fontane's realism, if we apply Goethe's well-known distinction to it, is no "simple imitation of nature," but "manner" and "style" or something between the two.

The old Fontane's receptive attitude toward the emergent movement of naturalism is well known. In a review of *Die Familie Selicke* by Holz and Schlaf (1890), he expresses the surmise that the future will belong to "these plays that according to the old view are not actually plays," "these 'slices' from life" (a translation of *tranches de vie*). But it is not so much this favorable judgment itself as its justification that makes us perk up our ears. He ends his review with the words: "For [!] there remains a huge differ-

[36] Mann, "Der alte Fontane," *Adel des Geistes*, p. 559.

ence between the image that life poses and the image that art poses; the transitional process that takes place creates a puzzling shape, and the artistic effect, the effect in general, is tied up with this shape. If I had seen little Lieschen Selicke die in the neighbor's apartment in the back of the house, I doubt if I would have cried; but I tearfully followed the little Lieschen who died on the stage yesterday. Art is a very special juice."[37] The autonomy of artistic creation claimed for the "consistent naturalism" of Holz and Schlaf can be attributed in much greater measure to Fontane's "realism." We wanted to reveal the new and unique realistic-mimetic power of Fontane's art of quoting, but at the same time to cast a proper light on the "puzzling shape" that alone makes a work of art.

[37] Hans Mayer, *Meisterwerke deutscher Literaturkritik*, Vol. 2 (1956), p. 896. The last sentence, freely adapted from *Faust I*, verse 1740, gives us an example of Fontane's predilection for parodistic quoting in his essayistic writings.

CHAPTER IX

Wilhelm Raabe

HASTENBECK

LET US begin this time with a few statistics. Without any exaggeration, it can be assumed that the number of quotations used by Wilhelm Raabe in his novels and stories amounts to at least five thousand.[1] If we consider that his narrative work in the complete edition[2] amounts to roughly ten thousand normal pages, this means that on the average at least every second page contains one quotation. This fact, which is in itself rather astonishing, is wholly in accord with the spontaneous impression that doubtless every reader gets when reading Raabe's works: the impression, namely,

[1] Fritz Jensch, *Wilhelm Raabes Zitatenschatz* (1925), contains 2,100 entries. This total refers to the number of literary passages, many of which are quoted repeatedly in various works. According to the calculations of Walther Scharrer, *Wilhelm Raabes literarische Symbolik dargestellt an Prinzessin Fisch* (Münster dissertation, 1927), who added several items to the material collected by Jensch, altogether 2,124 passages are quoted for a total of 3,600 references. The term "quotation" is understood quite broadly here and also includes references to literary works and the mentioning of titles. Both authors realize that these computations are of necessity quite incomplete because of the often very cryptic way in which Raabe smuggles quotations and quotation-like material into his works. In fact, the Raabe scholar often runs into literary passages that are not catalogued in Jensch's work. Scharrer goes so far as to suggest that in reality the number of quotations would amount to roughly double the number that he notes. And if one attempted to include the more or less clear leitmotific references to quotations already introduced—such as, for instance, the following references to Gottlieb Cober and Salomon Gessner in *Hastenbeck*—then one would never come to an end.

[2] Wilhelm Raabe, *Sämtliche Werke* (18 vols.). I cite *Hastenbeck* (Third Series, Vol. 6) according to this edition, which was published in three series of six volumes each. *Hastenbeck* has not yet been published in the currently appearing historical-critical edition by Karl Hoppe (1951ff.).

that this rampant wealth of quotations and other literary and cultural references plays a decisive part in determining the stylistic physiognomy of his narrative art, to a degree that probably can scarcely be equaled in the works of any other German or non-German narrator.

Consider the matter; but more: consider the means! In spite of this simple and unequivocal statistical finding, it turns out to be difficult to determine the precise nature of Raabe's use of quotations. For it is extraordinarily variegated and scintillates in many colors. One main element, however, strikes every reader, and it obtrudes particularly on one who comes, as we have just done, from Fontane. Raabe makes no attempt at all to limit the quotations to the dialogue of his characters. The narrator himself makes carefree use of them, with a freedom and largesse that can be compared only to that of Rabelais or Sterne. Whether this freedom, which becomes ever greater in the course of his development, is mere caprice or whether it is subject to a higher regularity—this is a tricky question that will concern us greatly.

In order to arrive at any clarity on this matter we must ask what artistic and structural effect the quotations achieve in Raabe's works.[3] Up to now this question has scarcely been posed by Raabe criticism; in many quarters there have even

[3] The most thorough separate study of Raabe's use of quotations is the one by Walther Scharrer cited above. He distinguishes between four functions of quotations in Raabe's works: characterizing, humoristic, mood-setting, and symbolic. These distinctions are useful, but the attempt to divide the quotations into four corresponding groups is misleading because Raabe's quotations generally have several of these functions at the same time. Despite this reservation it is clearly evident that the symbolic function increases in the course of Raabe's development. It is striking, by the way, that Scharrer does not notice and mention the structural-compositional function of the quotations. A brief but incisive passage on Raabe's art of quoting occurs in the valuable unpublished dissertation (Kiel, 1948) by Hermann Boekhoff, "Wilhelm Raabes Weltverhältnis in der Entwicklung seiner literarhistorischen und geistes-geschichtlichen Beziehungen," pp. 36-38. Regarding the symbolic quotation, see also Th. C. van Stockum, "Wilhelm Raabes *Schüdderump*: Komposition und Gehalt," *Von Friedrich Nicolai bis Thomas Mann* (Groningen, 1962), pp. 215-34.

been objections to the question itself. This is related to the notion, still quite widespread among Raabe enthusiasts, that Raabe's "deepest" significance is not to be found in the artistic realm, but in his ethical message and in the irrational depths of his own heart. This conception has been the predominant one for decades within the more devout Raabe congregation. But even in scholarly writing we can detect its traces. Thus in the preface to his splendid Raabe monograph Hermann Pongs writes:

> The secret lies in the depth of the emotional effects that go back much more to a kind of dark symbolic courage, to a sensitive organ for the relatedness of things, than to a highly conscious aesthetic sense. For that reason Raabe's work requires an exegete more than other writers, and one is faced with the necessity of interpreting every single work from its center, from Raabe's own heart.[4]

Far be it from me to say anything against Raabe's heart. But the alternative of irrational depth or aesthetic rationality that is implied here seems to me to be misleading. Precisely in Raabe's case it can be demonstrated in exemplary fashion how intimately both elements interpenetrate in his process of creation.[5] I, for my part, wish to adhere to this position in the course of our study at least as a heuristic point of view, not only because it strikes me as relevant in itself, but also because the special situation of Raabe scholarship makes it so urgently necessary. Namely, because the appeal to Raabe's heart has no defense against the sharp criticism which is sometimes leveled against Raabe's artistry and which can be magnified to a total denial of any artistic ability. This can probably be seen in its fiercest form in the voluminous work of Louis Kientz.[6] This is not the place to contradict systematically this crass indictment

[4] Hermann Pongs, *Wilhelm Raabe* (1958), p. 7.

[5] This interpenetration, by the way, is clear over and over again in Pongs's study, despite his programmatic preface.

[6] Louis Kientz, *Wilhelm Raabe. L'homme, la pensée et l'oeuvre* (Paris, 1939).

and the supposed unmasking of Raabe as a petty bourgeois pseudo-artist; I must content myself with the statement that this unmasking, in my opinion, is based on wholly false assumptions and amounts basically to a single gross misunderstanding.

But we do have to concern ourselves with Kientz's opinion regarding Raabe's treatment of quotations. He deals with it in a chapter on Raabe's style, which by the way bears the revealing title "Les faiblesses du style du Raabe." One of the many weaknesses of Raabe's style is supposed to be his immoderate quoting. According to Kientz's view, Raabe is not much more than a common cultural Philistine, and his broad culture, which is so complacently displayed, is taken to be nothing more than false insolence and a means of mystifying the reader. His terrible lack of taste and style is said to be related to this and to be caused by the avaricious hunger with which, during his whole life, he indiscriminately devoured popular literature of dubious *niveau*. Raabe is viewed as a miserable representative of the generation that believed blindly in the blessings of the encyclopedia. Raabe's own culture, claims Kientz, was a typical encyclopedia-culture: see *Abu Telfan*, where Leonard Hagebucher, who has returned home from African slavery, acclimates himself again to the German cultural world by means of the encyclopedia! The example could not have been more poorly chosen. For not only is it not permissible to draw, from a figure in a novel, general conclusions about its creator; but also it has apparently wholly eluded the critic that Raabe is here giving vent, with heavy-handed irony, specifically to his annoyance with German cultural Philistinism—no less sharply than he was later to do in *Stopfkuchen*. Moreover he permits his hero, Leonard Hagebucher himself, to participate in this irony. When Hagebucher, on one occasion, accompanies a pedantic cultural flourish with the words "Observe the fine classical quotation," this clear case of self-persiflage is taken by Kientz at face value and interpreted as Hagebucher's—and Raabe's—dour earnestness. But what ultimately concerns us most: in Kientz's opinion,

Raabe's quotations are not true components of the work of art but merely non-organic appendages.[7] One can be annoyed by Kientz's sarcastic and sometimes malicious claims or laugh at them, but one cannot simply ignore them. Their positive value consists in the fact that they challenge one to contradict them. Once again: The matter cannot be settled by a simple appeal to Raabe's irrational depths. We shall have to show what Raabe as a creating artist makes of his quotation material and what functional task he assigns to it in the final artistic form.

In Fontane's case it was possible to reveal the uniqueness

[7] A few characteristic sentences from Kientz's *Wilhelm Raabe*: "Le premier aspect du style de Raabe, qui frappe le lecteur dès qu'il aborde les 18 volumes touffus de l'oeuvre, est le manque d'unité et de goût dans un étalage hétérogène de science, la prétension à l'universalité en largeur et en profondeur. Il ne sait pas se limiter. . . . Cette impression d'encyclopédie est produite partout par la profusion des citations d'écrivains allemands et étrangers de toutes les époques, de toutes les catégories, citations en allemand, en latin, en grec, en français, en anglais, en italien" (p. 364). "C'est l'époque où les éditeurs allemands Brockhaus, Meyer, Herder, Wolff et d'autres diffusent avec un grand succès leurs encyclopédies, appelées Conversationslexikon für die gebildeten Stände. Raabe considère le dictionnaire encyclopédique et le recommande comme moyen de formation intellectuelle et de culture" (p. 365). "Rien n'est plus caractéristique pour les conceptions de Raabe que pareille assimilation du savoir encyclopédique avec la culture tout court, l'estime naive pour un savoir mal compris" (p. 366). "Après son retour dans sa cité natale, à côté des ouvrages d'inspiration centrale, les citations littéraires, qui n'ont que la fonction de simples hors d'oeuvre dans le texte, se multiplient à l'excès" (p. 367). And most astonishing: "Les fichiers de Jean-Paul Richter provenaient de lectures effectivement faites par l'auteur; Raabe par contre a lu sans prendre de notes, ses citations proviennent d'ailleurs" (p. 17). The artistic meaning that a quotation had for Raabe is illuminated vividly by a passage from a letter quoted in *In alls gedultig: Briefe Wilhelm Raabes aus den Jahren 1842-1910*, ed. Wilhelm Fehse (1940), p. 214. Adolf Kröner, the publisher of the popular journal *Gartenlaube*, had suggested to Raabe that he should cut from *Unruhige Gäste* a reference to Heine and a quotation from Sterne. There is no need to go into the ridiculous prudery of this suggestion. As far as Heine was concerned, Raabe reluctantly acceded. "But regarding the passage taken from *Tristram Shandy*, I cannot—cannot—cannot cut away at it and change it, and I implore you urgently to leave things as they are. . . . I beg you fervently, esteemed Sir, don't ruin all my pleasure in my work by such a mutilation of the ending!"

of his procedure in two novels, with the understanding that the findings held true essentially for his entire narrative work. In Raabe's case this does not seem to me to be possible. His quoting adapts itself, from one work to the next, to the richly shifting kaleidoscope of his narrative technique, becoming in the process enormously polymorphic. Since we cannot treat the works as a whole, it seems appropriate to focus our view on the work in which Raabe most highly intensified the uniqueness and capriciousness of his quoting art. There can be no doubt that this is the case in Raabe's last completed novel, *Hastenbeck* (1898), and in the fragment *Altershausen* which appeared posthumously in 1911. Because we are concerned above all with the structural function of the quoting in the totality of the novel, we must give the complete work precedence over the fragmentary one. For this reason I shall restrict myself to *Hastenbeck*—and I am delighted to do so because this novel, which has remained relatively unknown, belongs in my opinion among Raabe's most mature and meaningful creations.[8]

Let us first recapitulate the contents. *Hastenbeck* is a narrative related against a dark background, a story of blood and sorrow in the earthly vale of tears. The fact that it is at the same time a deeply serene story, and the reasons for this, will concern us later. It takes place in Lower Saxony, a subsidiary arena of the Seven Years' War. The war has just begun: the time is the fall of 1757. Raabe possesses and makes use of specialized information that he was able to acquire only by an exhaustive source study.[9] But the atrocious war events, which flare up in the background in the smol-

---

[8] I am not entirely alone in this conviction. Barker Fairley's "The Modernity of Wilhelm Raabe," in *German Studies*, Presented to Leonard Ashley Willoughby (Oxford, 1952), includes *Hastenbeck* among Raabe's five best works. Hermann Pongs, *op.cit.*, p. 612, compares *Hastenbeck*—as the product of Raabe's old age—to Fontane's *Stechlin*: "Es nimmt alle Züge der Altersreife in sich auf, nachdem Raabe drei Jahre 'daran gewürgt.'"

[9] Cf. Franz Hahne, "Das Odfeld und Hastenbeck," *Raabestudien*, ed. Constantin Bauer (1925), pp. 382-97.

dering colors of Grimmelshausen's *Simplicissimus*, remain confused and impenetrable for the reader as a political and strategic process. This confusion has a psychological and perspectivistic justification. For we do not experience the war from the perspective of the princes and generals, the politicians and strategists, but from the standpoint of the degraded, intimidated, and harassed populace. The men of power—Richelieu, Louis XV, King George II, the Duke of Cumberland, and their like—are mentioned constantly, but they appear only as sinister phantoms in the twilight of the distance. In the one case where Raabe considers politics and war from the lofty dynastic perspective (in the conversation between the Duke of Brunswick and his wife, in the twenty-second chapter), the depiction characteristically has a rather lackluster effect. The individual human being, the little man, is frightened and perplexed "like a flea on the bedsheets" (p. 135). Only this much becomes clear: that this is an ominous pause during the course of the war. The impenetrability of the situation helps to intensify the sense of imminent calamity in the air. The little man knows only that Germany is the battlefield of Europe. The British are allied with Prussia, the French with Austria. The Battle of Hastenbeck, which took place in July 1757, was won by the French; it was followed by the Convention of Kloster Zeven. Now the land between the Harz and the Weser is in the hands of the French.

In the center of the scene, in a specific sense, stands a parsonage that was known to the writer from his own experience: the parsonage in the village of Boffzen on the Weser, in the vicinity of Höxter.[10] The cast of characters is tossed together in a manner typical of Raabe. First of all there are the childless inhabitants of the parsonage: the pastor is kindhearted and gentle, but firm in his faith in God's Providence; his wife is basically also kindhearted, but over-energetic, self-righteous, and dogmatic. Then there is their adopted foundling Hannchen, the dear little

---

[10] Raabe's brother-in-law, Pastor Louis Tappe, had been a minister in Boffzen; see *In alls gedultig*, ed. Fehse, p. 25.

"Bienchen" or "Immeken" (both diminutives of "bee") of Boffzen, as she is called by the village inhabitants and especially by the young painters of the neighboring and recently established Fürstenberg Porcelain Works. Immeken is secretly engaged to Pold Wille, a young flower-painter at the porcelain works. But their love affair has not been blessed. The energetic foster mother caught up with them and slapped them, and in his fright and consternation the little flower-painter ran into the arms of the recruiters for the English Army and was cruelly impressed for war service. After the Convention of Zeven he deserted, and must now seek cover like a hunted animal. He finds sanctuary in the house of Old Wackerhahn, a beggarwoman decried as the village witch, but in reality the tutelary spirit of the two "children," Hannchen and Pold. This old woman is a figure of balladesque power and magnitude. At one time the rich and beautiful daughter of a peasant, she became the fiery wife of a forester and aided him in the life-and-death struggle against poachers. After his murder, she roamed through all Europe down as far as lower Italy and Sicily as a camp follower. Since her return she has been dwelling, ostracized and superstitiously feared, in the old Militia Tower. More dead than alive and with fever in his bones, Pold finds a first shabby sanctuary with her. Meanwhile, an uninvited guest is still living in the parsonage: the old and invalided Swiss captain Balthasar Uttenberger, who was wounded in the Battle of Hastenbeck and quartered here. He belongs to the "enemy," that is, to the French Army; but in this "enemy" the helpless young couple find their best helper. The old mercenary, after a life of hard and bloody experiences, has discovered in Immeken "the sweetness of the world." Pold is secretly brought to the parsonage and nursed back to health by the reluctant pastor's wife. But on all sides the deserter is threatened by imminent danger— running the gauntlet or worse. For this reason the lovers flee through night and fog, accompanied by Old Wackerhahn, who knows every path and crossing in the wild forest. She is able to arrange their marriage on the way by the

young pastor of Derenthal, who himself renounced Imme-
ken after long inner struggles. Finally, they find asylum
with the Duke of Brunswick on "neutral" territory in the
county of Blankenburg.

As far as the factual content is concerned, we seem to be
dealing here with a simple adventure story, but appear-
ances are deceiving. The plot alone with all its gloomy
earnestness, would scarcely lead us to believe that this is a
basically cheerful and even highly humorous work, con-
tinuing in the best sense the grand tradition of the humor-
ous novel. The sublime humor is based on the contrastive
harmony between the pragmatic narrative level and the
level of ideal meaning that transcends it. Raabe's narrative
style is not so much to recount as to illuminate. The nar-
rator is always explicitly present during his narrative. He
does not report, but talks about what is happening; he lets
the happenings develop by casting an interpreting light
upon them. He accomplishes this by creating firm points of
reference—symbols and similes—to an ideal realm, with re-
spect to which the meaning of events is measured and made
visible. These points of reference to the ideal may either be
set off sharply from the factual narrative content—think of
the hearse symbol that pervades the novel *Schüdderump*,
and even gives it its title, without playing any role in the
reality of the story—or they may emerge from the narrative
content. But in both cases they constitute the constellation,
as it were, by which the narrative orients itself and toward
which it charts its intellectual course.[11]

[11] It is deeply justified by the very nature of Raabe's work that
critics, in describing this state of affairs, repeatedly are forced to take
recourse to metaphors of light. "Immer wieder wird sie [= reality]
durch allgemeine Erfahrungen, durch literarische Hinweise, durch
geschichtliche Anspielungen, durch offene oder versteckte Vergleichun-
gen belichtet und damit so gegeben, wie sie sich im Dichter spiegelt";
Friedrich Neumann, "Wilhelm Raabes Schüdderump," *Zeitschrift für
deutsche Philologie*, 71 (1953), 294. "In der weit grösseren Zahl von
Fällen handelt es sich bei ihm . . . um dankbare Freude, mit der er
in dem Zitat geprägtes Leben entdeckt, das ihm eigenes Suchen und
Ringen deuten und klären hilft. In solchen Fällen kann es denn ge-
schehen, dass ein Zitat in seinem Werk zu einer Leuchte wird, an

The literary quotation plays, in the course of Raabe's development, an increasingly major part in this ideal upper realm. This highly unique art of quoting reaches its apex in *Hastenbeck*. Here Raabe creates something completely new and original—something that belongs legitimately to the tradition stemming from Cervantes and Sterne, but yet not actually prefigured by these great antecedents. Its uniqueness is characterized by the fact that here the structure of the narrative is not, or scarcely at all, determined by the pragmatic lower level, but rather by the ideal upper realm. This latter consists of two quotations or, better, two complexes of quotations which resound contrapuntally, which are constantly varied, and which form in their manifold interwovenness with each other and with the narrative content a heavy garland, as it were, extending through the whole book from beginning to end. I am speaking here of two books which are taken up as symbols in the context of the narrative and which also become visible at given intervals as actual objects, though they hardly play a role in the external action. In the inner action, however, their function is correspondingly greater. One is the book of devotions used by the pastor's family, a curious early-eighteenth-century prayer book from which the pastor reads every evening to the assembled members of the household: *Der Aufrichtige Kabinettsprediger* by Gottlieb Cober.[12] The other volume

---

der man nicht achtlos vorbeigehen darf, will man seinen tiefsten Sinn nicht verfehlen"; Wilhelm Fehse, *Wilhelm Raabe* (1937), p. 254.

[12] Gottlieb Cober (1682-1717), *Der aufrichtige Cabinett-Prediger* (Altenburg, 1711). "Einer der besten populär-theologischen Schriftsteller des 18. Jahrhunderts." "Das Buch machte ein ungemein grosses Aufsehen und wurde besonders vom gemeinen Manne stark gelesen und geliebt, weil es alle Schäden und Gebrechen, auch jene der höchsten Stände freimütig und schonungslos geisselte"; *Allgemeine deutsche Biographie*, Vol. 4 (1876), pp. 369ff. The work was repeatedly edited, even as late as 1854! Jean Paul's Schulmeisterlein Wutz reads the *Cabinett-Prediger*, and Jean Paul adds the note: "Cobers Kabinettprediger—in dem mehr Geist steckt (freilich oft ein närrischer) als in zwanzig ausgelaugten Predigthaufen." Raabe received the book at the end of 1891 as a gift from his friend and admirer Edmund Sträter, to whom he wrote words of happy gratitude

made its way to the house through the fortunes of war. It is an elegant little rococo book that bears the traces of battle. The original owner fell in the Battle of Hastenbeck. The Swiss captain picked up the duodecimo volume, with a bullet mark and bloodstains on its tattered cover, from the gory mud of the trampled field, and it now provides his favorite edifying reading. It is the *Idylls*—just published in 1756—of his Zurich compatriot Salomon Gessner, "who at the outbreak of the Seven Years' War struck on his lyre unaccustomed tones and sang into the thundering cannon his songs of the Golden Age, Arcadia, milk and honey, and Daphnis and Chloe" (p. 7).

Christian faith in divine providence and Arcadian bliss: bloody reality seems to mock these two dreams of salvation. The antithesis between upper and lower narrative levels seems to denote only a short circuit by revealing the events of war all the more vividly in their full horror. But this is not the case. In the humorous view of the world, reality is paradoxical and the seemingly incongruous is nevertheless forced into a unity. This is not expressed and discussed in theoretical reflections, but rather is made tangible by the power of artistic shaping—indeed, *as* aesthetic form—in the infinite interweaving of the quotations with the narrative content. This structure is so highly complicated that it is doubtful whether even the most intensive analysis can render it adequately visible. One peculiar difficulty with which all literary analysis has to struggle is particularly burdensome here. We can recognize the structure only by determining the individual structural elements; we cannot talk about the latter without singling them out, whether we want to or not. What in reality is simultaneous and interlaced, must necessarily be considered in the course of the analysis as successive and juxtaposed. Now in our novel the writer has undertaken to relate everything to everything else, to comprehend everything along with everything

---

(letter of 1 December 1891; in *In alls gedultig*, ed. Fehse, p. 271). In the following passages I quote from the edition of 1745.

else.[13] Despite the temporal succession to which all linguistic representation is committed, a kind of monistic simultaneity of the individual phenomena and statements is suggested by a tight network of references that establish points of contact in every conceivable direction. But because we must show first what sort of things are drawn into relationship, we must necessarily row against the current of the author's intention. We cannot avoid considering the two complexes of quotations, first, as separate—although their deepest meaning, as will become clear later, is related to their mutual interdependence.

It is in a remarkably cunning manner that Raabe causes the two complexes of quotations gradually to emerge and establish themselves in the opening chapters. The actual narrative gets under way only after the first chapter, which functions purely as a prologue. From the very start it is a highly idiosyncratic, jerky, and richly allusive form of narrative. First Raabe briefly refers to his earlier story "Höxter and Corvey," which has the same setting as *Hastenbeck*. In this connection all the emphasis is cast on the bridge over the Weser at Höxter, which constitutes the link between the two areas of action: "Once again, all summer long, it has often and miserably rumbled, groaned, moaned and bent under the military equipment of the war; but this time the axe and the petard have spared it, and so it will probably support our light tread on the trace of: 'God's Wonder Wagon'" (pp. 5f.). Unexpectedly, a puzzling phrase is tossed into the story. We are reminded of Raabe's frequent preference for symbols placed emphatically at the beginning of the narrative, for instance the cart in *Schüdderump* and the figure of young Fearless,

---

[13] This is a general compositional tendency in Raabe's works which reaches its apex in *Hastenbeck*. Cf. in this connection the excellent remarks by Barker Fairley, *op.cit.*, p. 73: "What we arrive at in our exploration of Raabe is an interdependence and an involvement—a richness of cross-reference—far in excess of what we expect in a novelist." Fritz Martini, "Wilhelm Raabes 'Prinzessin Fisch.'" *Der Deutschunterricht* (1959), pp. 31ff., writes in the same spirit and with particular attention to Raabe's art of quoting.

borrowed from Grimm's *Märchen*, in *Meister Autor*. The reader may or may not yet know what this "Wonder Wagon" is supposed to be; but he is all the more strongly moved by the suggestive power of the formula, which from this point on stretches through the whole narrative and holds it together. The very next sentence makes the connection somewhat clearer. Even before the characters are mentioned, a book is introduced. It is strangely identified with its author and made, as it were, the protagonist of the story:

> In his shabby Samar—that is to say, in his wellworn leather binding—he is lying this evening, too, in the light of the poor brass lamp in Boffzen, under the eyeglasses of the pastor loci, the honorable Gottlieb Holtnicker: the upstanding cabinet-preacher Gottlieb Cober from Altenburg, "who when he pays his visits, in a hundred sententious and agreeable discursive sermons knowledgeably discovers to persons of high and low standing their vices, faults and wishes along with the topsy-turvy course of the world today, warns them wellmeaningly, seriously admonishes, and vigorously consoles them," and we hear him discoursing about "God's Wonder Wagon" when we have stepped into the circle illuminated by this little lamp on the right bank of the Weser. (pp. 6ff.)

It is remarkable even here how the elements already interpenetrate each other. Who is it that we hear "discoursing" here: the pastor who is reading aloud or the "upstanding cabinet-preacher"? Probably it is both at the same time— one through the mouth of the other. Even more perplexing is the coalescence in the following paragraph, which imperceptibly switches over to Gessner's *Idylls*. (We will come back to this later.) But the narrator interrupts himself: "Honor to whom honor is due: first let the old cabinet-preacher from Altenburg speak and afterwards the worldly young poet from Zurich!" (p. 7). The narrator is still restraining himself; no real quotation has occurred, but already the puzzling expression "God's Wonder Wagon" is spreading out and the narrative content is established in

relationship to it. Of the foundling as well as of the invalid
Swiss captain, we hear that they "fell out of God's Wonder
Wagon" into the parsonage and "rolled to its feet" (p. 8).
So a tight network of interhuman references has already
been woven when we finally hear the pastor read the
twenty-fourth chapter of Cober's edifying book: "The Won-
der Wagon of God." The long quotation, only slightly ab-
breviated in comparison with the original text, is fre-
quently interrupted by the interpolated remarks of the lis-
teners and by the depiction of their varying reactions,
through which they are indirectly characterized. The key
sentences from Cober's chapter go as follows:

> People often want to go in this direction: but God
> leads them in that direction. He is wondrous in his deeds.
> God's Foresight is a Wonder Wagon. The four wheels are
> his Wisdom, Omnipotence, Fidelity, and Truth. God
> himself is the drayman who, in his wagon of Fortune
> and Misfortune, leads us only on byways. Never in
> a straight line. (p. 9)[14]

Now the reader knows what is going on, and he continues
to understand the image wherever the Wonder Wagon rolls
on through the story and human destiny is referred to it. At
the same time the most remarkable ties between symbol
and reality emerge through the effect of harmony and con-
trast. It is said of the old captain, for instance, that he was
"lifted down from cabinet-preacher Cober's Wonder Wagon
and left in the Boffzen parsonage to be cared for in life and
death," and in the same breath the passage explains un-
metaphorically: from the "baggage cart in the rearguard of
his Lord Marshall of Estrées" (p. 23). The identification is
carried so far that Old Wackerhahn even speaks, in an-

---

[14] *Cabinett-Prediger*, p. 103. Raabe does not quote with philological
exactitude. Cober's text reads: "Die vier Räder sind Seine Wahrheit,
Allmacht, Barmherzigkeit, Treue und Wahrheit." For understandable
reasons Raabe has reduced the number of predicate nouns to four.
The Reverend W. J. Manger of Baarn, Holland, kindly drew my at-
tention to the corresponding conception of the Wheel of Ezekiel
(Ezekiel 1:15-21; 10:9-17), which may underlie Cober's conception
of the Wonder Wagon.

other connection, of God's "wonder baggage wagon" (p. 88). In a still more paradoxical sense the Wonder Wagon is linked to the camp-followers' cart of Old Wackerhahn, and here the play between harmony and contrast is even more sharply pointed. To be sure, not everybody understands the paradox:

> If one had said to one's relatives in the year seventeen hundred and forty that even the forester's wife Wackerhahn had been unloaded again from God's Wonder Wagon in Boffzen, people would probably have answered: Satan himself had cast the errant female down from his cart and into the village. (p. 33)

But the narrator knows better:

> The Wackerhahn woman has traversed many a river through the wide world on the baggage wagon and with her camp-followers' cart; but it is better not to speak aloud of such things before honest wives and tender maidens. God's Wonder Wagon remains God's Wagon in any case! It is He Who gives His passengers their seats upon it, and that is also the best excuse that we have for the old woman in the Militia Tower. (p. 35)

In this way the author deals in sovereign freedom with his Wonder Wagon symbol, but at the same time it is also a constant item in the consciousness of the figures created by him and it is therefore modified according to their character. The pastor's wife, for instance, is much too energetic and self-righteous to surrender herself to the guidance of the Wonder Wagon. She prefers to take over the lead herself: "Here I know best, and when it is necessary I help the dear Lord to set His cart aright again" (p. 11). Because of this, her trust in God fails in the crisis of decision. She regards it as meaningless chance when the deserter Pold Wille comes to her house, and she reproaches the pastor for it: "O the naughty, naughty child with his foolish amour! . . . There you have your Wonder Wagon of God, that has carted *this* before my door in the peace of my old age!"

But at this point the mild-mannered pastor, remonstrating, opposes the power of his faith to her annoyance and irresolution: "Poor woman, say what you like to me, but do not try to obstruct the Lord's ways with idle chatter—not even in life's direst fear and distress! The roads of the earth are rutted, and indeed the wheels go through blood and tears, but leave me in the tracks of the wagon of Him Who makes everything right" (p. 67). In this manner the Wonder Wagon symbol determines the thinking and feeling of the figures of the novel and has a strong effect on their deepest decisions.

The same can be said, *mutatis mutandis*, of Salomon Gessner's *Idylls*. Here the case is even more striking. For the distress of life and surrender to God's wise guidance can always go well hand in hand, as is summed up by the proverb "Not lehrt Beten" ("Affliction teaches us to pray"). But between Gessner's lovely pastoral world and the bloody reality of our story there seems to be no connection at all unless it is that of sheer contrast. The Wonder Wagon symbol and the symbol of Daphnis and Chloe, however, must not be thought of as isolated from one another. Through their unification they bear witness to the conviction that, by God's will, "the sweetness of the world" cannot be destroyed by "the world's animality." In this sense Gessner's *Idylls* has no less power to institute symbols than does the book of devotions. Both complexes of quotations show a similar flow as they stretch out through the novel. Gessner's *Idylls* is first introduced gradually, heralded by a series of anticipatory notes. The very first hint, at the beginning of the second chapter, has an astonishing power of radiation. Remember: we neither know the persons as yet nor has the book of *Idylls* itself been named. Up to this point the cast of characters has only been hinted at typologically: pastor, pastor's wife, alien guest, pastor's daughter, and maid. Then the narrative continues:

After the evening prayers the guest too read a little piece from another book, which if not good was at least lovely.

It earned him a smiling inclination of the head from the spiritual shepherd, a suspicious headshake from the shepherdess, more than one astonished, glistening gaze from the wide-opened eyes of the shepherd girl, and from the stable girl, yard girl and house girl, Dortchen Krüger, an uninterrupted stare with gaping mouth. (p. 6)

This is an astonishing miracle of indirect characterization. Two unknown quantities—on the one hand the little book and on the other hand the assembled members of the household—are reflected in one another, illuminate each other reciprocally, and are preliminarily characterized by this art of illumination. The radiance spread by the still unnamed and still unknown book is like the play of colors in the sky before the sun itself appears. Only now is the book actually named by title and, at the same time, fitted into the meaning of the work:

It is a countryman of the Swiss captain Balthasar Uttenberger who, at the outbreak of the Seven Years' War strikes unaccustomed tones on his lyre and sings into the thundering cannon his songs of the Golden Age, Arcadia, milk and honey, and Daphnis and Chloe. Salomon Gessner . . . is his name, and the cultivated world from one end to the other listens to him despite the fire of large and small weapons. (pp. 6f.)

Gessner does not move into the center of our field of vision until the fourth chapter, which portrays Uttenberger's lonely nocturnal reading. The chapter ends with the first real quotation, which still has entirely an anticipatory character. It stems from the beginning of the idyll "Mirtil und Thyrsis" and contains the words with which Thyrsis exhorts Mirtil to sing him the story of Daphnis and Chloe. We then hear this song in the next chapter, again as a recapitulation of the captain's reading. The long quotation reproduces with a few cuts the entire text of Gessner's idyll—the stirring story of parting and the longing of love, of a miraculous rescue and happy reunion after dangers have been survived. The thematic agreement with the love story of Pold and Immeken is clear enough, but the element of mood and the lyrically elegiac tone have an even stronger impact than the contextual parallel. Mirtil's song begins with a lamenting exclamation, which is then repeated several times, echolike, as a refrain: "Mourn after me, you rocky cliffs! Sadly sound back my song, through the grove and from the shore!" (pp. 27ff.).[15] The elegiac power of this lament attracted Raabe particularly, and we have yet to see what an architectonic and at the same time lyrical use he makes of it.

While reading, the captain falls asleep. "Thank God! His Wonder Wagon rolled on after He had deposited Daphnis —the flower-painter Pold Wille—with Old Wackerhahn in the Militia Tower" (p. 28). The identification of Immeken and Chloe, of Pold and Daphnis, takes place both in the words of the narrator himself and in the consciousness of the captain. There are various lines of connection. The points of similarity between the rococo atmosphere of Gessner's *Idylls* and Fürstenberg porcelain are quite conspicuous. On one occasion Gessner's shepherds are called "porcelain dolls"; another time the willowy young flower-painter himself is simply called "Fürstenberg porcelain."[16] Further, the spiritual office of the pastor and his wife is related by a wordplay to the shepherds of the *Idylls* and their lambs. So on the one hand Immeken can be designated as the "shepherd girl" and as the "little lamb" entrusted to the spiritual shepherdess of Boffzen by God's Wonder Wagon; while on the other hand the two lovers are called "white lambs with a rose-red ribbon."[17]

But Gessner's idyll displays its revelatory symbolic power less in these surface affinities than in the great antithesis of "blood" and "flower," which constitutes the thematic center of our narrative and determines the form of utterance

[15] Salomon Gessner, *Sämtliche Schriften* (2 vols.; Reutlingen, 1789), pp. 71-74.
[16] *Hastenbeck*, pp. 69, 50.
[17] *Ibid.*, pp. 6, 45, 89.

from one page to the next. This antithesis, too, has a hidden quotational character, and it is possible to observe in detail how its elements are fitted together by the writer. Raabe borrowed the name of the flower-painter Johann Leopold Wille from a book about the Fürstenberg Porcelain Factory by his friend Heinrich Stegmann.[18] That was just a meager stimulus; but the suggestive words "flower-painter" ignited in the writer's fantasy and coalesced, crystal-like, with the inspiration that came from Gessner. The introductory sentence of the section "To Daphne," which opens the idylls, became in his mind the symbolic formula for the whole idyllic realm. He saves this sentence until the end of the fifteenth chapter, where it is quoted in harsh contrast to the misery of the war represented there: "Not the blood-spattered bold hero, not the desolate field of battle does the happy muse besing. Gentle and shy, she flees the tumult, her light flute in her hand." Gessner's text goes on to say, a few lines beyond this, that the muse walks "on flowers."[19]

Now we understand even more precisely the meaning of the paradoxical circumstance that Uttenberger picked up

[18] Heinrich Stegmann, *Die fürstlich braunschweigische Porzellanfabrik zu Fürstenberg. Ein Beitrag zur Geschichte des Kunstgewerbes und der wirtschaftlichen Zustände im 18. Jahrhundert* (1893). The dedication reads: "Seinen verehrten Freunden Wilhelm Raabe und Stadtarchivar Prof. Dr. Ludwig Hänselmann in herzlicher Zuneigung." This historical study by Raabe's companion from the Kleiderseller club surprises the reader through the quality of its writing and even through a certain narrative skill. The cosily subjective narrative attitude as well as the partly humorous, partly poetically animated tone are sometimes vaguely reminiscent of Raabe, and it is quite understandable that this work stimulated him—not merely as far as the facts are concerned, but also from the point of view of the cultural atmosphere. Stegmann writes with a lively vividness, especially when he is recounting the fate of porcelain manufacture during the Seven Years' War. In the "List of Painters Employed in Fürstenberg in 1759 and Their Monthly Wages" (p. 67), fourteen painters of figures, portraits, landscapes, flowers, and skies are mentioned; among them is the "Blumenmaler Johann Leopold Wille aus Braunschweig (26 Jahre)" along with his monthly pay of twelve *Reichstaler*. This sketchy reference is all that we know about Pold's historical model.
[19] Gessner, *op.cit.*, p. 13; *Hastenbeck*, p. 116.

this book of idylls from the slush and gore of the "desolate field of battle" and that it itself is "blood-spattered" and bears the traces of a bullet wound. We now also understand more deeply why Raabe outdoes himself with such expressions as "the bloodflecked shepherd's song of the dear Swiss poet," and why he repeats the designation "flowerpainter" throughout the whole novel with monomaniacal obstinacy. The words "blood" and "flower," along with their derivatives, wind garland-like through whole chapters and at times intertwine for a while in a taut tapestry of words. Let us see, for example, what a variety of things can be forced together in alternation on a single page: the "fleck of blood from the field near Hastenbeck," which "had laid itself over the Idyll about the 'Discovery of Gardens' and dripped down on to the page"; the quotation "flowery spring" from this very same idyll; the word "bloody" as a designation of the old mercenary soldier and the young deserter; and finally, once again, "in flowery spring" as a contrast to reality (pp. 76f.). All of this comes as a prelude to Uttenberger's confession that he has recognized in Immeken "the sweetness of the world":

> "I must take it to be a miracle: what our Lord God in his compassion has bestowed upon my old days, after so many marches in the service of so many masters, after so many small weapons, heavy cannon and murderous work with shining weapons, after so much blood and arson in the lands of many rulers—here under this roof, among these dear people, from this bloody flower-summer to this snow which is now coming down and attempting to cover the world's devilishness with white. There lies the little book that I also picked up out of the blood —what did I know, a Swiss herd boy, of the little sheep and little lambs on bright meadows? What did I know of the world's sweetness, until your little girl, little Immli, showed it all to me down there in her garden?" (p. 78)

A few pages later, to be sure, Old Wackerhahn has to explain the hard truth to her ward Immeken: "It is not a time when one can protect himself and his dearest in the world from the world's animality with love and kindness, with flower-sermons and flower painting . . ." (p. 88). In a painful recollection of the death of the young Spaniard who expired in her arms after running the gauntlet, she can even alternate the realms of blood and flower with caustic irony, allowing one to appear in place of the other. So she warns Pold Wille of the other kind of "flower painting" that awaits him threateningly: ". . . We, the ones in the camp as well as in the garrison, also understand something about flower painting! Blue-red, rose-red, blood-red! Guard your back against our paintbrushes, Musketeer Wille, and beg your friends and—enemies here in the house that they spare you, if only out of Christian mercy, the run through the alley, a lance in front, a lance in back, and a lead bullet in your mouth . . ." (p. 108). With these words she tosses on the table the bullet on which the Spaniard had gnashed his teeth and which now rolls toward the book of idylls.

In the symbolic figuration of blood and flower, Uttenberger and Old Wackerhahn have a similar position. Precisely these two, who have had most to do with "the world's animality," discover in the young couple "the sweetness of the world" and set themselves up as their protectors. One can speculate, and the author himself gives us every reason to do so, whether the "bloody widow" Wackerhahn is the mother of the lovely foundling, this flower from the Boffzen pastor's garden—not only in a metaphorical but also in a literal and physical sense. Raabe seems frequently to hint at this in a stealthy fashion, but he carefully restrains himself from ever revealing the secret through an unambivalent word. But even the unresolved and merely suspected secret enriches the symbolic content of blood and flower.[20]

[20] Pongs, *op.cit.*, p. 619, takes it for granted that Wackerhahn is the mother of Bienchen from Boffzen and he sees the father in the young Spaniard whose lovely teeth Wackerhahn rediscovers in Bienchen's features. For myself, I can testify that upon repeated readings and quite independent of Pongs I have been persuaded by the probability of the consanguinity. Particularly the temporal data concerning occurrences in the narrative past—Wackerhahn's return

While the two complexes of quotation have a clear symbolic function as far as meaning is concerned, they are subordinated formally to a structural principle that one might call—with proper caution—musical. Related contrapuntally to one another, they function in the linear extension of the novel as a theme with variations. This musical nature is already apparent when the narrator projects the quotations into the consciousness of his characters. But it manifests itself with full force whenever he plays with the quotations in free narrative sovereignty and, as it were, at his own expense. A remarkable example is offered by the lyrical lament from Gessner's idyll "Daphnis and Chloe." There, at brief intervals, the narrating shepherd intones a cry as a refrain and an integrating interruption of his story: "Mourn after me, you rocky cliffs! Sadly sound back my song, through the grove and from the shore!" Raabe appropriates this repetition—even its frequency is precisely the same— but he enlarges the intervals to correspond to the larger format of his story of Daphnis-Pold and Chloe-Immeken. Hence the refrain becomes in his hands a leitmotif extending over almost two hundred pages. First the lamentation is repeated as the final note of the fifth chapter. The factual relevance here is minimal; the writer is obviously concerned mainly with the lyrical, musical effect. Then, when Pold gets ready to tell the story of his sufferings in the Militia Tower in the eighth chapter, the writer lets the same cry resound again, quite suddenly and, as it were, from outside the specific context (p. 54). At the end of Gessner's idyll, finally, the lament is transformed into joy: "Now

---

from the war and the discovery of the child—seem to speak in favor of this assumption. But it is impossible to go any further. It seems to me to have been Raabe's conscious intention to let the secret remain a secret. Barker Fairley, in "A Misinterpretation of Raabe's *Hastenbeck,*" *Modern Language Review,* 57 (1962), 575-78, polemicizes against Walter Fröhlich, who was the first to attempt to prove the conclusiveness of the relationship: "Das Verhältnis der Wackerhahnschen zum Bienchen von Boffzen," *Mitteilungen der Raabe-Gesellschaft,* 44 (1957), 22-24. Fairley corroborates my opinion that the matter cannot be demonstrated with any certainty, but he does not convince me of the certainty of the opposite point of view.

mourn no more, you rocky cliffs! Let joy now sound back from the grove and from the shore."[21] Consistently, Raabe too concludes his series of leitmotifs with this reversal of the motif, when the refugees have reached the secure soil of County Blankenburg at the end of their odyssey (p. 184).

At this point a question automatically poses itself. What significance do the quotations have for the structure in a narrower sense, that is, for the composition and disposition of chapters in the novel? Clear organization does not seem to belong to the essence of Raabe's narrative art, and scholarship is rather inclined to apply to Raabe the reproach often leveled against Jean Paul—that he composes as systematically as a dog out for a walk. It should be immediately conceded that our novel often reveals little articulation from the point of view of the action. In some chapters the plot moves forward scarcely or not at all. A major disposition into several groups of chapters, however, can be readily recognized. The first two comprise ten chapters each and the last, five chapters. The first series closes with Pold's accommodation in the parsonage; the second relates the instigation to flee, describes the flight itself, and ends with the legitimate marriage of the lovers in the pastorage at Derenthal. These are units of plot that are clearly punctuated. The third section, for example, is set off from the preceding one by a conspicuous leap in time and space: at the beginning of the twenty-first chapter the refugees have reached the end of their vagaries, the secure land of County Blankenburg, and by far the greatest part of their odyssey is recapitulated retrospectively in brief images.[22]

How is the use of quotations related to this pragmatic disposition of material? Here it must be recalled, first of all, that the leitmotific series of the two quotational symbols

[21] Gessner, *op.cit.*, p. 74.

[22] Cf. Hahne, *op.cit.*; Raabe repeatedly calls *Hastenbeck* his "Lower Saxon" or "Duchy-of-Brunswick Odyssey" (letters to Karl Schönhardt, 30 December 1898, and to Robert Lange, 19 September 1898). It is not impossible that he had the *Odyssey* in mind as a model for the technique of retrospective recapitulation.

is maintained from their first appearance in the second chapter through all further chapters to the end of the novel. The single exception occurs when the series logically pauses for a short time—at the very moment when God's Wonder Wagon has finally brought Daphnis and Chloe into safety—in order to make room for a mass of other literary allusions.[23] It is striking, further, that the major disposition into three series of chapters is powerfully articulated by the quotational symbols. At the ending of the first group of ten, an exclamation of the narrator himself has the effect of a heavy pedal tone: "O Salomon Gessner! O Gottlieb Cober! . . . O God's Wonder Wagon—O Daphnis and Chloe!" (p. 72). The symbol can here be reduced to the barest cipher, because its entire content has already penetrated the consciousness of the reader. The boundary of the chapter is intensified even more by the fact that the beginning of the eleventh chapter has emphatically the character of a fresh start. The narrator has "to take a breath and wipe the sweat from his brow" after he has finally gotten Pold Wille "under a proper roof again" (p. 72). At the end of the second group of ten, a Biblical quotation serves to create a similarly weighty termination. The pastor of Derenthal sees the three fugitives trudging away in a snowstorm, into the perilous unknown, and murmurs after them the words of Jeremiah 10:23: "The way of man is not in himself: it is not in man that walketh to direct his steps" (p. 162). Together with the already mentioned gap in time and space between this and the following chapter, this quotation creates a sharp boundary articulation.

It has become clear that Raabe supports the organiza-

[23] These literary references have a certain coloristic value, but no symbolic value. The same holds true for the many insertions (Chap. 20) from Voss's *Luise*, by means of which the emergency marriage of Pold and Immeken is contrasted humoristically with the leisurely splendor of the wedding in the parsonage of Grünau. The reference is delightful and also has the function of indirect characterization; but in contrast to the use of Gessner's *Idylls*, it remains on the surface and does not expose any depths. The mysterious *coincidentia oppositorum* is lacking here. For that reason we do not need to go into these quotations more closely.

tion of content by these elements of form. But the forma-
tive power of the quotations extends even further. We have
already seen that the fifth chapter ends effectively with the
lamentation for the shepherd Mirtil. The next chapter
then begins with a quotation from the Psalms, which is at
the same time a self-quotation and hence weighs even more
heavily: "What a blessing and what a joy it is when men
dwell peacefully together; but how rarely is this the case!
The observation is not new. We made it in *Odfeld* [an
earlier novel by Raabe], and now we make it after the field
at Hastenbeck" (p. 32).[24] The same phenomenon—that
the chapter boundary is flanked on both sides by quota-
tions and hence fortified—is to be found again in the transi-
tion from the fifteenth to the sixteenth chapter. In neither
of the two last cases is this accentuation of the chapter
boundary actually suggested by the narrated content. But
the meaning of the phenomenon is clear. Over and beyond
the division into three groups of chapters, Raabe uses the
quotations in order to carry out a rhythmical organization
through which a balanced proportion of five groups of five
chapters is produced. In the case of a writer who is so often
and so expressly reproached with carelessness in the com-
position of his novels, this is a rather remarkable conclu-
sion to reach.[25]

If we reconsider the total achievement of Raabe's art of
quoting in *Hastenbeck*, we realize with respect what a pow-

[24] Freely adapted from Psalms 133:1.
[25] Kientz, *op.cit.*, treats Raabe's fictional composition under the
heading "Composition négligée (pp. 375ff.): "Les pratiques en usage
dans les rédactions de revues ont habitué Raabe à négliger la com-
position." "En écrivant pour des publications périodiques au fur
et à mesure de la livraison, Raabe a contracté des méthodes de tra-
vail déplorables" (pp. 375f.). The question of whether and to what
extent publication of serial novels in journals influenced the novelistic
structure of Raabe and others is interesting enough, but it can be
answered only through thorough analyses. In *Hastenbeck*, in any case,
there is no evidence of any such influence. It was only after its com-
pletion that the novel was published in five consecutive issues of the
Deutsche Roman-Zeitung—and, moreover, in five installments of
roughly equal length, which are closed units neither in content nor
in composition and which have no connection with the structure as
it has been demonstrated here.

erful aesthetic sense is at work here. Perhaps nowhere else
in the art of the novel has the literary quotation been raised
to a main structural element so radically and with such
experimental daring. *Hastenbeck* is a highly reflective and
heartfelt work, but its surpassing value is to be found in the
fact that its quality of reflection never becomes absolute
thought, but is revealed purely through the form. At one
point the narrator apostrophizes the Swiss poet of the
Idylls: "They can never dispute the fact that you once stood
like a lovely rainbow over the stormridden world!" (p. 69).
One is tempted to apply this image to Raabe's art of quot-
ing as well. Through it, an overarching constellation of
lower and upper realm, of the factual as well as the ideal
aspects of reality, is created. Factual reality is not volatil-
ized to the point of disappearing, but it does not have the
last word; it is valid only within this constellation and in
its relatedness to the other sphere of reality. Raabe does
not talk these delicate relationships to pieces dialectically,
but renders them in epic form. This is the wisdom of an
artist—yes, it is ultimately the wisdom of art.

CHAPTER X

Thomas Mann

THE MAGIC MOUNTAIN

AND

THE BELOVED RETURNS

IF THE *poeta doctus* can be regarded as a distinct type of writer, it is perhaps no exaggeration to say that Thomas Mann is the most significant representative of this type in our century. The characteristic greatness of his poetic vocation consists not least in the fact that he is simultaneously an innovator and a curator, the responsible executor of a mighty intellectual inheritance that constitutes the foundation on which his own writing builds. He achieves this in part by adapting to his own narrative works the cultural possessions that he has learned to be valid and authoritative, using them as a kind of meaningful upper stratum with which the narrative contents are coordinated and to which they are referred. It is well known that the structure of meaning even in his early works was greatly broadened and, as it were, brought to its peak by the adaptation and appropriation of preformed literary material. Consider, for example, Schopenhauer's chapter "Concerning Death and Its Relation to the Indestructibility of Our Being in Itself" in *Buddenbrooks*,[1] Wagner's *Tristan und Isolde* in the *Tristan* novella, and Plato's *Phaedrus* in *Death in Venice*. The sophisticated montage of authoritative preformed

---

[1] I quote the works of Thomas Mann according to the Stockholm edition (StA), noting that the new twelve-volume edition that S. Fischer Verlag of Frankfurt published in the summer of 1960 corresponds more or less to the pagination of the StA. *Buddenbrooks*, Part X, Chap. 5; StA (1959), pp. 642ff., esp. p. 655.

material—both quotations proper and whole complexes of meaning—in the late novels and above all in *Doctor Faustus* is probably even better known. It would be rewarding to trace Thomas Mann's art of quoting through his entire work with equal intensity. However, we must limit ourselves to a few central points.

First of all, *The Magic Mountain* (*Der Zauberberg*) offers itself as such a focal point. Hardly anywhere else does the literary quotation play such an important structural role in the musical "thematic texture," the *Themengewebe* —for this is the word which the writer himself chose to designate the main compositional characteristic of his narrative works—as in *The Magic Mountain*, and nowhere else can the leitmotific arabesques, into whose festoons the quotations are woven, be so clearly traced and so precisely reproduced in analysis as here. This may be related to the special position that *The Magic Mountain* occupies in the work of the author as a whole. The author himself has on various occasions emphasized the pivotal nature of this novel. In the lecture that Thomas Mann delivered to the students of Princeton University, and which he later added to his novel as an introduction, he accounts for the "intensification" (*Steigerung*) that *The Magic Mountain* represents in the course of his development. "His [Hans Castorp's] story is the story of an intensification . . . in itself as well, as a story and narrative. To be sure, it works with the means of the realistic novel, but it is not one; it constantly goes over and beyond the realistic by enhancing it symbolically and making it a transparent background for the spirit and idea."[2] This naturally should not be taken to mean that the author considered his preceding works as simply "realistic." In *The Reflections of a Non-Political Man* he emphasizes, in a slight variation of sentences from Grillparzer, the essentially musical-spiritual character of even his earlier works:

They were always good scores [Mann's italics], all of

[2] "Einführung in den Zauberberg," StA (1959), p. xi.

them . . . ; . . . art as Ethics in Sound, as *fuga* and *punctum contra punctum*, as a serene and earnest piety, as an edifice of non-profane vocation, where each thing is fitted into the rest, linked meaningfully, rationally, and without mortar, and held "by God's hand"—this *l'art pour l'art* is truly my ideal of art, which I in no way represent myself, but which I shall always endeavor to approach.[3]

In *The Magic Mountain*, however, and surely in connection with the mentioned "intensification" of meaning, the author posits an even more rigid requirement with regard to artistic form. This novel is supposed to be not only a "good score," but one in which the form itself has wholly become meaning. The Princeton lecture expresses this suggestively: it is supposed to be the ambition of this work "to bring content and form, essence and appearance together in full congruity, and always simultaneously to *be* that which it is dealing with and talking about." In this connection the author is rightfully thinking above all of the relation between the experience of time and the structuring of time:

> The book itself *is* that of which it speaks; for by depicting the hermetic enchantment of its young hero in timelessness, it strives by its artistic means to annul time through the attempt to bestow full presence in every instant upon the musical and hypothetical world that it embraces and to create a magical "nunc stans." (p. xi)

Escalation of the real into the symbolic by means of the technique of realism therefore goes hand in hand with a formally strict merging of meaning and form here; they are different aspects of one and the same substance.

This is possible, however, only through a third basic characteristic of this work which we have more cause than usual to emphasize: *The Magic Mountain* is Thomas Mann's first entirely humorous work. This quality, too, is touched upon by the self-reviewer, though only in passing; he speaks

[3] *Betrachtungen eines Unpolitischen* (1st-6th ed., 1918), p. 310; StA (1956), p. 311.

of the "expansive style of English humorists in which I recuperated from the severity of *Death in Venice*" (p. vii). We must not allow ourselves to be led astray by the word "recuperate." Naturally one can imagine that the humorous narrative attitude was refreshing and relaxing for the writer, if only by virtue of variety after the objective conciseness of the novella. *Varietas delectat*. But in essence the expansive style of humor is no less "strict" than the other. It has a strictness all its own; yes, it alone enables this work "to be that of which it speaks." The countless places where the narrator, on his own, turns to the reader and urges him to actively participate in completing the structure of the narrative work; and especially the many short and long subjective digressions, particularly about the relationship between subjective and objective time and between the experience of time and the narrative shaping of time—these elements insure that the reader will become consciously aware of the unity of content and form intended by the writer and that the reader will thus help to bring about this unity. It is astonishing with what sovereignty Thomas Mann here appropriates in one stroke the sophisticated means of humorous narration once practiced by Fielding and Sterne. He has fused not only individual techniques but the entire integral process of humorous narrative. This fusion, which constitutes a new unity with his previously developed realistic-symbolic musical technique, has far-reaching consequences for his entire subsequent work.

Like Fielding and Sterne, Thomas Mann makes the *act* of narrative as such into an integrating *element of form*, by discussing with the reader the disposition and development of his story and by urging the reader to join in judging it. Like them, he integrates the essayistic digression on the narrative process into the entire narrative sequence by means of a sublimely complicated system of interlockings.[4] It would lead too far afield if we tried to demonstrate this in specific detail here. It should only be recalled, by way of

[4] Cf. my essay "Zum Problem der epischen Integration," *Trivium*, 8 (1950), 299-318.

suggestion, that Fielding once illuminated his method of procedure in one of his theoretical digressions[5] by discussing the free sovereignty of the narrator in the use of compression and extension of time. Sterne, basing his ideas on Locke's conception of "duration," posits the subjective experience of time as the determining factor for narrative shaping of time[6] just as Thomas Mann subsequently did, the latter in historical proximity to Bergson's philosophy and probably under the direct or indirect influence of it. Was Thomas Mann aware of this kinship with the English humorists while he was working on *The Magic Mountain?* Did a hidden elective affinity prevail here—or at least a "dark sense of tradition" like the one mentioned in the Princeton lecture in another connection (p. xiv)? *Tristram Shandy* is not documented by Mann as "fortifying reading" until the time of the composition of the Joseph novels. "Sterne's inventions and wealth of humorous phrases, his possession of a genuine comic technique attracted me to him; for I needed something like that to enliven my work."[7] Be that as it may, in *The Magic Mountain* Thomas Mann proves himself to be the legitimate heir of the great Englishman, whether he himself knew it or not.[8]

Unity of realistic profusion and supra-realistic symbolism, and all of this in a work bearing an overall humorous stamp: this is the point of view from which Thomas Mann's richly variegated art of quoting becomes clear. He combines the strengths of Fontane's use of quotations for realistic characterization and of Raabe's for musical symbolization. And in this union the quotations form an upper stratum of ideas which is interpretively linked with a lower level

[5] *Tom Jones*, Bk. 2, Chap. 1.

[6] *Tristram Shandy*, Bk. II, Chap. 8.

[7] *Neue Studien* (Stockholm, 1948), p. 179.

[8] Concerning Thomas Mann and Sterne, see Oskar Seidlin's imaginative essay, "Laurence Sterne's *Tristram Shandy* and Thomas Mann's *Joseph the Provider*," *Modern Language Review*, 8 (1947), 101-18; a German version, "Ironische Brüderschaft: Thomas Mann Joseph der Ernährer und Laurence Sternes Tristram Shandy," can be found in *Orbis Litterarum*, 13 (1958), 44-63, and is also included in Seidlin's *Von Goethe zu Thomas Mann* (Göttingen, 1963), pp. 185-207.

of pragmatic narrative content. Through this interplay between the realms of meaning and fact, there arises that stratification of narration that has been of basic significance for the humorous novel ever since Cervantes. This does not hold true, naturally, for all quotations in equal measure. Sometimes their effect contributes, as in Fontane, only to the direct characterization of the speakers. However, a gradually shifting scale emerges that ultimately leads from mere realism, by way of the symbolic enhancement of the realistic, to a purely hypothetical symbolism. In the following pages we want to attempt to make these gradations visible. We can restrict ourselves essentially to the small circle of main figures. The large circle of secondary figures in *The Magic Mountain*, a generally stupid and disorderly company, is too dull to ornament its conversations. Even if a quotation occurs from time to time, it is only an impertinently chatty one bearing the mark of Fontane—"not even a dog would like to live much longer like this, or something like that" (p. 308)[9]—which is only supposed to disclose the limp insubstantiality of the speaker.

Even the quotation-like phrases of Dr. Behrens often do not transcend mere empty flourishes, and always remain a subordinate element of his "many-tongued expressiveness" and of his brilliant humorous gift of gab. Instead of a simple "Look here!" he says (borrowing from Schiller's familiar ballad "Die Kraniche des Ibikus") "Look here, look here, Timotheus!" (p. 353); or when he releases Hans Castorp from his confinement in bed he uses the Biblical words: "Stand up and walk, man!" (p. 285). The borderline between an actual quotation and a general saying ("the will of man is his Kingdom of Heaven," "to slaughter the fatted calf") is fluid here. When Hans Castorp discloses to Dr. Behrens the news that Joachim is going to return to the sanatorium, the doctor answers: "So now you have it. For nine months he's had his heart's desire and his kingdom of heaven. But a kingdom of heaven that has not been com-

---

[9] Goethe, *Faust I*, verse 376: "Es möchte kein Hund so länger leben!" ("No dog would like to live much longer like this!").

pletely decontaminated, that is no blessing. . . ." But he does not hold it against Joachim; "he would open his arms paternally and be prepared to kill a calf for the runaway" (pp. 692f.). And even when the literary quotations are genuine, they all have this general appearance of figures of speech. Take, for example, the doctor's first encounter with Hans Castorp: "But *you* ought to get a little more color, you know, otherwise you will be less appealing to the ladies. The golden tree of life is green, as the poet says, but green is not quite the right thing for the complexion. Totally anemic, of course" (p. 69). The sense of what has been quoted is wantonly distorted[10]—that is where the humorous spice lies—and this distortion always amounts at the same time to a banalization. This holds true even in serious discussions, as for instance when Dr. Behrens answers Hans, who has dared to inquire about the condition of his "moribund" cousin, with a snatch of the Parable of the Rings from Lessing's *Nathan der Weise*, in this fashion: "You rather like mixing once in awhile in matters that are not so harmless, but then you treat them as though they were harmless, and think *to find favor in the eyes of God and man*. You're a bit of a hypocrite and a bit of a coward . . ." (p. 731; italics mine). If Theodor Fontane had had the opportunity to read *The Magic Mountain*, he would surely have taken great pleasure in the brilliantly clever language of the doctor, which is so closely related to his own.

Conversational and mimetic quotation in the manner of Fontane, however, is only one among many possibilities here, and a relatively subordinate one at that. This becomes quite clear if we turn to the character in whose mouth Thomas Mann's art of quoting attains its highest sophistication, the humanist Ludovico Settembrini. Only in his language does the literary quotation also receive a contextually symbolic significance in unending leitmotific variation. Set-

[10] *Ibid.*, verses 2038f.: "Grau, teurer Freund, ist alle Theorie,/ Und grün des Lebens goldner Baum" ("All theory, dear friend, is gray/ And green is the golden tree of life").

tembrini is the only person in this novel to whose manner of speaking the quotation belongs in essence, constituting as it were the precipitation of his humanistic credo. We know what to make of this much-vaunted "humanism": Settembrini is the incarnated "Zivilisationsliterat" who had been attacked a few years earlier in *The Reflections of a Non-Political Man*. The word *Zivilisationsliterat* as such does not occur in the novel, but it is present in a clever disguise, for in one of his first discourses Settembrini attributes to himself the honorary title *Literat* (man of letters) and immediately thereafter offers a toast to *Zivilisation* (pp. 223-25). The main article of his credo (which is taken generally, and in part verbatim, from *The Reflections of a Non-Political Man*, where it occurs within ironic quotation marks) is to the effect that the "word" constitutes the honor and dignity of man, that "literature" is the source of all human breeding and morality, and that the "beautiful word" produces the "beautiful deed" (p. 224).[11] As far as his basic conviction is concerned, from the beginning of the novel to the end Settembrini remains consistently in character and true to himself.

It is another matter altogether that the light in which Settembrini appears becomes noticeably more favorable in the course of the novel and that his petty and all too human traits, his gossipy, wicked tongue, and his bombast, gradually recede into the background. It is not Settembrini who changes during the seven year period of action. His creator was transformed deeply during the lengthy period of composition, and specifically in such a way that he himself moved perceptibly closer to Settembrini's brand of humanism. Many of his explanatory utterances about *The Magic Mountain* immediately after its appearance—for instance in the essay "On the Spirit of Medicine"[12]—could have stemmed directly from Settembrini's mouth. The general pleasure that Settembrini takes in language must be even keener

[11] Cf. also *Betrachtungen eines Unpolitischen*, StA (1956), p. 65.
[12] "Vom Geist der Medizin. Offener Brief an den Herausgeber der 'Deutschen Medizinischen Wochenschrift'" (1925); in *Altes und Neues* (1956), pp. 727-32.

when he employs the "word" in its most heightened sense: the poetic expression that is already formulated, polished, and beautifully valid! What a joy it must be for him to reach into the treasure-house of his literary culture and lend brilliance and breadth to his speeches through choice quotations—not unlike his creator who, after all, is himself a grand master of the art of quoting in his essays. His quotations have nothing comfortably folksy about them; they are his personal cultural possessions and are applied with astonishing accuracy whether they are intended ironically or whether a serious philosophical pathos vibrates in them. In a droll mood, Settembrini warns Hans Castorp *sub rosa* against Councillor Behrens and his proposals: "How does it go, that opera of yours: 'A fowler bold you see in me, forever laughing merrily!'" ("Der Vogelfänger bin ich ja, stets lustig, heisa, hopsassa!" p. 88; from Mozart's opera *The Magic Flute*). And a Heine quotation is worked in aptly when with impassioned words he portrays his father, the brilliant humanist: "from the very beginning he advocated the cause of man, earthly interests, freedom of thought and joy of life, and he was of the opinion that 'the heavens might well be left to the sparrows'" (p. 223). How does he express his delight at the lovely spring weather? "'Joyfulness,' he said, 'held court brilliantly in the halls of his breast' as Aretino put it, and that was spring's merit, a spring of which he approved" (p. 518).

These and similar quotations serve nicely for occasional characterization and in general do not stand in any leitmotific connection. The case is different when the author makes Settembrini the bearer of a *Faust* quotation that is of key significance for the entire novel. The intimate connection between *The Magic Mountain* and Goethe's *Faust* has been emphasized in various places, first of all probably by Hermann J. Weigand and subsequently by the novelist himself in his Princeton lecture. Weigand writes that "Hans Castorp's surrendering to disease has the same symbolic significance as Faust's concluding his pact with the devil,"[13] and the author confirms this. *The Magic Mountain,* according to Thomas Mann, is located in the world tradition of the "quester legend," which has its most famous manifestation in German in Goethe's *Faust.* "Its hero . . . is the seeker and questioner who . . . challenges heaven and hell and makes a pact with mystery, with illness, evil, death, . . . on his search for . . . the highest, for knowledge, cognition, initiation . . ." (p. xiv). Now in order to infuse the world of *The Magic Mountain* with the meanings of Goethe's *Faust,* the author uses the quotation-intoxicated man of letters as his mouthpiece. He bestows upon Settembrini something of the role of Mephisto, but by an ironic and paradoxical switch it turns out that the humanistic pedagogue endeavors to restrain his experiment-minded protégé from making any pacts with disease and with evil.

This state of affairs is revealed by a great number of widely distributed quotations, which gain their coherence only if the receptive reader independently unites them into a chain of motifs. As so often is the case with motifs in the works of Thomas Mann, the devil motif is first introduced very unobtrusively; it is catalyzed by an insignificant word tossed off at random. Immediately upon their first acquaintance, Hans Castorp responds to Settembrini's general observation that all real work is difficult with the thoughtless everyday expression: "Yes, the Devil only knows!" But the man of letters takes the word literally: "You even summon the devil . . . to corroborate that? Satan in person?" and he finds himself compelled to quote the hymn of his great teacher Carducci: "O salute, o Satana, o ribellione, o forza vindice della ragione . . ." (p. 86). This devil of course has nothing to do with Mephisto; he is simply the idol of Settembrini's rational humanism and is on excellent terms with the spirit of work, of progress, and of enlightened criticism, so that "Satana" (the title of this chapter) can rightfully stand for "Settembrini." In the chap-

[13] Hermann J. Weigand, *Thomas Mann's Novel Der Zauberberg* (New York and London, 1933), p. 47.

ter that follows shortly thereafter—"Satana Makes Proposals That Touch Our Honor"—the references become more complicated. This title, which corresponds directly to the preceding one, refers only superficially to Settembrini's proposal—inspired by his pedagogical apprehension —that Hans should get away as soon as possible, before the spirit of the Magic Mountain has completely ensnared him. Hans Castorp, however, rejects this imputation: "I would be ashamed, I would seem to myself actually to be a coward" (p. 124). But this rejection of what is ostensibly dishonorable is only a figurative sophistry: as he speaks, his eye comes to rest by chance on the figure of the Russian patient Madame Chauchat. The true Satan, who makes the opposite proposal, is the adventurously extravagant "feeling of dissolute sweetness" that is aroused in him by the lasciviously bold speeches of a certain Herr Albin and intensified by the presence of the charming Russian patient; it is the temptation to find out what life is like without the "pressure of honor" and with the "boundless advantage of shame." The chapter immediately preceding "Satana Makes Proposals That Touch Our Honor" closes with these words, so that they collide sharply with the title that follows. The "Proposals" chapter then ends with precisely the same words in leitmotific repetition. Though it is never explicit, the double significance of "Satana" is expressed hiddenly through this artful figuration of the vocables "honor" (*Ehre*), "shame" (*Schande*), and "touching upon honor" (*ehrrührig*), as well as through the hint implicit in the plural form "Proposals."

Settembrini's art of quoting reaches its high point in the chapter "Walpurgis Night." Through his brilliant *Faust* quotations, which always have an ingenious bearing on the concrete situation, he manages from the very start to view the improvised Mardi Gras entertainment of the sanatorium guests from the perspective of the Blocksberg, so important to the author because of its wealth of symbolic associations as the scene of the Walpurgis Night revelries in *Faust*. The association of Blocksberg and Magic Mountain can be

heard in the words of the will-o'-the-wisp that Settem-
brini jots down on a scrap of paper:

> "But then, reflect: the *mountain's magic*-mad today,
> And if a will-o'-the-wisp must guide you on the way,
> You musn't take things too precisely."[14]

At first these quotations have no important narrative con-
sequences. But then Thomas Mann executes a masterstroke
by making the quotation intercede in and precipitate the
action. Once again Settembrini wants to warn Hans Cas-
torp figuratively against the devilish charms of the lovely
Russian, and to this end he uses a quotation from Mephisto.
At this point the assimilation is so artful that we must re-
produce the relevant passages word for word. The *Faust*
passage goes:

Faust: But who is that?
Mephistopheles: Note her especially,
          'Tis Lilith.
Faust: Who?
Mephistopheles: Adam's first wife is she.
     Beware the lure within her lovely tresses,
     The splendid sole adornment of her hair.[15]

Out of this Thomas Mann makes the following:

> "Note her especially!" Hans Castorp heard Herr Settem-
> brini say as though from afar, while his gaze followed her
> as she walked on, toward the glass door, out of the room.
> "'Tis Lilith."
> "Who?" asked Hans Castorp.
> The man of letters rejoiced. He replied:
> "Adam's first wife. Beware...." (p. 456)

The narrative joke arises, of course, from the fact that
Hans Castorp fails to recognize the choice quotation as
such but nevertheless, in his monosyllabic question, sticks

[14] *Der Zauberberg*, StA, p. 452; Goethe, *Faust I*, verses 3868ff.
(trans. by Bayard Taylor; italics mine).
[15] *Ibid.*, verses 4118ff.

precisely to Goethe's wording. His "Who?" supplies the man of letters, who overestimates the literary education of his problem child, with the cue to continue the quotation. But the misunderstanding does not stop at this point. Since Hans Castorp does not recognize the quotation, he takes the familiar form of address (the *du* of the German text) to be a license of the Carnival atmosphere and replies in the same form, whereupon Herr Settembrini calls him to terms in the name of civilization and good breeding. This inspires Hans Castorp to deliver his long and alcoholically candid speech that combines thanks with dismissal. One thing affects the other. The misunderstood quotation prepares the way for an important step in the plot: Hans Castorp approaches Clavdia Chauchat and asks her for a pencil, an action prepared long in advance as a leitmotif. And this in turn is the overture to the love adventure, the actual Walpurgis Night which, however, is not rendered in the narrative, but—a magnificent example of aposiopesis on a large scale—falls into the "interval that is wordless on our part" (p. 483) between the first and second part of the novel.

The unrecognized quotation as a motive of the plot: here we see something of Thomas Mann's subsequent predilection for the cryptic use of quotations, particularly conspicuous in *Doctor Faustus* and in *The Holy Sinner*. In his essay *The Composition of Doctor Faustus*[16] the author drolly reveals that Leverkühn once, in a conversation with Serenus Zeitblom, uses an image from *Much Ado About Nothing* to which the latter unwittingly responds by continuing the quotation. This device is anticipated in the "Walpurgis Night" chapter. Even a proper cryptic quotation occurs, by exception, on one occasion in *The Magic Mountain*. When Hans Castorp posits the "scope" of Mynheer Peeperkorn's blurred "personality" as an absolute value, Herr Settembrini rejects it as mystical drivel. "Only despise discrimination, precision, and logic, the coherent language of man. Only despise them for the sake of some hocus-pocus of intimation and emotional charlatanry—if

---

[16] *Die Entstehung des Doktor Faustus* (1949), pp. 35f.

you will, the devil already has you fast and sure . . ."
(p. 811). As far as the precise wording is concerned, only
the opening and concluding words correspond to Me-
phisto's ironic admonition, but in its tenor and flow the
whole reprimand agrees with Goethe's pattern, though it
has been narrowed down to a certain extent in its adapta-
tion by the man of letters:

> Reason and knowledge only thou despise,
> The highest strength in man that lies!
> Let but the lying Spirit bind thee
> With magic works and shows that blind thee,
> And I shall have thee fast and sure![17]

In contrast to Thomas Mann's late works, here the psycho-
logical justification of the cryptic quotation can easily be
perceived. Literature is so much a part of Herr Settem-
brini's constitution that one can easily believe that he might
on occasion unconsciously paraphrase a literary passage
that stuck in his memory.

How do matters stand with his ideological adversary, the
Jewish Jesuit Leo Naphta, who out of a fundamental anti-
humanism combines medieval theocracy and communistic
terror with one another in a daring dialectic? His quota-
tions are no less effective than Settembrini's, but they are
more one-sided in their quality. Beauty and language con-
stitute for him no autonomous value, no guarantee for the
dignity and honor of man. For him, generally speaking, the
word is meaningful and valuable only as a weapon in intel-
lectual conflict, as a means of proving that there is no hu-
man honor and dignity at all, but only divine dignity and
human corruption. The same, of course, holds true of his
quotations as well: whether he appeals to Augustine's
(actually Anselmus of Canterbury's) "credo ut intellegam"
(p. 550) or to Gregory the Great's "Cursed be the man who
restrains his sword from blood!" (p. 557), always and in
every case the quotations have exclusively a polemical
character. Also, the debater's favorite trick of anticipating

---

[17] *Faust I*, verses 1851ff.

his opponent is not absent here. In a dispute about church
and state he interrupts his partner after only a few words
("The State, sir,—") in a very abrupt manner: "I know what
you think about the national state. 'Above all things goes
the love of fatherland and limitless desire for fame.' That's
Vergil. You correct him through a somewhat liberal individ-
ualism, and that is democracy; but your basic attitude to-
ward the state is completely untouched by it" (p. 556). It
is evident how he takes the quotation that would have fit
legitimately into his opponent's train of thought and snaps
it out of his mouth, as it were, and then immediately de-
stroys it. The following malicious thrust is even more art-
fully constructed. Hans Castorp, albeit unwittingly,
turns Settembrini's own words against him when he recalls
the latter's statement that the great day for the unification
of all peoples will come "if not on Dove's feet, then
on eagle's pinions."[18] Naphta instantly perceives the oppor-
tunity for an attack. "There you have been convicted by
your own protégé of martial inclinations. *Assument pen-
nas ut aquilae . . .*"(p. 530).[19] The introduction of this quo-
tation is just as malicious as it is brilliant, and it has a dou-
ble basis. Whereas on the one hand it only seems to mod-
ify Settembrini's statement (eagle's pinions versus dove's
feet), it affirms at the same time with secret malice the
fact that Hans Castorp's mind has become independent
and threatens to free itself from the pedagogue.

Next to these two powerfully articulate fighting cocks—
or actually above them in his capacity as a magnificent
"personality"—stands Mynheer Peeperkorn. As far as choice
rhetorical embellishments are concerned, the regal stam-
merer of course has nothing to offer with which he could
in any way compete with those two. But when he quotes,
and this happens only a single time, it is entirely in keep-
ing with his superhuman personality. In the course of his

[18] The "Dove's feet" perhaps go back to a memory of the chapter
"Die stillste Stunde" in *Also sprach Zarathustra*; cf. Erika A. Wirtz,
"Zitat und Leitmotiv bei Thomas Mann," *German Life and Letters*,
New Series 7 (1953-54), 126-36, esp. 134.

[19] Isaiah 40:31.

nocturnal bacchanalia the desire for sleep overcomes his less robust guests. At this point he delivers his magnificently confused speech, which however is not entirely lacking in structure. First he praises sleep as a "classic gift of life." But then, in a sudden switch to the present situation, there follows a monstrosity:

> "Would you, however, observe and recall Gethsemane! 'And took to himself Peter and the two sons of Zebadiah. And said unto them: Remain here and wake with me.' Do you remember? 'And came to them and found them asleep, and said unto Peter: Can you not wake with me for an hour?' Intensive, ladies and gentlemen. Penetrating. Heartmoving. 'And came and found them asleep, and their eyes were full of sleep. And said unto them: O do you want now to sleep and rest? Lo, the hour is upon us—' Ladies and gentlemen: piercing, heart-consuming." (p. 789)

To be sure, this is a grotesque blasphemy, confused and offensive like his whole "blurred personality," that weird mixture of man of sorrows and immodest heathen priest. But precisely in its monstrosity it is at the same time an explosively laden symbolic expression for his tragically endangered existence. The "simple" but also "crafty" Hans Castorp understands it intuitively: the "apprehension about his emotions," that is to say the "fear of the breakdown of feeling" (pp. 829f.), is really a Gethsemane in which he cannot desert Peeperkorn. For that reason he forms a bond of friendship with Clavdia Chauchat "for" Peeperkorn, but even this cannot prevent the Dutchman from taking his life voluntarily. "He was built on such a grand scale that he considered it a blasphemy, a cosmic catastrophe to be found wanting in spirit. For he regarded himself as the instrument of God's marriage organ, you should know . . ." (p. 867). Even if we hesitate to call Peeperkorn a "religious" man (despite the well-known layers of the montage: Gerhart Hauptmann and Tolstoy), it is still remarkable that there is a line of connection between his Dionysian vitalism and the religious virtuosity of Jaakob in the Joseph tetralogy. The absolutism of feeling of the coffee-king corresponds somehow to the arrogant "authoritarianism of feeling," the "emotional splendor" of the patriarch.[20] It was not by chance that Thomas Mann wrote to Kerényi, confirming the latter's *aperçu* that in *The Magic Mountain* "the interests and motifs are involved peripherally, which then in the *Joseph* novel become the exclusive objects of the narrative." *The Magic Mountain* is a link between the realistic *Buddenbrooks* and the manifestly mythological Biblical novel.[21] This consideration also tends to make us understand the symbolic transparency of Peeperkorn's blasphemous Biblical quotation.

Everything treated thus far stands in a significant and effective, but still more or less indirect, relationship to the innermost heart of our "hermetic story," to the inner development of Hans Castorp. For his story, according to Thomas Mann's subsequent statement, is supposed to represent not only a single destiny but "the *homo dei*, man himself with his religious question regarding himself, regarding his source and his destination, his essence and goal, his position in the universe, the secret of his existence, the eternal riddle of humanity."[22] Does the author's art of quoting also penetrate into this innermost realm? Does it have, here too, a symbolically illuminating function?

The answer could be affirmative only in a very limited sense if we restricted ourselves to the words that the author puts into the mouths of his protagonists in the conversations. In articulateness, our young and "simple" cultural traveler stands far behind Settembrini and Naphta, and in comparison with them his art of quoting is also not very advanced. His behavior is receptive rather than productive. Only out of a desire to please and to play up to Herr Settembrini does he once try to emulate him by citing Heine's "Belsazar," "Ich bin der König von Babylon!" ("I

[20] *Die Geschichten Jaakobs* (1933), pp. 316f.

[21] Letter to Karl Kerényi on 20 February 1934; in *Altes und Neues*, p. 736.

[22] *Neue Studien*, p. 169.

am the King of Babylon!"), as the embodiment of outrageous *hybris* (p. 495). Or, "crafty" (*verschlagen*) as he is, he turns the words of Settembrini against him. In one of the first conversations Settembrini finds the fitting symbolic expression for Hans Castorp's pleasure in philosophical experimentation: Petrarch's motto "Placet experiri," which from that point on resounds throughout the entire novel as a leitmotif. But when the apprehensive pedagogue feels that he must warn his protégé against the "intellectual delusions" of the sophistic fanatic Naphta, Hans Castorp replies with an innocent mien: "But in answer one could cite Petrarch with his motto, Mr. Settembrini already knew, and what Naphta came out with was worth listening to under any circumstances . . ." (p. 565). In the same way he reaches back to Settembrini's Carducci quotation, when his teacher once reproaches him with his tendency "to make confessions to the devil" (where, of course, the teachings of Naphta are meant by "the devil"). Here, too, he gives a quasi-innocent answer: "Well, they had discoursed about the devil exactly a year ago, Herr Settembrini and he, Hans Castorp. 'O Satana, o ribellione!' Which devil is he supposed to have made concessions to? The one that talked about rebellions, work and criticism, or the other one? It was mortally dangerous—devils to the right and devils to the left! How in the devil was one supposed to get through!" (p. 640). All of this is psychologically illuminating, charming, and even amusing. But as far as its evocative symbolic power is concerned, this conversational use of quotations remains peripheral and of slight importance.

The case is completely different with another series of leitmotific figures of a quotational nature which, characteristically enough, occur and have their effect not in the *speeches* of the protagonist, but silently and wordlessly in his consciousness, or, more precisely still, in his more or less conscious emotional life, in the labyrinth of his breast. They all stem, again characteristically, not from the realm of pure literature but from music, which the humanistic perspective regards as "suspect" and which, in opera and song at least, makes use of words for its purposes. These quotational figures have their focal point toward the end of the second volume in the chapter centering on music, "Abundance of Euphony" ("Fülle des Wohllauts"). Their entire symbolic power becomes wholly clear, however, only when one traces them in their breadth and extent throughout the entire novel, from their first and generally inconspicuous occurrence all the way to their point of culmination.

One of these figures, to which we shall devote our most particular attention, seems at the beginning not even to refer to Hans Castorp at all, but only to his cousin Joachim, that gentle and correct person with his military idiosyncrasy. At the beginning of the second part Joachim has made a "wild departure"; as Hans Castorp puts it dreamily, he has "deserted to the flag." But after nine months he must return to the sanatorium. The chapter beginning with his return is entitled "As a Soldier and Brave." The quotation is half-cryptic: it serves to prepare the perspicacious reader figuratively for Joachim's death. For this purpose it is necessary, first of all, that the reader recognize the quotation as such and also recall the situation in which the words occur. The words are those with which Valentin, in *Faust*, expires:

> Ich gehe durch den Todesschlaf
> Zu Gott ein als Soldat und brav.
>
> (Now through the slumber of the grave
> I go to God as a soldier and brave.)[23]

And in order to apply the quotation to Joachim, the reader must have a good memory for the subtle hints with which the author has prepared the way for the hypothetical Joachim-Valentin relationship. There is only a fleeting hint, which is exceptionally artful precisely because of its indirectness. In the chapter "Walpurgis Night" Hans Castorp invites Madame Chauchat to dance, but she declines with gentle ridicule. " 'That's less well-behaved than I thought

[23] Goethe, *Faust I*, verses 3774f.

you are,' she said, and since he laughed disparagingly, she added: 'Your cousin has already gone'" (p. 466). The single word *brav* (which in German means both "brave" and "well-behaved") here refers only indirectly and *a contrario* to Joachim, and is then concealed in Clavdia's judgment formulated in French: "C'est un jeune homme très étroit, très honnête, très allemand"; whereupon Hans Castorp tries to explain to her that Joachim's *honnêteté* is not *bourgeoise* but *militaire* (pp. 466ff.). By this means the other referential word, "soldier," has been subtly introduced. As a complete quotation, however, Valentin's words are not used conversationally; but in their capacity as chapter heading they are loosely integrated into the narrative as the symbolically transcendent formula that sums up the essence and meaning of Joachim's life and his quietly heroic death.

But this quotational leitmotif reaches its full development only after Joachim's death, in the chapter "Abundance of Euphony." Here the excessive affable talk stops, and music draws the young sorcerer's apprentice into its magical enchantment in the lonely night. One of his favorite gramophone records is the "Prayer" from Gounod's *Faust*. "Someone appeared, someone extremely appealing, called Valentin, but to whom Hans Castorp secretly gave another name, a more familiar melancholy name, whose bearer he identified to a high degree with the person speaking out of the cabinet although the latter had a much lovelier voice" (p. 902). Not until this point does the symbolic identification of Joachim and Valentin fulfill itself in Hans Castorp's consciousness, and specifically in a way that would not be possible merely on the basis of Goethe's text. Goethe's over-virtuous soldier is obsessed only with mundane and bourgeois honor; he says explicitly "Leave our Lord God out of the matter"[24] and curses his sister, who in his opinion has become a whore. In Gounod's opera, by contrast, Valentin sets himself up as his sister's protective spirit even beyond death. "But if God summons him to heavenly heights, he sang, then he wanted to gaze down protectively

[24] *Ibid.*, verse 3733.

upon 'you' from above. This 'you' meant his sister; but nevertheless it stirred Hans Castorp in the depths of his soul . . ." (p. 902). Why this emotion? Because he relates this "you" directly to himself, because he imagines that the deceased Joachim is gazing protectively down upon him, as Valentin looks down upon his sister who is threatened by disgrace. Joachim had been the last tie that linked him with the solidity of the world "down below," a counterbalance to metaphysical excesses and the "boundless advantages of shame" (pp. 116, 131). Hans was deeply shocked when it was decided that the cousin would return to the flatland below and that he would remain alone: "Then it's forever and eternally, for on my own I shall never and never more find the way back into the flatland . . ." (p. 575). The feeling that ties the orphaned child Hans Castorp to his cousin—latent during Joachim's life, but aroused to consciousness after his death—is a kind of substitute father-bond, because Joachim embodies for him, at least by representation, the world of his heritage and his forefathers. For this reason the dead Joachim, even more than the living one, is the support to which Hans Castorp clings. And this fact contains a certain excuse for what follows.

For the recording of Valentin's "Prayer" has not yet played out its role. In conclusion, in the immediately following chapter, "Highly Questionable" ("Fragwürdigstes"), the recording serves in the strictest sense of the word to precipitate real action, and specifically a happening of a highly scandalous sort. This may come as a surprise. "Does Hans Castorp degenerate? Does he come down in the world? He comes up!" Thus Thomas Mann, in his essay "On the Spirit of Medicine," defends his hero and his novel.[25] But one must not imagine this "coming up" as a simple and straightforward rise, as an expression of the direct realization of the "idea." Hans Castorp's hermetic course of development reveals all the vacillations and all the inconsistencies of life as it is lived. Notable in this respect is the func-

[25] "Vom Geist der Medizin," *Altes und Neues*, p. 732.

tion of the chapter "Snow," where the hero is granted the grand insight which the author italicizes to emphasize its validity as a maxim: *"For the sake of love and goodness, man shall let death have no sovereignty over his thoughts"* (p. 686). If *The Magic Mountain* were a *roman à thèse* and nothing else, it could end here. No more pacts with disease and death. Fortunately, however, the epic conception of the novel is richer than the ideological maxim. Lived life consists of falling and getting up again. It must be regarded as life, not as ideology, when Hans Castorp falls back into his pact-making even after the "Snow" chapter. Prefiguring Joseph in the later novel, Hans Castorp falls into the "pit" two times: in "Walpurgis Night" and in "Highly Questionable." And the second pit is deeper! The free license of Carnival was only to a limited extent "an objectionable wildness, a flirtation with primitive circumstances, a foul game" (p. 457)—only in the eyes of the ethical rigorist Settembrini. But the spiritistic exercises undertaken by the psychoanalytical intriguer Doctor Krokowski are, not only in Settembrini's opinon but also in the author's, a much more disreputable form of pact-making, a flirting with the underworldly and with the forbidden.[26] Even the relatively innocent levitation of the table is an "impure play with nature" (p. 918), and even in Hans Castorp's eyes it is "in bad taste, incomprehensible and without human dignity" (p. 914). And nevertheless, in his "amicably conceding and rather lax way" (p. 926), he lets himself in for a much crasser bit of squalor, the "materialization" of a dead man—not just any dead man, but his cousin Joachim Ziemssen.

The experiment succeeds, but it is not the "very lovely adventure" (p. 931) that Hans had promised himself. The "scandalous delivery" (p. 943) of the young patient who is

[26] Cf. also the value judgment regarding pacts with the occult in the roughly contemporary essay "Okkulte Erlebnisse" (1923), in *Altes und Neues*, pp. 102ff.: "a kind of decay" ("eine Art von Verderbnis") emanates from the occult world (p. 103); it is "the spiritual slough" ("der geistige Pfuhl") to which one succumbs "depravedly" ("lasterhafterweise").

misused as medium, perhaps the eeriest portrayal in the whole of *The Magic Mountain,* is unequivocally a sinful degradation of man. And in this act of sin Hans Castorp becomes an accomplice when, prostituting his innermost treasure of feeling, he proposes during the seance that they play that specific gramophone record. It is Valentin's prayer —"Und ruft mich Gott zu Himmelshöhn, Will Schützend auf dich herniedersehn!"—which forces the beloved departed one to return to the earthly world. Hans Castorp had already arranged matters in his subconscious before he arrived consciously at this thought. The accident whereby the record in question, contrary to all order and rule, happens to be in Doctor Krokowski's analytical cabinet, is a textbook case of a *Fehlleistung.* Here Hans Castorp acts instinctively—in "the torpor's passion" ("der Dumpfheit Leidenschaft") of the first part of *Faust,* and not the "pleasure with consciousness" ("Genuss mit Bewusstsein") of the second part. It is unmistakable that the spiritistic seance, too, stands in an analogical relation to the *Faust* story. It has already been mentioned that the adventure in the snow reveals certain correspondences to Faust's journey to the Mothers and to the conjuration of Helena. Thomas Mann has split the theme, so to speak, into two contrasting parts. In "Snow" the positive aspect is revealed: the deep insight into the nature of life and death that Hans Castorp achieves through his contact with the elements. In "Highly Questionable," on the other hand, the crass negation of the same theme occurs. The impure magic of the spiritistic conjuration of the dead, inasmuch as it is a flirtation with the forbidden, stands in a compelling analogy to the conjuration of Helena. Here, however, one is more likely to think involuntarily of Faust's blackest infamy in the chapbook[27] than of the episode in Goethe's drama, which has been aesthetically purified.

Let us recapitulate once again the course of this leitmotif,

---

[27] *Das Volksbuch vom Doktor Faust* (1587), Chap. 59: "Von der Helena auss Griechenland, so dem Fausto Beywohnung gethan in seinem letzten Jahre" (Neudrucke, Vols. 7-8 [1878], p. 106).

which by means of a complex of quotations assembled from Goethe's text and the opera libretto brings about the symbolic identification of Joachim and Valentin. Anticipated by the merest haphazard word (*brav*), the identification is at first carried out only in a free symbolization that transcends the level of reality of the narrative (through the title "As a Soldier and Brave"). After Joachim's death, it becomes the central content of Hans Castorp's consciousness and thus a significant empirical element of the narrative ("Abundance of Euphony"). Finally, it even intercedes as an active element in the shaping of the action ("Highly Questionable"). This is what a single thread of this gigantic narrative tapestry looks like when it is examined under the microscope. A main characteristic of this sophisticated weavery turns out to be its intertwining of reality and symbol in a single pattern. The use of quotations proves to be a significant means of symbolic intensification above and beyond the realistic.

WE MUST forego the pleasure of drawing Thomas Mann's entire later work into our investigation. What quotations and allusions accomplish in these late works—somewhat restrainedly in the Joseph tetralogy and then in voluptuous application in *The Beloved Returns*, *Doctor Faustus*, and *The Holy Sinner*—could be made clear only through a detailed monographic description, whereby considerable differences between the individual works would be revealed. Despite all differences, however, one important common trait would emerge clearly. In *The Magic Mountain*, with few exceptions, the literary quotation is wholly apparent; its aesthetic effect is based on the fact that it is recognized as such by the reader and that it contributes, by being recognized, to a disclosure of the contextual and formal structure of the work. In the late works, by contrast, the quoting procedure becomes more and more cryptic. In *Doctor Faustus* literary and historical data are forced together and interwoven in a manner which the author himself designates as "montage technique": "A hitherto unknown ruthlessness in the assembling of factual, historical, personal, even literary data, that in its fantastic mechanics has continually confounded me. . . ."[28] In this connection he also speaks of the "quotation," by which, however, he understands not only the verbatim appropriation of what has been literarily formed, but more generally the appropriation of literary and historical contents. "Quotation," as Thomas Mann explains, is the appropriation of Tschaikovsky's invisible friend Frau von Meck as Madame de Tolna. The triangle of Adrian Leverkühn, Marie Godeau, and Rudi Schwerdtfeger is a "quotation" of Nietzsche's indirect marriage proposals, but at the same time it is a "quotation" of the motif of treacherous wooing in Shakespeare's sonnets and dramas—and so forth.

In the course of such appropriation of contents it can happen that a preformed expression is fused in as well, but in that case the fusion is generally so free that the quotation as such becomes unrecognizable. To give one example, Shakespeare's verses from *Two Gentlemen of Verona,* "Who should be trusted, when one's own right hand/ Is perjured to the bosom?" (Act V, Scene 4), are made into a prose sentence: "It is bitter to be sure, and one asks oneself whom one should trust if our own right hand turns itself against our breast."[29] Good Zeitblom can do little about the fact that he, like the reader, fails to recognize the quotation. The same holds true for a long series of archaic expressions that are borrowed from the chapbook of Doctor Faustus, Luther's correspondence, Grimmelshausen's novel *Simplicissimus,* et cetera, and woven into Leverkühn's archaistically artificial language. "For I thought: he that wants to bowl must set up the pins, and one must venerate the Devil today because for great undertakings and work one can else use and have no one but him."[30] One senses the old-fashioned quality of the phraseology used here, but it is scarcely to be expected that the reader will recognize the thought

[28] *Die Entstehung des Doktor Faustus,* p. 33.
[29] *Ibid.,* p. 35; *Doktor Faustus* (Stockholm, 1947), p. 671.
[30] *Doktor Faustus,* p. 754.

as a quotation from the chapbook, where it is written: "Accordingly as one bowls, he must set them up."[31] In addition to a series of quotations that are specified as such, there stands a much larger number of borrowings that remain anonymous and that are supposed to create, through their very anonymity, a certain atmosphere of apprehension. The situation is similar with regard to the many quotational borrowings from Middle High German literary sources (Hartmann, Gottfried, *Nibelungenlied*, Wolfram, Freidank, and so forth), which together with Old French, Low German, English, and American tags constitute the variegated linguistic garb of *The Holy Sinner*, Mann's novel about the legendary Pope Gregorius. Here it is a matter not for the average reader, but solely for the sharp-minded and well-read philologist to ferret out the author's tricks and track down his sources.[32]

However, we have a particular reason for singling out *The Beloved Returns* (*Lotte in Weimar*) from the late works for special consideration. This should be mentioned briefly lest, otherwise, the image of Thomas Mann's art of quoting remain all too incomplete. The quoting procedure in *The Magic Mountain* attested to the sovereign freedom of the narrator. Since he was not restricted to a specific area of literature which the content of the narrative compellingly prescribed, he was free in principle to appropriate his quotations from whatever source he desired. The same holds true, despite all other differences, for *Doctor Faustus* as well. The art of quoting in *The Holy Sinner* is tied down somewhat more tightly to a specific contextual realm, but it turns out on close consideration that the author nevertheless has reserved for himself even here an astonishingly great area of mobility. As far as *Lotte in Weimar* is concerned, the case is basically different. What we

[31] *Das Volksbuch vom Doktor Faust*, p. 112.

[32] See Hermann J. Weigand, "Thomas Mann's Gregorius," *Germanic Review*, 27 (1952), 10-30 and 83-95, both because of the astonishingly acute detection of many borrowings and because of the sensitive interpretation of the "transmutation into an integrated new work of art."

have here is an historical novel which takes Goethe as its subject, and this means that the author is somehow bound to the given facts of historical reality; and not to any reality he might choose, but specifically to that "exemplary" reality that Goethe's existence had represented in his eyes for decades. It is forbidden to mix reality and phantasy with one another in an unscrupulously subjective way. Cognition of truth on the basis of broad experience—this is the lofty goal toward which the author is striving here. The philologist can only gape in astonishment at the extent of Thomas Mann's historical knowledge.[33] His material is Goethe's total work in its broadest circumference, in addition to the whole wealth of documentary evidence that has come down to us from Goethe's contemporary world. One can speak here of "dilettantism" only in the sense in which Goethe liked to use this designation for himself. No less astonishing is the way in which Thomas Mann presides over this material, the way in which it is present in his mind at every moment and at his service. Even more decisive for the structure of this novel is the circumstance that Goethe's own words, as well as documents from the age of Goethe, constitute rather exhaustively the material basis on which Mann constructs his work. This is the specific asceticism of this otherwise so overflowingly rich work.

Fortunately this does not mean that the author renounces his sovereignty as narrator. In a deeper sense this highly restricted novel is also—after the title of Goethe's autobiography—"poetry and truth"; not in the sense of being a mix-

---

[33] Gerhard Lange, in "Der Goethe-Roman Thomas Manns im Vergleich zu den Quellen" (Bonn dissertation, 1954), has investigated Thomas Mann's knowledge of the works by and about Goethe very thoroughly and with fruitful results. Unfortunately, I was still unaware of this dissertation when the present section on *Lotte in Weimar* originally appeared in the Festschrift for Hermann J. Weigand, *Wächter und Hüter* (New Haven: Yale University Press, 1957). Lange ascertains that "Thomas Mann's reading in Goethe's writings was so extensive that it could probably be matched only in the circles of professional Germanists: and moreover a knowledge of *all* aspects of Goethe's total output, even counting the meteorological notes and the various paralipomena" (p. 34).

ture of what has been made up and what is real, but in the sense that here truth is revealed in the manner of poetry.[34] Even though the novel is based extensively on insights that the author had established in his earlier essays ("Goethe and Tolstoy," 1922; "Goethe as a Representative of the Bourgeois Age," 1932), it is by no means merely a fictionally embellished repetition of those essays. The procedure is radically different: not essayistic discussion, but narrative shaping. It is the author's task to live up to Goethe's behest "to transform the past into an image." With regard to factual matters, Thomas Mann creates for himself a certain area of free play by choosing from Goethe's so completely "known" life an insignificant and only sparsely documented incident: the visit of the privy councillor's widow Charlotte Kestner, née Buff, to Weimar in the fall of 1816. In Goethe's life this incident was not epoch-making in the least. His extremely laconic journal entry for the twenty-fifth of September shows no trace of emotional engagement, and the same is true of the short letter of the ninth of October in which he offers to his old friend Lotte his place in the theater. The annoyed tone of Lotte's equally brief letter to her son August, and of Klara Kestner's letter to him, bears this out in full.[35] But Thomas Mann's narrative art proves itself precisely within the framework of this skeletal event. The individual circumstances of the reception in Goethe's house are developed freely. The series of visits on the day of arrival is completely fictional, as is also the dialogue in Goethe's carriage that concludes the novel. (In

[34] It is well known that, after 1945, verbatim quotations from the seventh chapter of *Lotte in Weimar* were circulating widely as authentic utterances of Goethe regarding the German character; during the war they had even been passed about by the enemies of the regime as a leaflet with the cover-title *Aus Goethes Gesprächen mit Riemer*. Regarding this comedy of errors and its spectacular culmination in the final statement of the British Chief Prosecutor at the Nuremberg Trials (July 1946), cf. Mann, *Die Entstehung des Doktor Faustus*, p. 169, and the meticulous collation of the material in Lange, *op.cit.*, pp. 24-29.

[35] Biedermann, *Goethes Gespräche* (new ed., Flodoard von Biedermann; Leipzig, 1909), Vol. 2, pp. 367f.

connection with the latter there is a unique turn of affairs that must still be discussed.) It is not the reality of the factual that provides the norm here; the truth of the potential is a no less strict criterion to which the freedom of the narrator is obligated.

Now this potential truth is constituted essentially and wholly by its artistic shaping. For this reason we cannot avoid considering, first, the total shape of the novel, and asking what it accomplishes as an expression of meaning. What strikes us first of all is the very unequal proportion of narrative time and narrated time. Lotte's stay in Weimar lasted several weeks. But the main substance of the story—more than four-fifths of its volume and seven of the nine chapters—serves to represent only the merest fraction of that expanse of time: namely the first half of the day of arrival (about which, as it happens, the documents have nothing to say). The remainder is dealt with in two rather short chapters. The structuring of time *within* the period of time represented in those seven chapters is even more willful. Let us visualize the situation. Shortly before eight o'clock in the morning, Lotte arrives at the inn in Weimar with her daughter and maid. She wants to go to her sister on the same morning, but due to a series of unexpected visits her departure is delayed until late in the afternoon. The long conversations with her visitors—an English lady who is a painter, Riemer, Adele Schopenhauer, and August von Goethe—are continued for six chapters, or for far more than half of the novel. In the seventh chapter, with a mighty jerk, the narrator sets the clock back to a moment that lies an hour *before* the beginning of the action in the first chapter! We are present when Goethe wakes up at seven o'clock on the morning of this same day. At the end of this long chapter, while the narrative time is already moving toward its close, but still—or again—in the course of that first morning, Goethe commissions his son August to pay a visit to the friend and love of his youth. But the reader has already witnessed the execution of this commission in the sixth chapter!

This technique of hysteron proteron, which at first glance seems to be quite violent, has its reason and its justification in the sophisticated perspectivistic art of which the narrator here makes use. Only after the reader has already worked his way through two-thirds of the book does Goethe appear in person. Up to this point Goethe appeared only by an indirect illumination, mirrored through the experience of the society surrounding him. This experience is subjectively conditioned and narrowed; the rays of light are broken, colored, and also obscured by the medium through which they pass.[36] Here too, of course, there are gradations and intensifications. But the many statements and opinions cannot be focused into a pure picture; there emerges a contradictory and almost tormenting total view. After this long preparation, the seventh chapter allows us to draw a deep breath of relief. We enter the innermost circle of the novel. The number seven is certainly not a matter of chance, any more than is the case when it occurs in *The Magic Mountain* and in the Joseph novels. In addition, the author has distinguished this chapter with a roguishly cryptic hint, which probably only a few readers notice, at its special place. Whereas otherwise the headings read "First Chapter," "Second Chapter," and so forth, here he emphatically adds the definite article: "The Seventh Chapter." Goethe himself becomes visible, no longer from outside, but purely and unveiledly in his intimate monologue. Now the question is no longer: How is Goethe reflected in the eyes of the world? It becomes: How are the world and his own ego reflected in Goethe's mind? And this signifies an intensification that leads above and beyond the preceding chapters. The intensity and consonance of the image that now arises does not refute what has preceded it, to be sure, but reveals its merely relative validity. One can scarcely speak any longer of an "image." An image is some-

[36] See Ernst Cassirer, "Thomas Manns Goethe-Bild. Eine Studie über Lotte in Weimar," *Germanic Review*, 20 (1945). In a highly illuminating manner Cassirer applies Goethe's notion of "repeated mirroring" to Thomas Mann's own narrative procedure.

thing facing us; representation by means of reproduction of the inner stream of consciousness, however, transposes the reader's intellectual point of view into Goethe's consciousness itself. Because of this there arises an almost oppressive and yet delightful immediacy of the object. What does the procedure of quoting add to this aesthetic exercise in perspectives and to this intensifying shift from distance to proximity?

This important element of form, the quotation, is equally efficacious at all levels of this gradation: the quotation proper functions harmonically in the total linguistic milieu of this novel. The homogeneous coloring of language from the age of Goethe produces the pleasant illusion of an authentic atmosphere to which the reader willingly submits. An ascending scale can be set up for the stylistic means that produce this veracious illusion, and at its peak stands the full quotation. It begins with the light archaicization of orthography, morphology, and idiom ("Ächtheit"; "Ein zweischläfrig Zimmer"; "erbötig"). From these unobtrusive atmospheric assimilations the scale moves imperceptibly up to idiomatic and syntactical phrases in which a reminiscence of specific sayings of Goethe gently reverberates. Here Thomas Mann's mimetic art celebrates true triumphs. When August's designation of certain auctorial secrets of his father as "that which is unpublished, not to be published" ("das Unveröffentlichte, nicht zu Veröffentlichende," p. 241)[37] strikes us as so familiar and authentic, this is because this figure of *annominatio* is reminiscent of Mephistopheles' words: "To the Unreachable, ne'er to be reached; ... to the Unbeseechable, ne'er to be besought" ("Ins Unbetretene, Nicht zu Betretende; ... ans Unerbetene, Nicht zu Erbittende").[38] In a similar vein, it is not a true quotation when, on one occasion in the reproduction of Goethe's inner monologue, it is said: "This spirit of the millennium is also related to tradition, whoever only understood it"

[37] *Lotte in Weimar*, StA (1958). All following quotations are taken from this edition.
[38] *Faust II*, verses 6222f.

("Hat freilich auch mit der Tradition zu tun, der Jahrtausendgeist, wer sich auf die nur verstünde," p. 284). But the conditional use of the relative pronoun is modeled after Alba's words, "Freedom! A lovely word, whoever understood it properly" ("Freiheit! Ein schönes Wort, wer's recht verstünde").[39] The case is scarcely different with such phrases as "and so from this time forth" ("Und so fortan!"), "May God have mercy!" ("Dass Gott erbarm!"), and similar ones, which one might take as quotations, to be sure, but which can more rightfully be regarded as Goethe's general idiom.

From here, again, an imperceptibly small step leads to the quotation fragment. When August attempts to suggest to Lotte the character of the poems of *West-östlicher Divan*: "It is the most personal and yet bears attributes of the firmament, so that the cosmos acquires a human visage, while the self gazes with starry eyes" (p. 231), there is no doubt that he has in mind the Hafis poem "Unbegrenzt" ("Your song revolves like the firmament": "Dein Lied ist drehend wie das Sterngewölbe"), and applies it to his father. One small step further brings us to the paraphrastic use of the same line, when Goethe reluctantly excerpts a few lines from the nascent *West-östlicher Divan* for a ladies' journal: "It is not the specific, it is the whole; it is after all a revolving vault and orrery . . ." (p. 314). The flowing nuances of this scale of stylistic variations on the quotation condition the impact of the full quotation, with which we shall concern ourselves principally in what follows. Nowhere does the quotation leap out at us, but rather is gently bedded in the homogeneous linguistic milieu which permeates the whole.

Here too we want to trace the gradual intensification of effects in the course of the novel. The Goethe quotations in the mouth of the waiter Mager have scarcely any existential substance, although he uses much droll skill to weave the fruits of his reading into his speech. Remarkably enough, even the quotations put in the mouth of the heroine

---

[39] *Egmont*, Act IV, Scene 2.

have little true substance. When the author allows her to speak in quotations, he prefers to do so with a playful wit of which she is unaware. Thus she tells Riemer about Goethe's Wetzlar days: "Big Merck also came once on a visit to Wetzlar,—his friend, I didn't like him, always looked on cynically and half angrily, a repulsive face that constricted me inside . . ." (p. 109). These, of course, are all tags from the scene in Martha's garden, from Gretchen's words regarding Mephisto.[40] It is not Lotte, but the philologically well-versed author who is aware of the "identity" of Merck and Mephisto and plays with it here. Lotte's unconscious quoting is also delightful when she says to August: "That you are loved in return—I don't doubt it. Your congenital merits offer me the most convincing guarantee for it" (p. 253). The "congenital merits" ("angeborene Verdienste")—that is *the* Goethe phrase that Thomas Mann had had on his lips for years as a proper symbolic expression whenever he happened to talk about Goethe.[41]

Goethean expressions have a completely different weight in the mouth of Goethe's learned collaborator, the philologist Friedrich Wilhelm Riemer.[42] Here the writer and psychologist Thomas Mann has succeeded in producing a psychological portrait of astonishing subtlety and depth. One realizes what a superb achievement of mimetic art and integrative capacity is presented here when one goes back to the documents that he had at his disposal. With great acuity he transposed Schmeller's portrait of Riemer into words and made the physical appearance of this man into a tangible reality which expressed his spirit. Virtuoso mimicry can also be sensed in Mann's rendering of the speech patterns of this man—which skill, by the way, can be demonstrated only by a precise stylistic comparison with Riemer's *Observations on Goethe*. The extreme incapsulation characteristic of Riemer's style in writing and speaking, his fussy

[40] *Faust I*, verses 3471-493.
[41] As early as "Goethe und Tolstoi" (1922); in *Adel des Geistes*, p. 230.
[42] See Hans Wahl and Anton Kippenberg, *Goethe und seine Welt* (1932), p. 169.

exactness and his peculiarly repressed dynamism are, as the author makes clear, the expression of a rich but highly precarious spirit and an equally precarious spiritual situation. Riemer venerates Goethe to the point of idolatry, but bound up inexorably with this are his inner reservations and moral scruples. Thomas Mann allows him to say so himself. For him, Goethe is far too great an object, a disquieting and even somewhat offensive riddle. Hence his unhappy emotional ambivalence, his doubts; hence also the a priori state of vexation, which runs through his *Mitteilungen über Goethe* as a quiet undertone, and the "pouting" expression around his mouth. As far as the latter is concerned, Thomas Mann was obviously impressed by the fact that Goethe, according to a remark of Kanzler von Müller, developed "a regular theory of dissatisfaction" from the example of Riemer.[43] Thus certain quotations take on, in Riemer's mouth, an ungratifyingly derogatory note: for example, when he uses the words of Gretchen—"I don't understand what he finds in me"[44]—slightly modifying them to make fun of Goethe's liking for his friend Zelter (p. 70). At one point Thomas Mann finds a quotational symbol of great revelatory power. With enthusiastic words Riemer is elaborating on the divine greatness of Goethe's poetic genius. Merely "by way of an example" he recites the beginning of the parable of the fly's death (p. 77):

> Sie saugt mit Gier verrätrisches Getränke,
> Unabgesetzt, vom ersten Zug verführt;
> Sie fühlt sich wohl, und längst sind die Gelenke
> Der zarten Beinchen schon paralysiert. . . .

> (It sucks with greed the treacherous potion,
> Unceasingly, at the first draught betrayed;
> How pleasant 'tis—and yet the motion
> Is lamed in its fine limbs and powerless made. . . .)[45]

He then immediately asserts that it was only "ridiculous

---

[43] Biedermann, *op.cit.*, Vol. 2, p. 615.
[44] *Faust I*, verse 3216.   [45] JA, Vol. 2, p. 142.

chance, blind caprice" that he had chosen precisely this ex-
ample and none other. But the reader is supposed to un-
derstand that Riemer himself (he declined a professorship
at the University of Rostock in order to be able to stay close
to Goethe) is the fly that is "paralyzed" by Goethe's over-
powering presence.

What Riemer has to say about Goethe, about his divine
greatness and, even more, about its negative secondary
phenomena—all of this has the unmistakable mark of his
own complicated personality. His opinions are not pasted
on, but are components of the total profile of his character.
Nevertheless, if one frees them from their narrative struc-
ture and traces them back to their "empirical" level, then
one realizes with astonishment that it is precisely these fas-
tidiously negative utterances that are, part and parcel,
Thomas Mann's most personal possession in the book. They
constitute an essential part of his earlier essays "Goethe and
Tolstoy" (1922) and "Goethe as a Representative of the
Bourgeois Age" (1932). It is particularly the piercing and
almost anguished reflections on Goethe's "constitution so
hostile to ideas" in the second essay that Mann now trans-
poses to Riemer. Goethe's "objective poetic attitude that is
void of views and valuations," his "destructive equanim-
ity," his "tolerance without gentleness," his "coldness" and
"médisance," his "nihilism," and even such a unique formu-
lation as that of Goethe's "elfin" lack of principle—all these
formulations crop up here verbatim as secret self-quota-
tions (pp. 80ff.).[46] What is this supposed to mean? Is
Thomas Mann simply making Riemer into his own mouth-
piece? And do the latter's utterances have his approval, as
attested by the earlier essays? The true state of affairs is
rather the opposite. By putting his own earlier statements
into the mouth of this intelligent but cramped man, who
inwardly simply cannot come to terms with Goethe, he rel-
ativizes their validity. They have a certain content of truth,
now as before, so that they can continue to resound even in

[46] See in this connection especially "Goethe als Repräsentant des
bürgerlichen Zeitalters"; in Adel des Geistes, esp. pp. 126-30.

a later work such as the "Fantasy on Goethe."[47] But it is a truth that has been perspectivistically limited and emotionally narrowed. This becomes completely clear if we confront Riemer's image of Goethe with the one in the seventh chapter.

Here, in the innermost circle of the orrery, the quotations are heaped up in an incomparable way. Whereas the author conscientiously strewed a relatively moderate number of Goethean expressions among the preceding conversations, he now weaves a tight net of Goethean language in which the authentic Goethe phrase, the contemporary document, and free composition in the spirit of the sources are inextricably interwoven with one another. The justification of this procedure in factual terms is evident. After all, it is Goethe's own thoughts and words that we are supposed to overhear here in this long interior monologue, and it is felt as almost an undesirable disturbance when this monologue is interrupted by conversations with the manservant Carl, the secretary John, and the son August. It seems only natural that in the stream of Goethe's thought, in which the past is marvelously present, previously formulated ideas and poetic expressions emerge again and again, adapting themselves to the thoughts of the moment or even initiating or advancing them. This is the enchantment that Thomas Mann achieves here through his art of weaving, and the streaming wealth of this thought is based not least on this interwovenness of past and present, thanks to the grace of the goddess Mnemosyne. This structure of Goethe's thinking, which effaces the boundaries of time, reflects everything, as we shall see, that constitutes the principal thematic content of his thoughts: duration in the midst of change, the overcoming of corrosive time by an enhancing repetition. Goethe's thinking is constructive and associative at the same time. The thought-factory is really like a loom where one tread moves a thousand threads. Through the creative use of his knowledge of source materials, Thomas Mann was able to make a living reality

[47] In *Neue Studien*, pp. 9ff.

of this simultaneously roving and purposeful thinking, which is largely identical with the process of poetic creation.

At the beginning of the chapter Goethe wakes up. His mind extricates itself from a delightful vision of heathen-antique stamp: Venus and Adonis, with their alert hound at their side. Through the association of this hound with the dog of Saint Gotthard, the legend of Saint Rochus emerges and, along with it, the daily task: the work on the essay about the Rochus festival in Bingen. "Today the peasant saws must be added to the Rochus fest. Where is the notebook? Left-hand drawer of the secretaire. When April's dry the peasants sigh. When the willow-wren sings ere the vine doth sprout—a poem" (p. 260). In reality, of course, these lines constitute no poem at all. The essay contains simply the prose maxim: "If the willow-wren sings before the grapevine sprouts, it signals a good year."[48] But Thomas Mann causes Goethe to sense in the peasant maxim its own underlying poetic rhythm. This is potential reality: How many of Goethe's rhymed maxims might not have arisen in this manner? In the serene ceremony of the elements in the course of his morning ablutions, reminiscences of "Pandora" are linked with the closing verses of the "Classical Walpurgis Night."[49] Thus the shuttles shoot back and forth, between experienced and imagined reality, between the old poem and the new, from Timur to Napoleon, from Saint Helena to Helena in *Faust*, from the *Divan* back to *Werther*. It would be a boundless undertaking to unravel this tight web and to separate it into its single elements. Even these few examples leave no doubt as to the richness of the system of associations at play here. Rather, one might ask apprehensively if Thomas Mann does not here become the victim of his own erudition. Will he not succumb before the mass of his material? If one tread here stirs a thousand

[48] JA, Vol. 29, p. 211.

[49] This is, to be sure, a bold anticipation, for the "Classical Walpurgis Night" was not conceived until 1826 and was written down in 1830.

threads, does it not remain in the last analysis a tread that simply marks time without moving forward?

The author escapes this danger by virtue of the fact that he subordinates the wealth of material and thoughts tyrannically to the one main theme that is hinted at in the Goethean formulas "duration in change" ("Dauer im Wechsel"); "intensification" ("Steigerung"); and "metamorphosis"—the theme which in the novel is generally called "repetition" ("Wiederholung") for short. In Goethe's interior monologue it is said: "Animals have but a short existence, while man knows the repetition of his conditions: youth in age, age as youth, to him it is given to live his experience once again, intensified by the mind; his is a heightened rejuvenation which is a victory over youthful fear, powerlessness and unkindness, the rounding of the circle that bans all death . . ." (pp. 284f.). It is scarcely necessary to mention how thoroughly Thomas Mann was prepared for this very theme by his struggles with the time problem and through his conception of the central idea of the mythic annihilation of time in *The Magic Mountain* and in the Joseph novels. And it is no less apparent that the choice of subject—the reappearance of Goethe's youthful love on his horizon—was dictated by this main thought. Now from the point of view of Goethe scholarship one could naturally say that this is an important and correct idea, but not earthshakingly new. Is it worthwhile to write a whole novel for the sake of this idea? But this is to put the question in the wrong way. For here it is not the bare idea that matters, but rather the manner in which it is realized in the specifically narrative structure. How does this novel transform into narrative the "philological" insight that the Marianne-experience and the *Divan* constitute an intensified repetition of the Lotte-experience and *Werther*?

Sulpiz Boisserée provides us with a vivid report of an evening spent together at the Tannery Mill, Willemer's country house near Frankfurt. Marianne sings Goethe's songs, Goethe reads his Suleika poems aloud. "Willemer fell asleep and was made a mock for it. We stayed together that much longer, until one o'clock. It was a lovely moonlit night."[50] How does the corresponding passage in the novel go? "The moon was full, the night grew late. Albert fell asleep, Willemer fell asleep with his hands folded across his stomach, good fellow, and was made a mock. It was one o'clock when we parted" (pp. 270ff.). This is a rather faithful paraphrase, with the exception of that one short extra sentence: "Albert fell asleep." Along with the Tannery Mill, all at once, Wetzlar is evoked from the well of the past as Goethe's inner monologue continues. Not in the course of his conscious thinking but in the labyrinth of his breast there emerges the parallelism between the House of the German Order and the tanner's mill, between Kestner (the model for "Albert" in *Werther*) and Willemer. For the time being, matters do not go beyond this scant hint; the servant Carl enters and the interior monologue gives way to the conversation of the day.

After his morning toilette, Goethe's memory strays back again to the trip that he had taken on the Main and Rhine the year before. On that occasion he had kissed the young waitress in the inn garden at Hardtheim—a detail which also comes from Boisserée's journal. And then, in an apparently unconnected transition: "Raspberries, with the sun on them, unmistakable smell of warm fruit. Are they canning in the house? But it is not the right season" (p. 287). No, they are not canning in the house, but we understand why Goethe suddenly has this aroma in his nose—from half a century in the past. But to understand this the reader must also have a good memory and must be able to recall a short hint at the beginning of the novel, almost three hundred pages back. At that point Lotte thought back to the Wetzlar days: "He had kissed her roundly, half whirlwind, half hypochondriac, while they were gathering raspberries in the sun,—had kissed her quickly and ardently, with rapture and tender desire, and she had permitted it" (p. 30). In this way, too, Goethe's play of thoughts now wanders on from the raspberries to the woman's lips. "If love is the best part

[50] Biedermann, *op.cit.*, Vol. 2, p. 341.

of life, then in love the best part is the kiss—poetry of love, seal of ardor, sensual and platonic, the sacrament midway between a spiritual beginning and a fleshly end, sweet act, carried out in a higher sphere than that . . ." (p. 287). This, too, has been prepared for by a leitmotif. In his conversation with Lotte, Riemer cited a verbal utterance of Goethe, interpreting it as a symptom of Goethe's "nihilism"—exactly as the author of "Goethe as a Representative of the Bourgeois Age" had already done, by the way: "A poem, you know, is like a kiss that one gives all the world. But no children come of kisses" (p. 86).[51] But what a magnificent positive turn this expression now undergoes in Goethe's monologue. "Kiss is bliss, procreation is lust, God gave it to the worms . . . also it is the difference between art and life, for the consummation of life for the human being, producing children, is not the affair of poetry, of the spiritual kiss on the raspberry lips of the world" (p. 288). And now the name is mentioned directly and for the first time: "Lotte's lip-play with the canary bird, how dearly the little animal presses itself into the sweet lips . . . Well done, gifted young fool who already knew as much of art as of love and secretly meant the former when he was playing at the latter . . ." (p. 287). Only now, after the roving play of associations, does Goethe's conscious reflection about the law of repetition begin. In the spring the first edition of *Werther* fell into his hands. "It was no accident, it had to happen, reading it supplied the final link of all that began with Sulpiz's visit, it belongs to the recurring phase, to the renovation of life, intensified by intellect, to the blithe celebration of repetition . . . *Divan* and *Faust*, all right, but *Divan* and *Werther* are even more closely related, or better: the same thing on different levels, an intensification, a refined repetition of life" (p. 288). Poetry as the expression of life, life and poetry equally subject to the law of heightened repetition and of the rejuvenation that overcomes time—with this sequence of thoughts the comprehensive validity of this law seems to be summed up.

[51] This corresponds almost verbatim to a passage in *Adel des Geistes*, p. 129.

Nevertheless a remnant is left over that must be dealt with. As a poetic figure the beloved of his youth has become "exemplary." But what about the real Lotte? Goethe grants this thought only fleeting attention and then immediately shakes it off. "Indeed, it is rather haunting to think that she still lives somewhere, even on the periphery, old, her form subject to time—not quite so comforting and attractive as the idea that *Werther* lives on side by side with the *Divan*" (p. 289). So there is an abyss between life and poetry, here still half-obscured, but suddenly completely revealed when August brings the note from Lotte. How does Goethe react? At first he does not react at all; he guides the conversation to other matters that interest him more strongly, to questions of mineralogy, to the difference between crystal, animal, and man in their relation to temporality. The thematics of these observations—duration in the midst of change, the past and the present—is connected only in a subterranean manner with the "curious occurrence." But August comes back to this, and then Goethe answers with a choice bit of heartlessness. He puts before August a strophe that he has just written for the *Divan* (p. 332):

> Man sagt, die Gänse waren dumm!—
> O, glaubt mir nicht den Leuten:—
> Denn eine sieht einmal sich rum—
> Mich rückwärts zu bedeuten.

> (They say that geese are silly things!—
> The proverb is but hollow:—
> For one of them just turned around—
> And beckoned me to follow.)[52]

A priceless find, charming precisely because of the witty twist given to the meaning of the strophe wrenched out of its context. For in Thomas Mann's usage the expression "rückwärts bedeuten" means something like: to be confronted with the empirical past that has not been poetically rejuvenated. Despite Goethe's ostensible phlegm, we sense

[52] JA, Vol. 5, p. 39.

that this confrontation has given him a well-nigh elemental fright and poses a hard test precisely for his basic conviction of life and art. "When past and present become one— they have always tended to do that, with me—the present easily takes on a ghostly character. That can have a lovely effect in a poem, but in life it is rather terrifying" (p. 333). (The passage alludes to the poems "Dauer im Wechsel" and "Im Gegenwärtigen Vergangenes," and it is in addition a rather faithful paraphrase, with darker associations, of a passage in his autobiography *Poetry and Truth*.)[53] Will Goethe become master of his "trouble and disorder"?

In the eighth chapter, which depicts Lotte's reception in his house, nothing seems to indicate that Goethe has come to terms inwardly with her visit. He receives her with impersonal politeness, his demeanor is conventional, as befits a privy councillor. One senses that this is the means by which Goethe wards off the "apprehension" that he has not mastered. If this were the final chapter, the novel would end on a totally negative and dissonant note. But the author had something else in mind. The ninth chapter reproduces the conversation between Lotte and Goethe in a carriage after Lotte's visit to the theater. From the historical point of view the conversation is completely fictitious, as is so much else in this novel; but there is something remarkable about its novelistic reality. Is Goethe "really" sitting beside Lotte in the carriage? Much speaks against this assumption, and the ambiguity is surely also the author's intention. Is the conversation supposed to be Lotte's subjective imagining, a hallucination, and hence a merely psychological reality? That, too, seems impossible, for how

[53] This passage, to which Hans-Egon Haas called my attention, goes as follows: "A feeling, however, that increased mightily within me and seemed unable to express itself marvelously enough, was the sensation of past and present in One: a view that brought something ghostly into the present. It is expressed in many of my major and lesser works, and it always has a benevolent effect in poems although—in the instant when it might be expressed directly through life and in life itself—it necessarily struck everyone as strange, inexplicable, perhaps unpleasant" (*Dichtung und Wahrheit*, Bk. III, Chap. 14; JA, Vol. 24, p. 213).

then could Goethe quote verses from the *Divan* that are completely unknown to her? Or is this rather a conversation among spirits, a heightening above and beyond the level of reality like that which occurs in, let us say, the "Book of Paradise" with which the *Divan* concludes?[54] This bold narrative trick—leaving the degree of reality of the conversation so much up in the air—surely does not mean that we are dealing here with a pure play of phantasy that has no further meaning. The author makes it clear to us figuratively that if it did not actually happen this way, then it in any case could have. It is not the reality that matters, but the potential truth.

During the conversation in the carriage, the strictures of convention fall away. Both participants reveal themselves in their true essence. They unlock their souls. Using the image of the gnat and the candle, Lotte speaks of the bitterness of the sacrifices that she and others have made for his sake. Then Goethe explains to her the deeper meaning of his existence: the identity, in his life, of sacrificing and being sacrificed—of gnat, candle, and flame. The continuing sacrifice is inextricably bound up with what he calls his "dearest and most inward, his great hope, his deepest craving": metamorphosis (p. 404). The game of transformation that encompasses life and poetry is so powerful that it can no longer be impaired by the continuing existence of the past. So he is inwardly reconciled with Lotte's coming: "so rest assured that it meant much to me and was in keeping with my own thinking, that you thought of it and came to me, the figure of your old age decked out with youthful signs" (p. 404). Life and poetry, which at first were in conflict, give way here to complete harmony.

[54] Here one should take into account Thomas Mann's commentary in a letter to Hans Eichner: "Lotte's need to attain some sort of conciliatory conclusion to this late reencounter is so strong that it causes her to imagine Goethe's presence in the carriage. And one may assume a similar need on Goethe's part, so that we are dealing with a kind of encounter of souls." Quoted by Hans Eichner in his unpublished London dissertation, "Thomas Mann's Relation to Goethe and its Significance for his own Development," p. 321; and quoted by Lange, *op.cit.*, p. 243.

In this brief closing conversation Thomas Mann makes sublime use of the art of quoting in order to summon up, once again, all the symbolic motifs of the novel in concentrated form and to attain one last intensification of the main motif. This intensification is made possible because the great confessional poems—especially "Eins und Alles," "Dauer im Wechsel," and "Selige Sehnsucht"—continuously resound, pouring their own significance into the novel. But the phrase that can be regarded as the key quotation of the entire novel comes from the final poem of the "Book Suleika" of *West-östlicher Divan*, from the ghazel "In tausend Formen magst du dich verstecken" ("You hide yourself behind a thousand forms"). With a bright chord this phrase concludes the leitmotific theme, sketched above, that began with that interpolated recollection, "Albert fell asleep." It was fully intentional when the author so emphatically wove into the content of the novel, as early as the beginning of the seventh chapter, the series of poems "Howards Ehrengedächtnis" with its vivid image of Kamaruza, the goddess of the clouds who constantly changes her shape. For it is the symbol of the cloud that he now seizes from the ghazel, from the strophe:

> Wenn steigend sich der Wasserstrahl entfaltet,
> Allspielende, wie froh erkenn' ich dich;
> Wenn Wolke sich gestaltend umgestaltet,
> Allmannigfalt'ge, dort erkenn' ich dich.

> (When water, rising, gushes up,
> Playful one, how joyously I recognize thee;
> When cloud, in motion, transforms itself,
> Most varied one, there I recognize thee.)

Goethe consciously takes the line out of its context and gives it a different meaning, but one that is highly appropriate for him. Lotte has confessed her fear to Goethe: she wonders whether it will be she or Friederike, his other youthful love, who will take the place beside Goethe as his "real one" in the blissful meadows of fame, like Laura beside Petrarch.

Smiling, Goethe asks: "Jealousy? Is Laura's then the only name that shall be sung by all tender lips? Jealous of whom? Of your sister, nay, your mirror-image and other you? When the cloud, in motion, transforms itself, is it not still the same cloud?" (p. 402). Certainly this shift is daring, but it is no sacrilege because it does justice amazingly well to the total meaning of the ghazel. Through this productive addition, Thomas Mann has found the authoritative key phrase through which the leitmotif dominating the entire novel can be resolved in a full pure chord.

Let us summarize the meaning and achievement of the art of quoting in this novel. At one point, when Thomas Mann reproduces Goethe's thoughts on his "scholarly" concern with Oriental literature with special reference to the *Divan*, he uses words that apply equally well to himself. "Making contact—a meaningful word, says a lot about our method, this boring and burrowing in the sphere and object, without it one could do nothing, bury yourself and dig away with the secret understanding of a man possessed, it makes you an initiate of the world you've seized with a loving grasp, so that you speak its language with ease and no one can distinguish the fact you've learned from the one you've invented" (p. 302). One could scarcely imagine a better characterization of the narrative procedure at work in *The Beloved Returns*. The complete fusing of "learned" and "invented" does in fact determine the hallmark of this work. At the beginning of this study of *The Beloved Returns* we mentioned how greatly the author is restricted in his creation by his material. Yet, as we saw, this restriction implies no bondage. The analysis of quotations aptly shows that the author masters his material without becoming its victim. Through his sovereign control of artistic form, which manifests itself particularly in the creation of symbols by means of literary quotations, Thomas Mann is able to remain true to his sources and, at the same time, to maintain that freedom which is the true life-element of art.

274

INDEX

Gottfried von Strassburg, 255
Gottsched, Johann Christoph, 108, 116, 117
Gounod, Charles François, 249
Gregory the Great, 243
Greuze, Jean Baptiste, 114
Grillparzer, Franz, 231
Grimm, Jacob and Wilhelm, 216
Grimmelshausen, Hans Jacob Christoffel von, 14, 210, 254
Grootaers, Jan, 9
Grünewald, Mathias, 197
Gutzkow, Karl, 155

Haas, Hans E., 271
Habert, François, 51
Hahne, Franz, 209, 226
Haller, Albrecht von, 195
Hamburger, Käte, 55
Harenberg, Johann Christoph, 123
Harper, Kenneth E., 73
Hartmann, von Aue, 255
Hatzfeld, Helmut, 52, 60, 69
Hauptmann, Gerhardt, 245
Hazard, Paul, 65
Hegel, Georg Wilhelm Friedrich, 135, 162
Heine, Heinrich, 134, 208, 238, 246
Helvetius, Claude Adrien, 119-20, 121
Herbelot, Barthélemy d', 110, 111
Héroët, Antoine, 49
Hesse, Rudolph, 122
Hettner, Hermann, 123
Heyse, Paul, 19, 181
Hoffmann, Ernst Theodor Amadeus, 18, 21, 125-46, 149, 156-57, 162, 196
Holz, Arno, 202, 203
Homer, 77
Horace, 76-77, 112, 122, 165
Hume, David, 117-18
Hutten, Ulrich von, 34

Immermann, Karl Leberecht, 18, 148-68, 196

Jean Paul (pseud. for Jean Paul Friedrich Richter), 7, 11, 15-17, 30, 78, 100, 104, 125, 126, 129, 140, 141, 151, 213, 226
Jefferson, D. W., 75
Jens, Walter, 22
Jensch, Fritz, 204
Jöcher, 123
John of Salisbury, 150
Joyce, James, 22, 73

Kant, Immanuel, 117, 135, 136
Kayser, Wolfgang, 11, 124
Keller, Gottfried, 202
Kientz, Louis, 206-208, 228
Kippenberg, Anton, 262
Kleist, Heinrich von, 136
Klemperer, Victor, 60
Knigge, Adolph Franz Friedrich, Freiherr von, 129
Kohlschmidt, Werner, 126
Krieg, Walter, 19

La Borderie, Bertrand de, 49
Lafontaine, August Heinrich Julius, 129
Lange, Gerhard, 256, 272
La Rochefoucauld, François, 103
Lefranc, Abel, 26, 37, 38, 41, 42, 45, 48, 50
Lehmann, Paul, 41
Leibniz, Gottfried Wilhelm von, 137
Lempicki, Sigmund von, 143
Lessing, Gotthold Ephraim, 18, 117, 129, 236
Lichtenberg, Georg Christoph, 103
Locke, John, 74, 77, 78, 79-80, 234
Lohenstein, Daniel Casper von, 11
Lote, Georges, 25, 26, 28-29, 30, 50
Lucian, 38
Lucretius, 38
Luther, Martin, 26, 197, 198, 254

Maack, Rodolph, 81, 83
Madariaga, Salvador de, 56
Mann, Thomas, 8, 10, 11, 20, 22, 60, 64, 104, 149, 202, 230-74